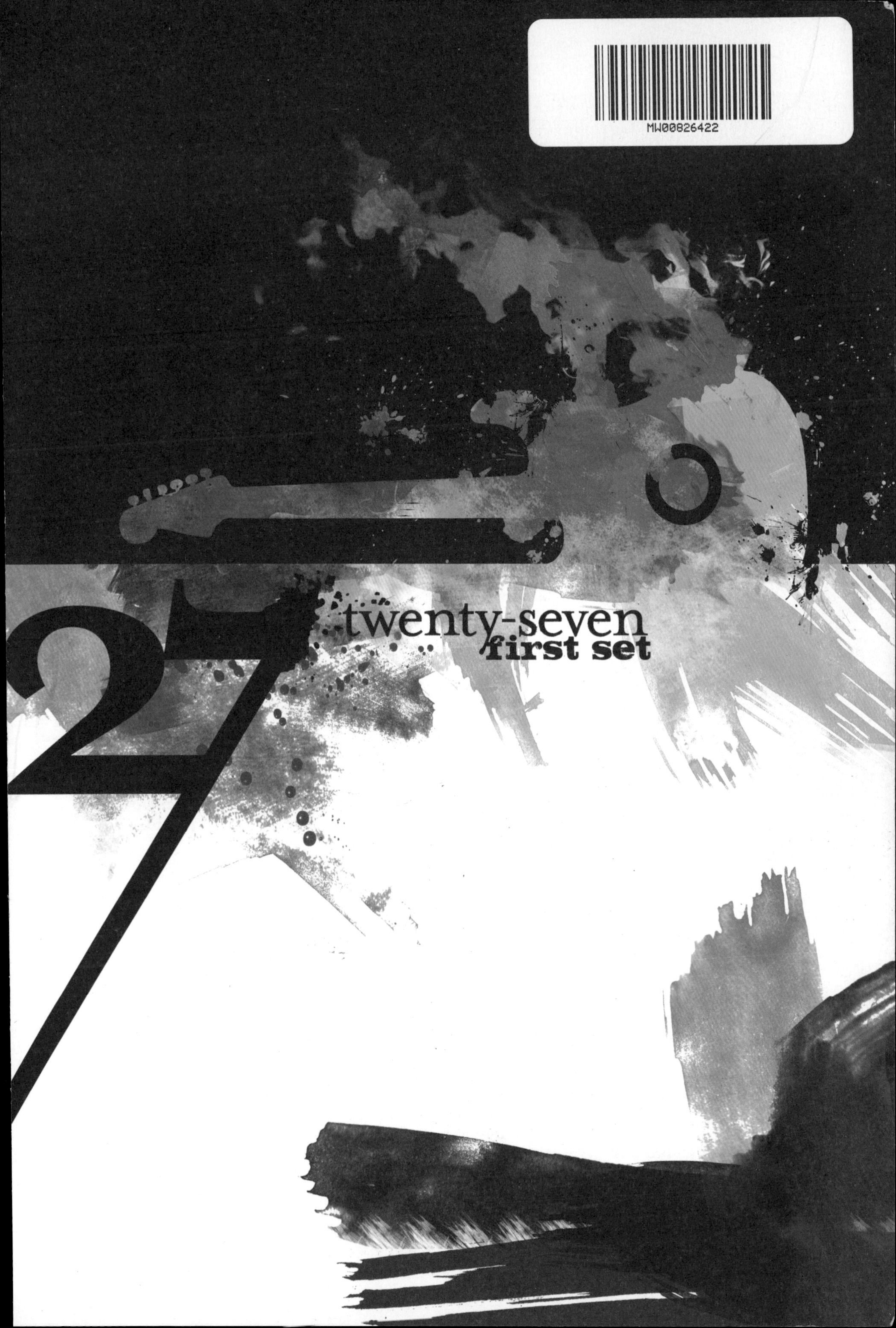
27
twenty-seven
first set

TWENTY SEVEN: FIRST SET, VOL. 1. First Printing. Published by Image
Comics, Inc. Office of publication: 2134 Allston Way, Second Floor, Berkeley, California 94704. Copyright © 2011 CHARLES SOULE. Originally published in single magazine form as TWENTY SEVEN #1-4. All rights reserved. TWENTY SEVEN™ (including all prominent characters featured
herein), its logo and all character likenesses are trademarks of CHARLES
SOULE, unless otherwise noted. Image Comics® and its logos are registered trademarks of Image Comics, Inc. Shadowline and its logos are ™
and © 2011 Jim Valentino. No part of this publication may be reproduced
or transmitted, in any form or by any means (except for short excerpts
for review purposes) without the express written permission of Image
Comics, Inc. All names, characters, events and locales in this publication
are entirely fictional. Any resemblance to actual persons (living or
dead), events or places, without satiric intent, is coincidental.
PRINTED IN KOREA. ISBN: 978-1-60706-382-7

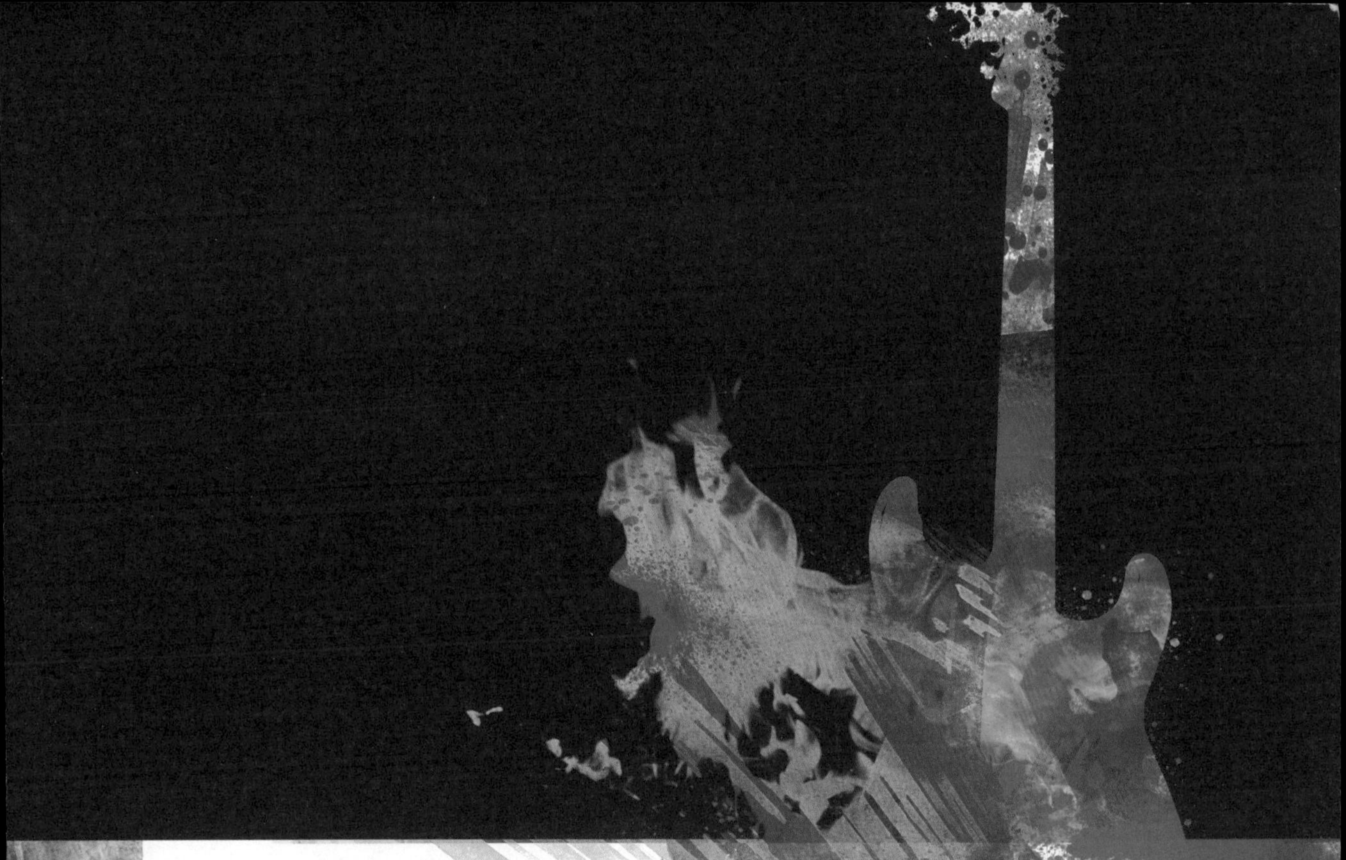

charles soule

WORDS

renzo podesta

ART

shawn depasquale

LETTERS

w. scott forbes

COVER//SERIES COVERS

tim daniel

DESIGN

jade dodge

EDITS

jim valentino

PUBLISHER

image comics, inc.//www.imagecomics.com

IMAGE COMICS, INC.

Robert Kirkman - chief operating officer
Erik Larsen - chief financial officer
Todd McFarlane - president
Marc Silvestri - chief executive officer
Jim Valentino - vice-president
Eric Stephenson - publisher

Todd Martinez - sales & licensing coordinator
Sarah deLaine - pr & marketing coordinator
Branwyn Bigglestone - accounts manager
Emily Miller - administrative assistant
Jamie Parreno - marketing assistant
Kevin Yuen - digital rights coordinator

Tyler Shainline - production manager
Drew Gill - art director
Jonathan Chan - senior production artist
Monica Garcia - production artist
Vincent Kukua - production artist
Jana Cook - production artist

dedications

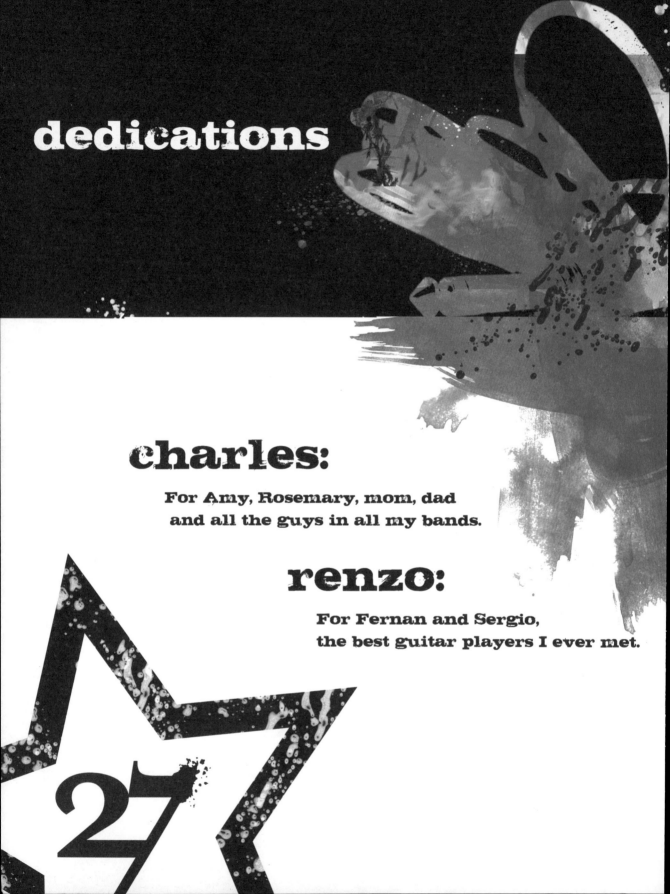

charles:

For Amy, Rosemary, mom, dad
and all the guys in all my bands.

renzo:

For Fernan and Sergio,
the best guitar players I ever met.

27

intro

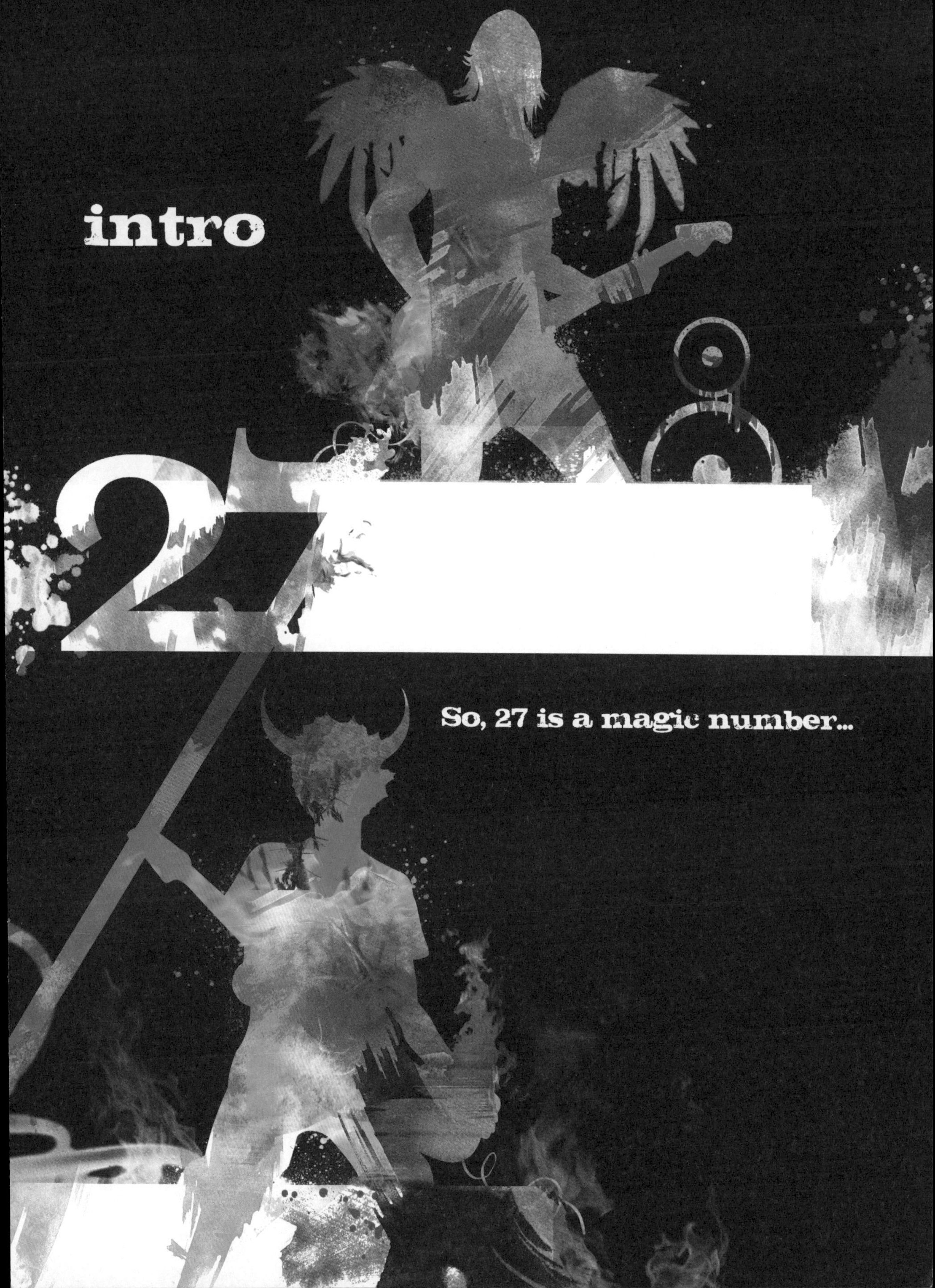

27

So, 27 is a magic number...

At some point a couple of years back, Charles Soule dropped into my lap a book he'd written called
STRONGMAN. And I read it, and it was good. The voice was unique, and the story went in its own direction.
Charles wasn't stomping around in someone else's well-worn boot steps, and I sensed an emerging talent
with the potential to do some special things in comics. So it's no real surprise to me that 27 is a strong step
in the evolution of a rising talent.

Any music fan can tell you how old Jim Morrison, Jimi Hendrix, Janis Joplin and Kurt Cobain were when
they died. One of those fascinating coincidences that can spur conversation about wasted potential and the
consequences of the rock and roll lifestyle.

Luckily for us, Charles Soule had the creative drive to extend that conversation in new directions. 27 is one
of those books that does exactly what creator-owned comics should do. There's no question when reading
this book that Charles is personally invested in music, in creativity, in the nature of the muse, and in numbers. He's tossed all of these elements, each one near and dear to his heart, into a cocktail shaker and what
tumbled out is a fascinating speculation on the nature of creativity.

But more than just presenting an argument for a deeper metaphysical debate on inspiration and the creative curve, 27 gives us a protagonist we're interested in following. A flawed personality whose personal
growth is spurred by his being thrust into a situation that only a rock star's ego could handle. A character
we wouldn't mind revisiting down the road to see which buttons get pushed next. And each supporting
character is clearly defined, working to advance the journey in logical directions and hook the reader a
little more firmly.

b. clay moore

MARCH 2011

More than anything, 27 makes something that's very difficult to do look very easy. Charles and Renzo Podesta have stuffed a four issue mini-series with enough ideas to spawn multiple dissertations, yet the story
never once gets derailed, as each new layer reveals itself, expanding the world (worlds?) by new and more
complex degrees.

The magnificent thing about comics is that there are no limits on how far you can travel on whatever road
you choose. Ultimately, the highest praise I can muster is that 27 is the kind of book that spurs me to find
new maps of my own.

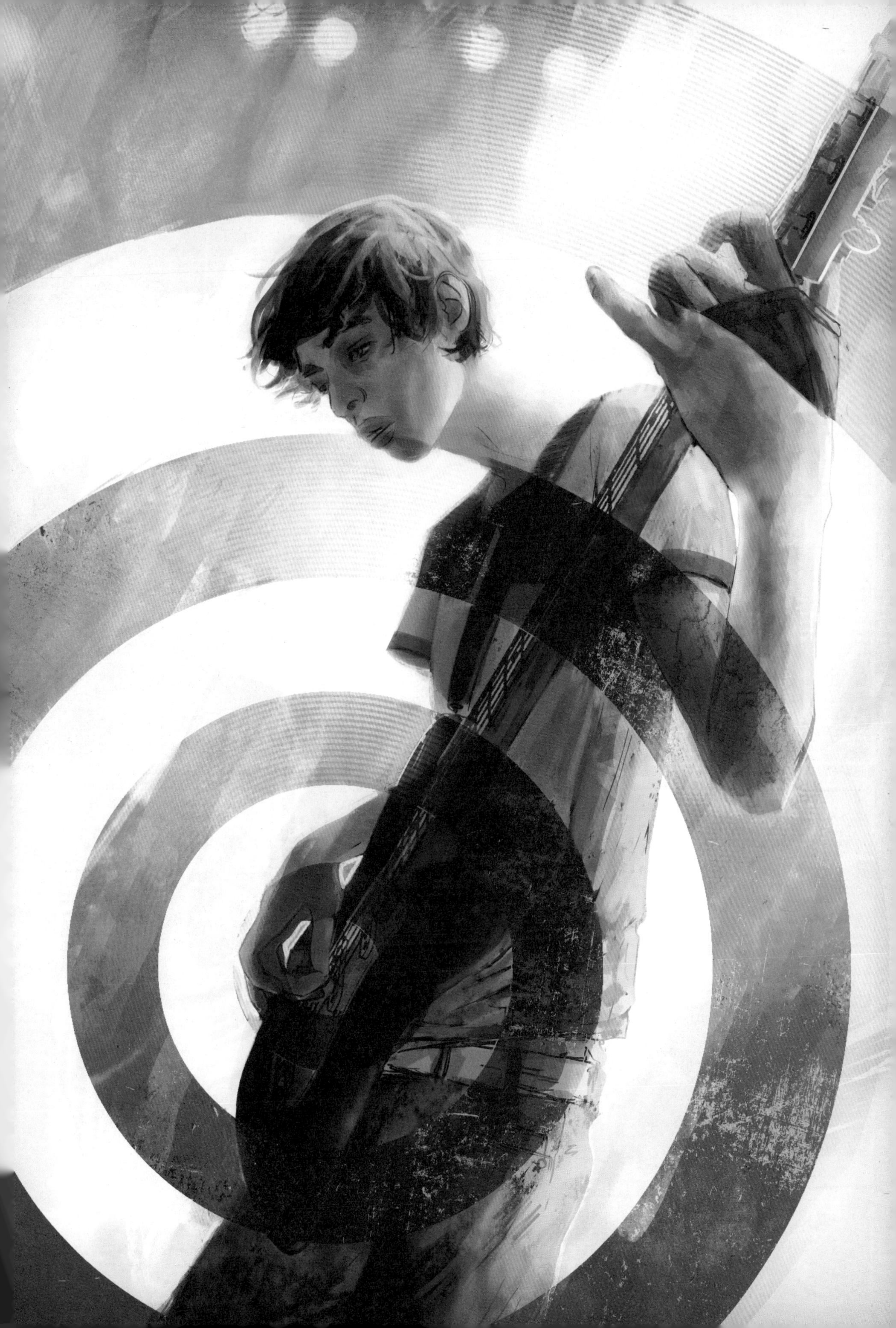

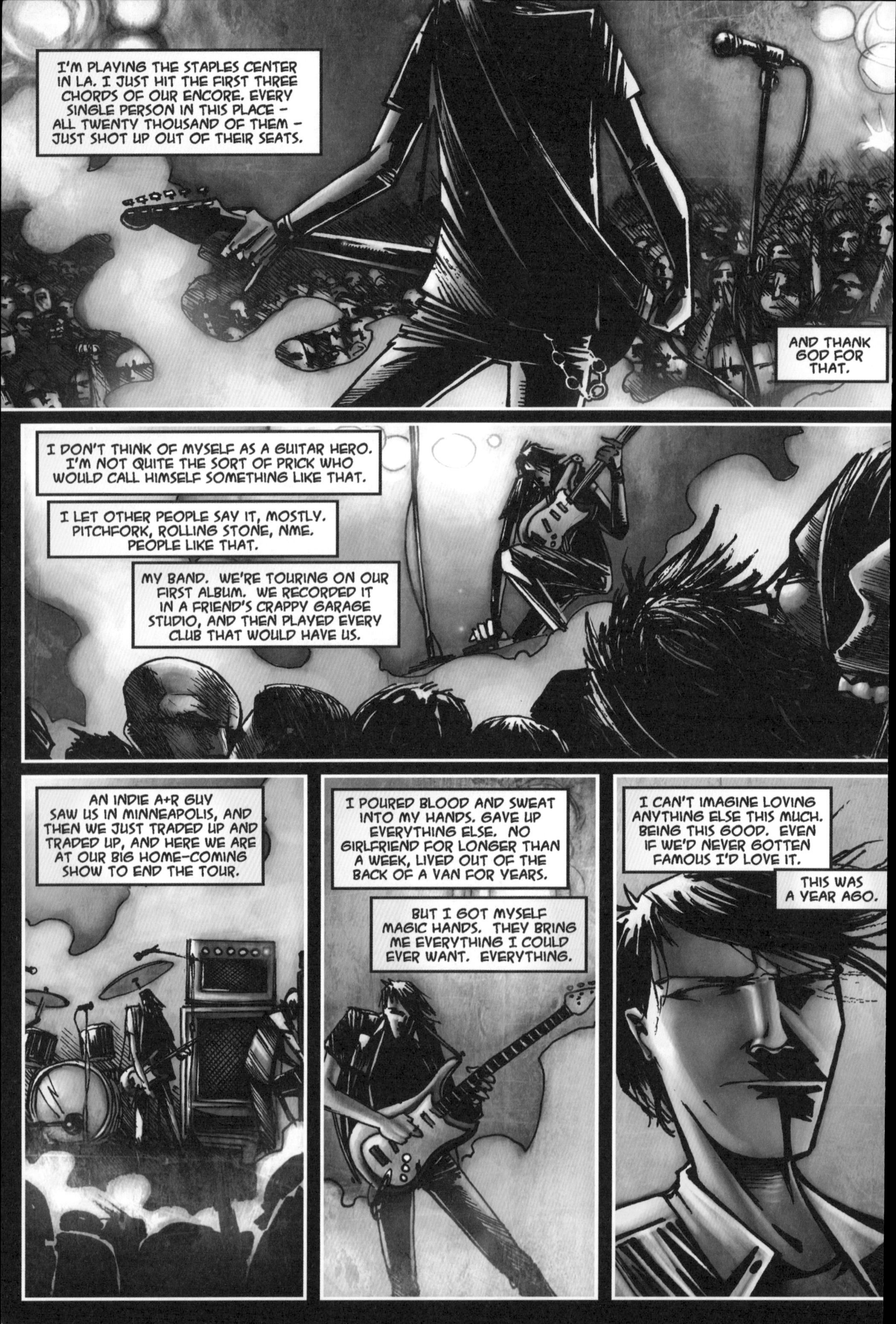
I'M PLAYING THE STAPLES CENTER IN LA. I JUST HIT THE FIRST THREE CHORDS OF OUR ENCORE. EVERY SINGLE PERSON IN THIS PLACE - ALL TWENTY THOUSAND OF THEM - JUST SHOT UP OUT OF THEIR SEATS.
AND THANK GOD FOR THAT.
I DON'T THINK OF MYSELF AS A GUITAR HERO. I'M NOT QUITE THE SORT OF PRICK WHO WOULD CALL HIMSELF SOMETHING LIKE THAT.
I LET OTHER PEOPLE SAY IT, MOSTLY. PITCHFORK, ROLLING STONE, NME. PEOPLE LIKE THAT.
MY BAND. WE'RE TOURING ON OUR FIRST ALBUM. WE RECORDED IT IN A FRIEND'S CRAPPY GARAGE STUDIO, AND THEN PLAYED EVERY CLUB THAT WOULD HAVE US.
AN INDIE A+R GUY SAW US IN MINNEAPOLIS, AND THEN WE JUST TRADED UP AND TRADED UP, AND HERE WE ARE AT OUR BIG HOME-COMING SHOW TO END THE TOUR.
I POURED BLOOD AND SWEAT INTO MY HANDS. GAVE UP EVERYTHING ELSE. NO GIRLFRIEND FOR LONGER THAN A WEEK, LIVED OUT OF THE BACK OF A VAN FOR YEARS.
BUT I GOT MYSELF MAGIC HANDS. THEY BRING ME EVERYTHING I COULD EVER WANT. EVERYTHING.
I CAN'T IMAGINE LOVING ANYTHING ELSE THIS MUCH. BEING THIS GOOD. EVEN IF WE'D NEVER GOTTEN FAMOUS I'D LOVE IT.
THIS WAS A YEAR AGO.

AND THIS IS TODAY.

ABOUT SIX MONTHS AGO, MY MAGIC HANDS LOST THEIR MAGIC. MY LEFT HAND, MY FRETBOARD HAND, STARTED TO HURT ANY TIME I TOUCHED THE STRINGS.

EVENTUALLY, MY HAND FELT LIKE I DIPPED IT IN BATTERY ACID ANY TIME I USED IT. MY RIGHT HAND STILL WORKS, BUT SO WHAT?

YOU CAN'T PLAY GUITAR WITH ONE HAND.

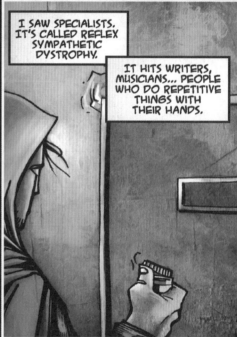

I SAW SPECIALISTS. IT'S CALLED REFLEX SYMPATHETIC DYSTROPHY.

IT HITS WRITERS, MUSICIANS... PEOPLE WHO DO REPETITIVE THINGS WITH THEIR HANDS.

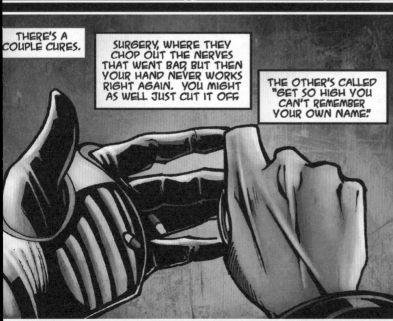

THERE'S A COUPLE CURES.

SURGERY, WHERE THEY CHOP OUT THE NERVES THAT WENT BAD, BUT THEN YOUR HAND NEVER WORKS RIGHT AGAIN. YOU MIGHT AS WELL JUST CUT IT OFF.

THE OTHER'S CALLED "GET SO HIGH YOU CAN'T REMEMBER YOUR OWN NAME."

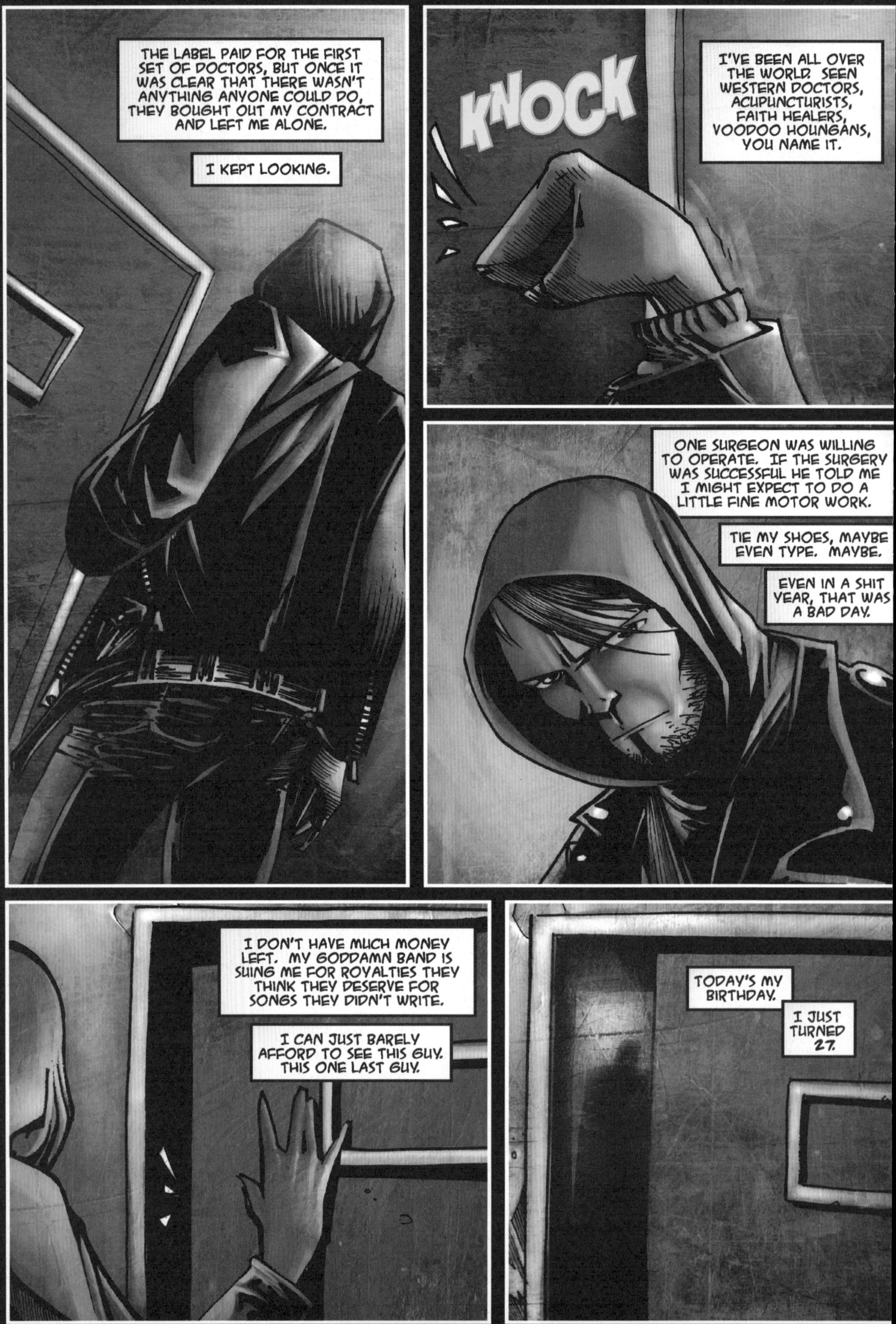
THE LABEL PAID FOR THE FIRST SET OF DOCTORS, BUT ONCE IT WAS CLEAR THAT THERE WASN'T ANYTHING ANYONE COULD DO, THEY BOUGHT OUT MY CONTRACT AND LEFT ME ALONE.
I KEPT LOOKING.
KNOCK
I'VE BEEN ALL OVER THE WORLD. SEEN WESTERN DOCTORS, ACUPUNCTURISTS, FAITH HEALERS, VOODOO HOUNGANS, YOU NAME IT.
ONE SURGEON WAS WILLING TO OPERATE. IF THE SURGERY WAS SUCCESSFUL HE TOLD ME I MIGHT EXPECT TO DO A LITTLE FINE MOTOR WORK.
TIE MY SHOES, MAYBE EVEN TYPE. MAYBE.
EVEN IN A SHIT YEAR, THAT WAS A BAD DAY.
I DON'T HAVE MUCH MONEY LEFT. MY GODDAMN BAND IS SUING ME FOR ROYALTIES THEY THINK THEY DESERVE FOR SONGS THEY DIDN'T WRITE.
I CAN JUST BARELY AFFORD TO SEE THIS GUY. THIS ONE LAST GUY.
TODAY'S MY BIRTHDAY.
I JUST TURNED 27.

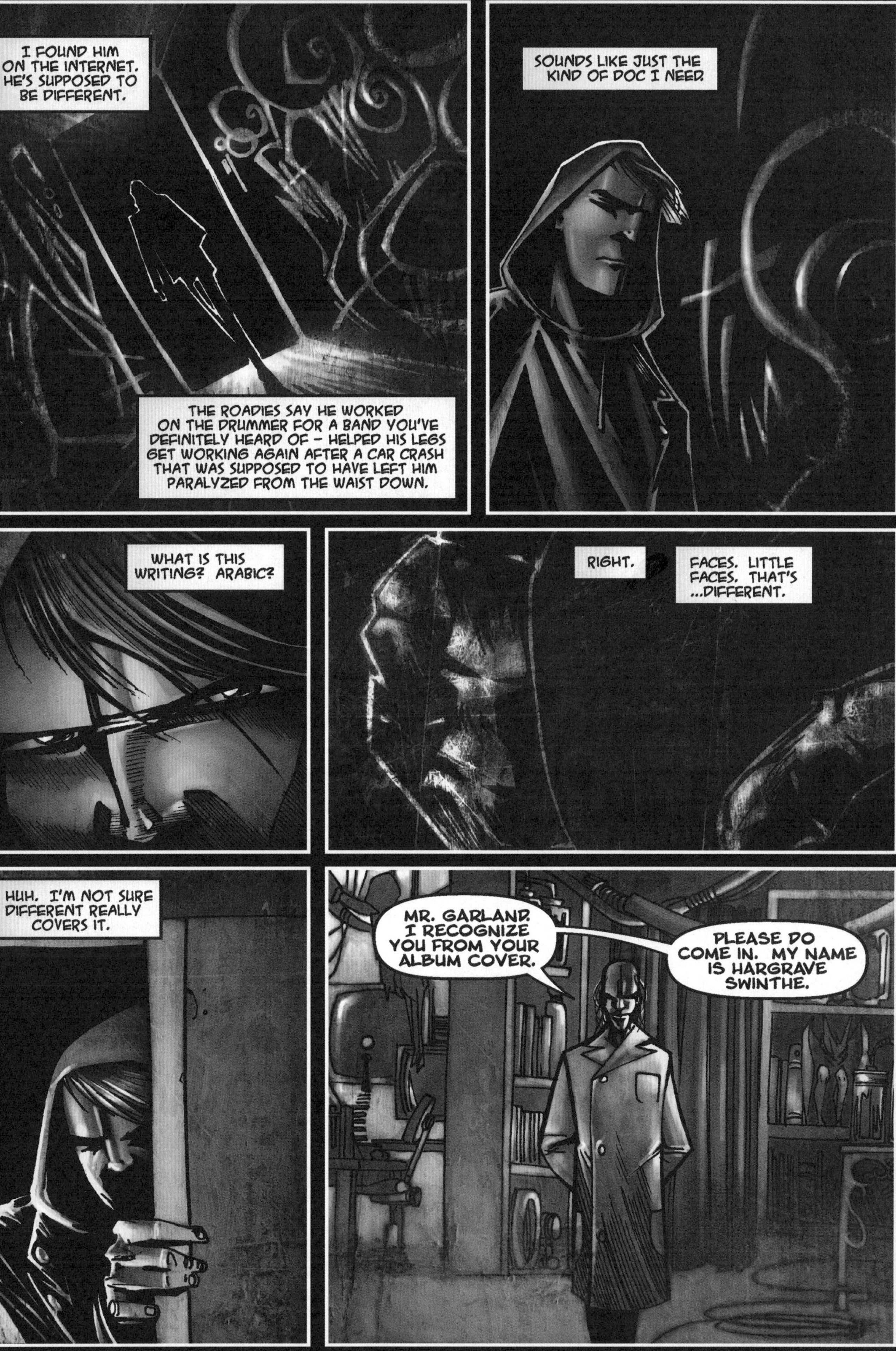
I FOUND HIM ON THE INTERNET. HE'S SUPPOSED TO BE DIFFERENT.
THE ROADIES SAY HE WORKED ON THE DRUMMER FOR A BAND YOU'VE DEFINITELY HEARD OF – HELPED HIS LEGS GET WORKING AGAIN AFTER A CAR CRASH THAT WAS SUPPOSED TO HAVE LEFT HIM PARALYZED FROM THE WAIST DOWN.
SOUNDS LIKE JUST THE KIND OF DOC I NEED.
WHAT IS THIS WRITING? ARABIC?
RIGHT.
FACES. LITTLE FACES. THAT'S ...DIFFERENT.
HUH. I'M NOT SURE DIFFERENT REALLY COVERS IT.
MR. GARLAND. I RECOGNIZE YOU FROM YOUR ALBUM COVER.
PLEASE DO COME IN. MY NAME IS HARGRAVE SWINTHE.

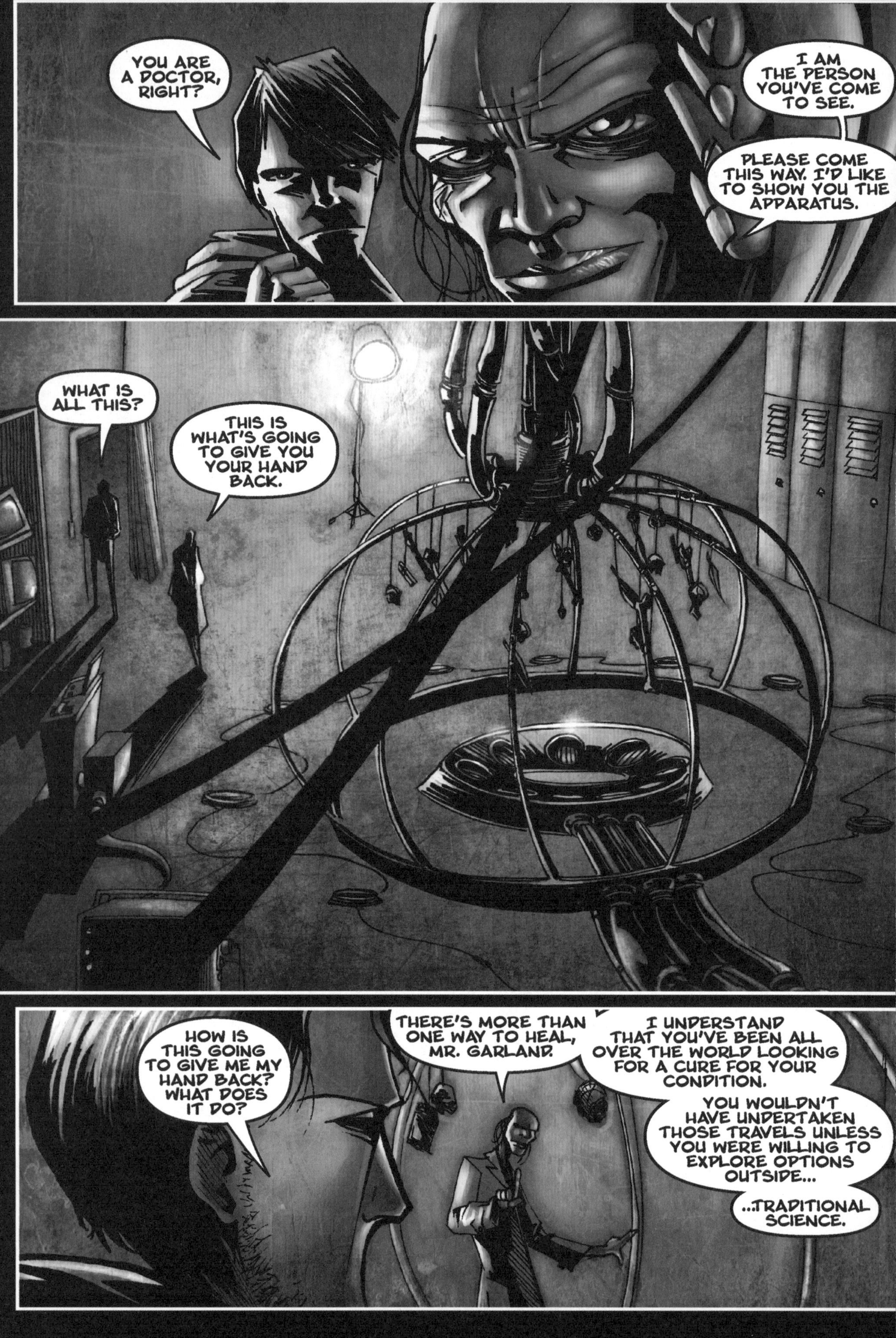
YOU ARE A DOCTOR, RIGHT?
I AM THE PERSON YOU'VE COME TO SEE.
PLEASE COME THIS WAY. I'D LIKE TO SHOW YOU THE APPARATUS.
WHAT IS ALL THIS?
THIS IS WHAT'S GOING TO GIVE YOU YOUR HAND BACK.
HOW IS THIS GOING TO GIVE ME MY HAND BACK? WHAT DOES IT DO?
THERE'S MORE THAN ONE WAY TO HEAL, MR. GARLAND.
I UNDERSTAND THAT YOU'VE BEEN ALL OVER THE WORLD LOOKING FOR A CURE FOR YOUR CONDITION.
YOU WOULDN'T HAVE UNDERTAKEN THOSE TRAVELS UNLESS YOU WERE WILLING TO EXPLORE OPTIONS OUTSIDE...
...TRADITIONAL SCIENCE.

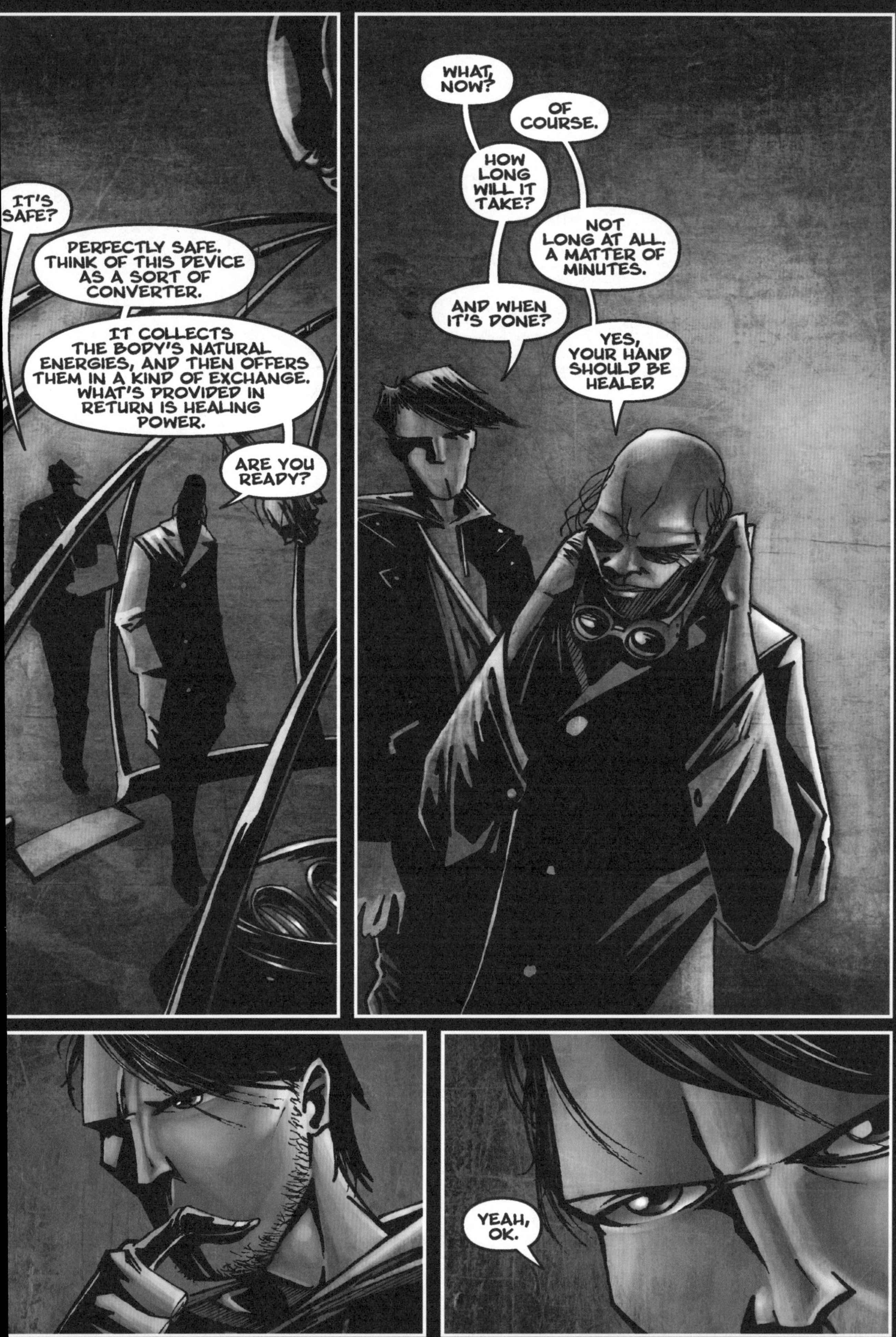
IT'S SAFE?
PERFECTLY SAFE. THINK OF THIS DEVICE AS A SORT OF CONVERTER.
IT COLLECTS THE BODY'S NATURAL ENERGIES, AND THEN OFFERS THEM IN A KIND OF EXCHANGE. WHAT'S PROVIDED IN RETURN IS HEALING POWER.
ARE YOU READY?
WHAT, NOW?
OF COURSE.
HOW LONG WILL IT TAKE?
NOT LONG AT ALL. A MATTER OF MINUTES.
AND WHEN IT'S DONE?
YES, YOUR HAND SHOULD BE HEALED.
YEAH, OK.

CAN WE HURRY THIS UP, DOC? IT'S COLD AS HELL.

JUST A FEW MORE MOMENTS.

WHAT'S WITH THE CATS?

CATS ARE POWERFULLY ASSOCIATED WITH THE NUMBER NINE. NINE CATS, NINE LIVES EACH, 81 LIVES IN ALL. EIGHT PLUS ONE EQUALS NINE.

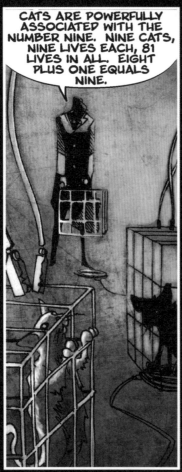

HOLD ON, WHAT ARE YOU DOING?

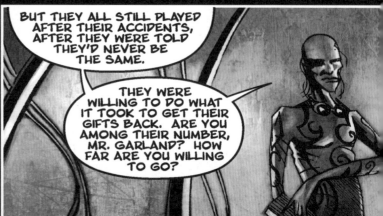

BUT THEY ALL STILL PLAYED AFTER THEIR ACCIDENTS, AFTER THEY WERE TOLD THEY'D NEVER BE THE SAME.

THEY WERE WILLING TO DO WHAT IT TOOK TO GET THEIR GIFTS BACK. ARE YOU AMONG THEIR NUMBER, MR. GARLAND? HOW FAR ARE YOU WILLING TO GO?

I HAD TO BE NAKED, HE SAID, SO NOTHING WOULD INTERFERE WITH THE ENERGIES. PERSONALLY, I'M MORE WORRIED THAT HE MADE ME TAKE MY BRACE OFF. I'VE GOT ABOUT FIVE MINUTES BEFORE I START TO SCREAM.

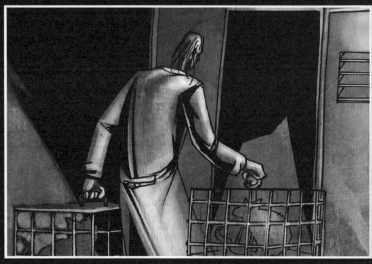

COME ON, WHAT THE HELL IS THIS? LET ME OUT OF HERE.

HOW FAR ARE YOU WILLING TO GO TO HAVE YOUR HAND BACK?

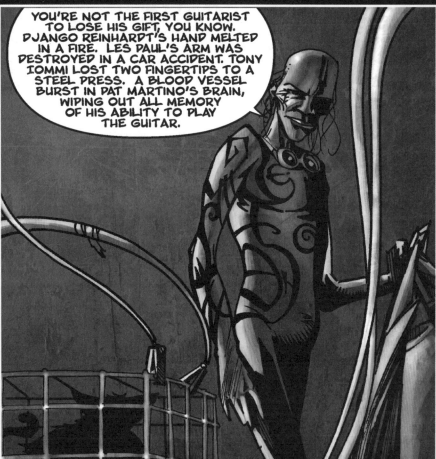

YOU'RE NOT THE FIRST GUITARIST TO LOSE HIS GIFT, YOU KNOW. DJANGO REINHARDT'S HAND MELTED IN A FIRE. LES PAUL'S ARM WAS DESTROYED IN A CAR ACCIDENT. TONY IOMMI LOST TWO FINGERTIPS TO A STEEL PRESS. A BLOOD VESSEL BURST IN PAT MARTINO'S BRAIN, WIPING OUT ALL MEMORY OF HIS ABILITY TO PLAY THE GUITAR.

JUST TELL ME WHAT'S HAPPENING!

I'VE ALWAYS LOVED YOUR MUSIC.

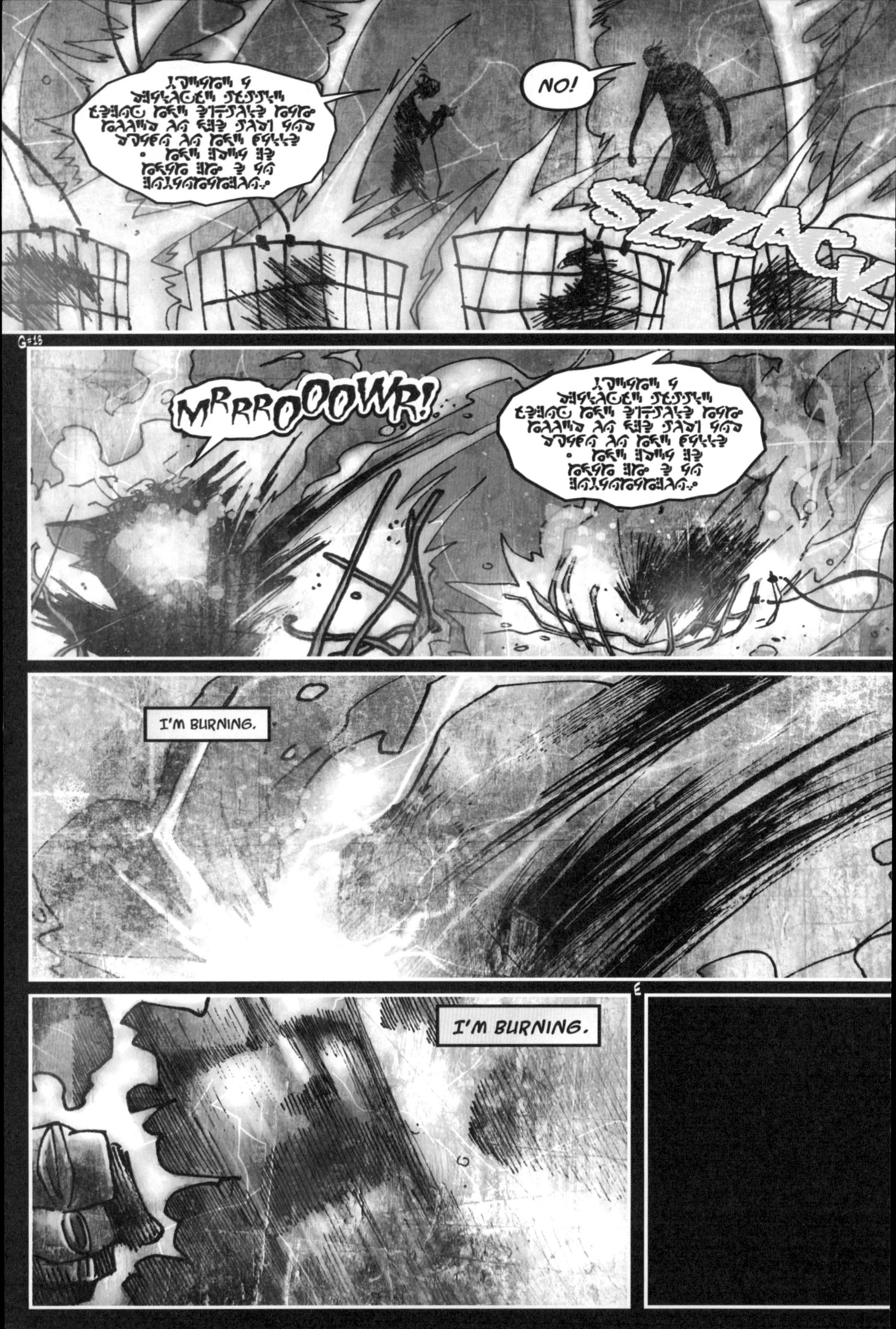
NO!
SZZZACK
MRRROOOOWR!
I'M BURNING.
I'M BURNING.

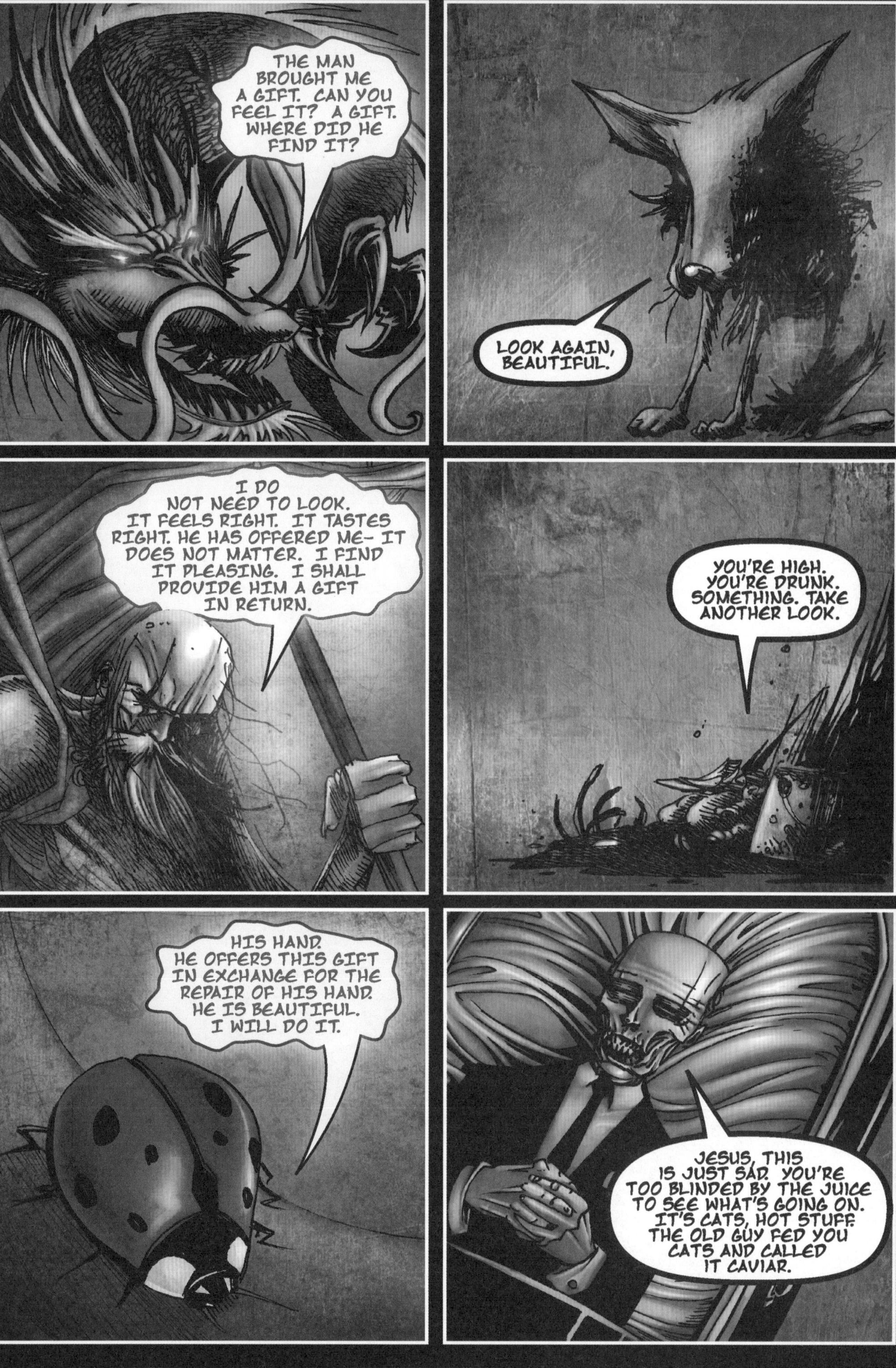
THE MAN BROUGHT ME A GIFT. CAN YOU FEEL IT? A GIFT. WHERE DID HE FIND IT?
LOOK AGAIN, BEAUTIFUL.
I DO NOT NEED TO LOOK. IT FEELS RIGHT. IT TASTES RIGHT. HE HAS OFFERED ME- IT DOES NOT MATTER. I FIND IT PLEASING. I SHALL PROVIDE HIM A GIFT IN RETURN.
YOU'RE HIGH. YOU'RE DRUNK. SOMETHING. TAKE ANOTHER LOOK.
HIS HAND. HE OFFERS THIS GIFT IN EXCHANGE FOR THE REPAIR OF HIS HAND. HE IS BEAUTIFUL. I WILL DO IT.
JESUS, THIS IS JUST SAD. YOU'RE TOO BLINDED BY THE JUICE TO SEE WHAT'S GOING ON. IT'S CATS, HOT STUFF. THE OLD GUY FED YOU CATS AND CALLED IT CAVIAR.

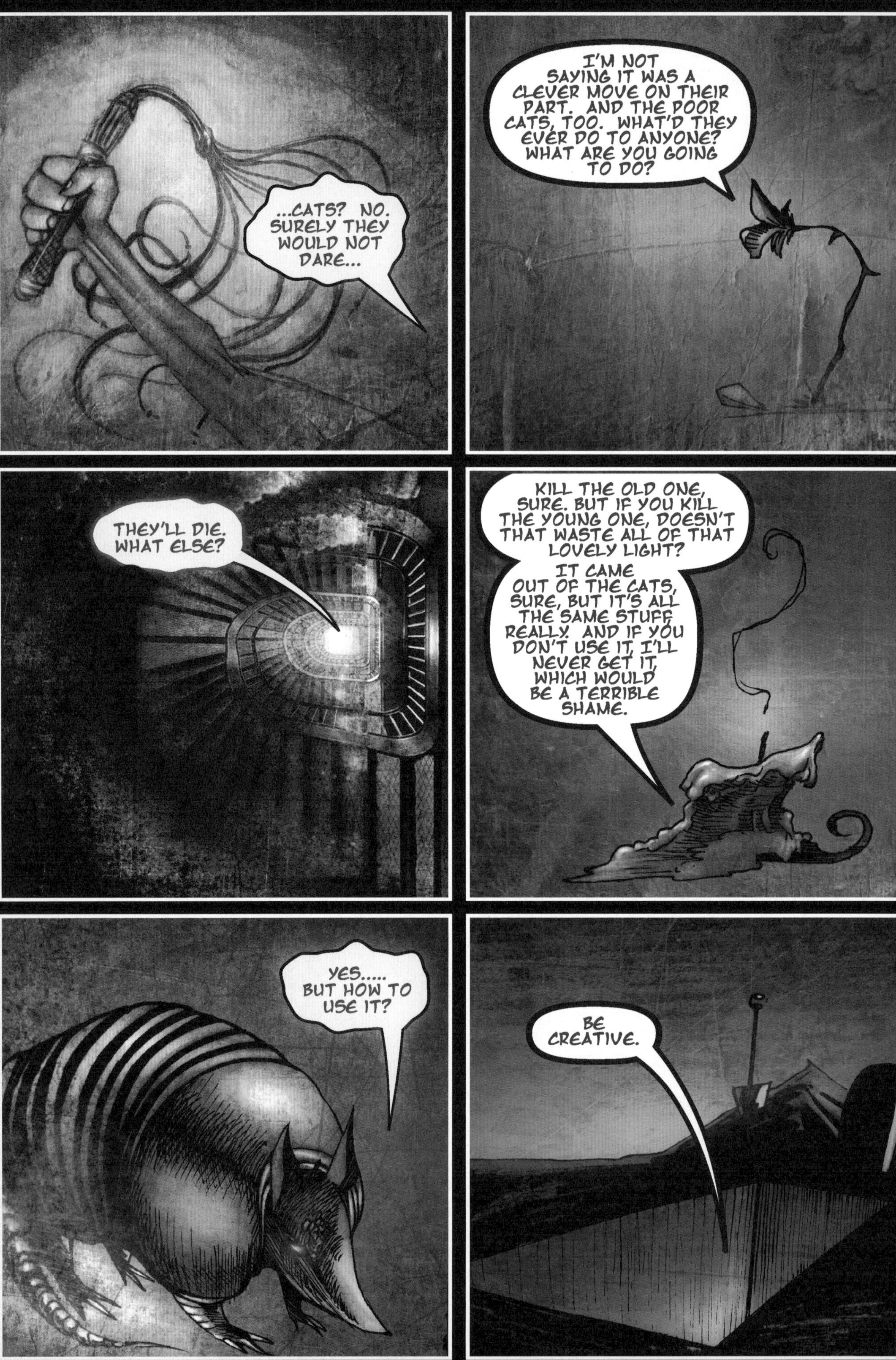
...CATS? NO. SURELY THEY WOULD NOT DARE...
I'M NOT SAYING IT WAS A CLEVER MOVE ON THEIR PART. AND THE POOR CATS, TOO. WHAT'D THEY EVER DO TO ANYONE? WHAT ARE YOU GOING TO DO?
THEY'LL DIE. WHAT ELSE?
KILL THE OLD ONE, SURE. BUT IF YOU KILL THE YOUNG ONE, DOESN'T THAT WASTE ALL OF THAT LOVELY LIGHT?
IT CAME OUT OF THE CATS, SURE, BUT IT'S ALL THE SAME STUFF REALLY. AND IF YOU DON'T USE IT, I'LL NEVER GET IT, WHICH WOULD BE A TERRIBLE SHAME.
YES..... BUT HOW TO USE IT?
BE CREATIVE.

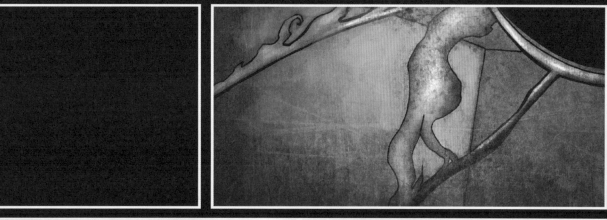

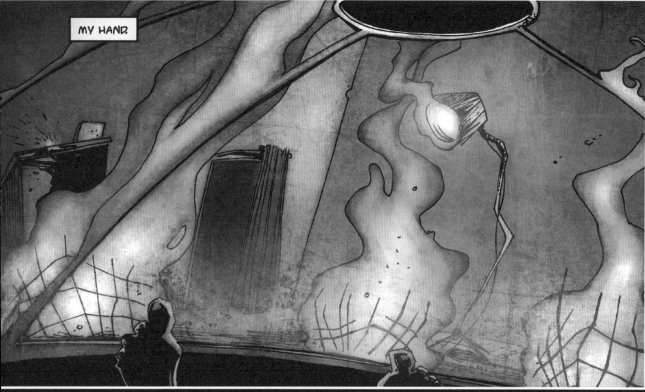

MY HAND

IT HURTS. HOLY GOD, IT HURTS.

WHAT..?

OH, GOD...

WHERE'S MY BRACE? I CAN'T THINK.

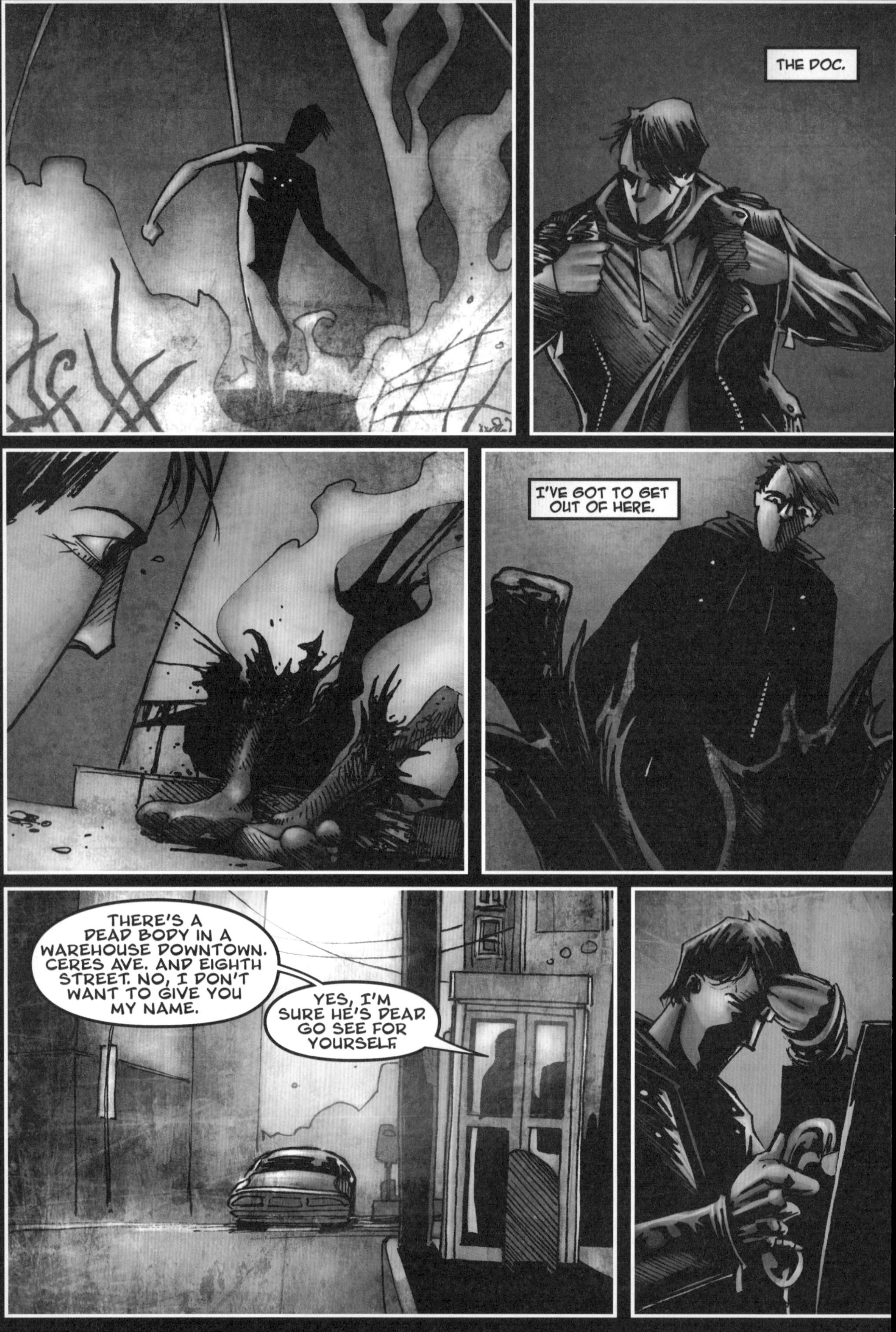
THE DOC.
I'VE GOT TO GET OUT OF HERE.
THERE'S A DEAD BODY IN A WAREHOUSE DOWNTOWN. CERES AVE. AND EIGHTH STREET. NO, I DON'T WANT TO GIVE YOU MY NAME.
YES, I'M SURE HE'S DEAD. GO SEE FOR YOURSELF.

CAME HOME.

YEAH, I TRIED TO PLAY. FIRST THING I DID.

NO, SECOND.

FIRST, MY SISTER CALLED. SHE CALLS ME CONSTANTLY, LIKE TEN TIMES A DAY. I CAN UNDERSTAND THAT – SHE'S FREAKING OUT.

I DON'T KNOW WHAT SHE EXPECTS ME TO DO. IT'S NOT LIKE I DON'T FEEL SHITTY ABOUT IT TOO. ANYWAY, THEN I TRIED TO PLAY.

DIDN'T WORK. MY HAND DOESN'T FEEL ANY DIFFERENT. MAYBE A LITTLE WORSE, EVEN. STILL CAN'T PLAY.

...FINAL COUNT ON CHILDREN HELD CAPTIVE...

EXTREMISTS DEMAN

twenty seven bodies were

WHAT THE HELL WAS I EXPECTING? THIS ISN'T GOING TO GET FIXED. EVERYTHING'S JUST...

18 CHILDRE HELD B

...BROKEN.

GODDAMMIT.

WHAT IS THIS THING? WHAT DID THAT FREAK DO TO ME?

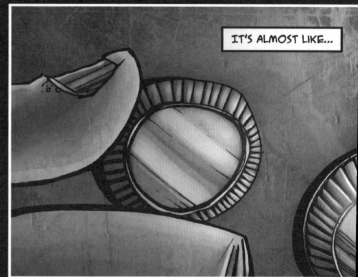

IT'S ALMOST LIKE...

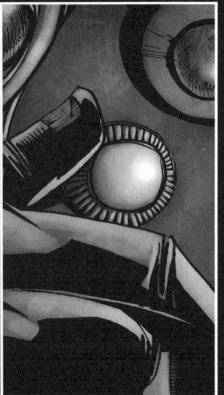

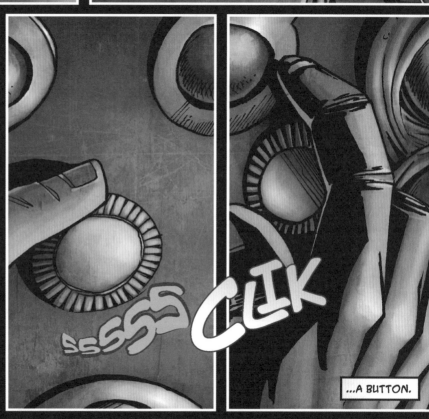

SSSSS CLIK

...A BUTTON.

HUH.

FEELS... WEIRD.

PLEASE...

IT DOESN'T HURT.

IT DOESN'T **FUCKING** HURT!

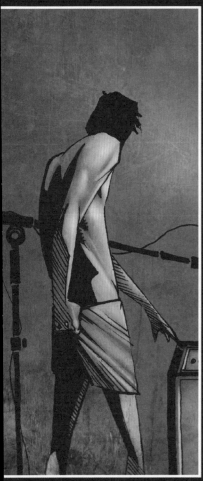

I DON'T EVEN FEEL DRUNK ANYMORE.

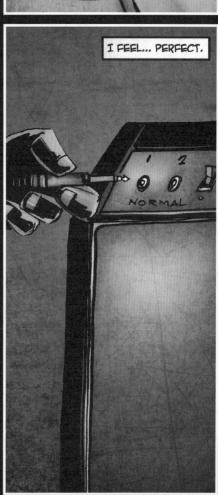

I FEEL... PERFECT.

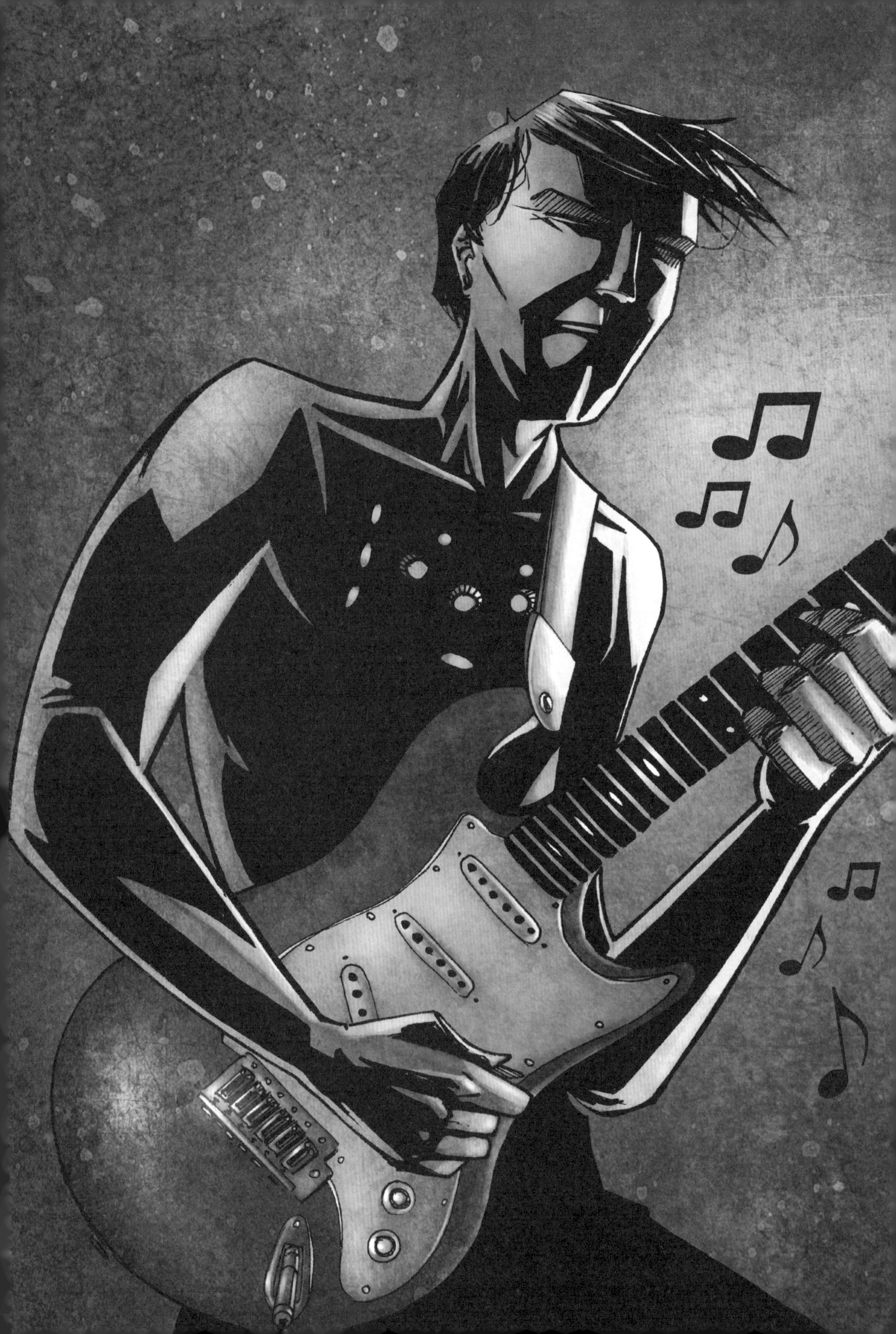

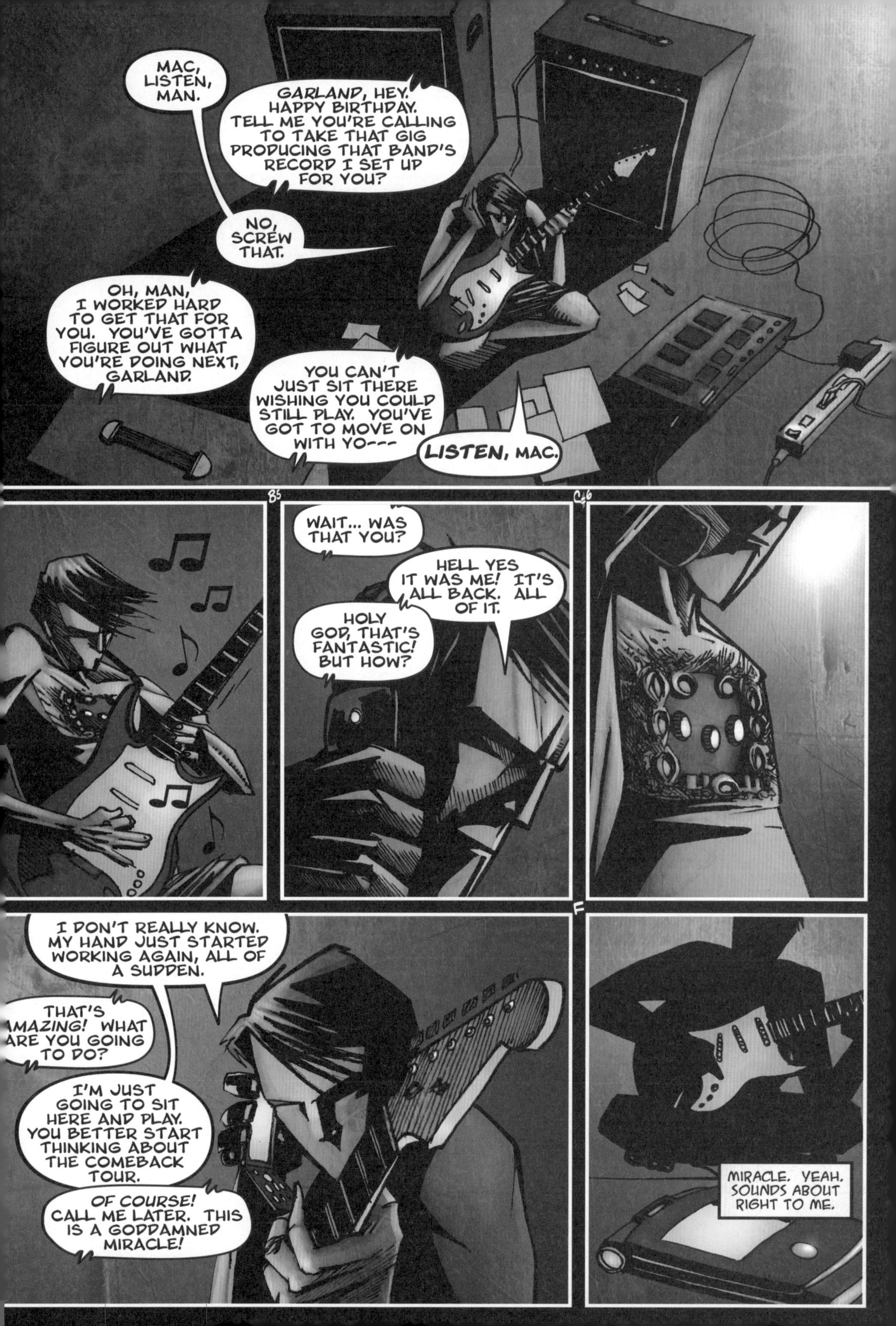
MAC, LISTEN, MAN.
GARLAND, HEY. HAPPY BIRTHDAY. TELL ME YOU'RE CALLING TO TAKE THAT GIG PRODUCING THAT BAND'S RECORD I SET UP FOR YOU?
NO, SCREW THAT.
OH, MAN, I WORKED HARD TO GET THAT FOR YOU. YOU'VE GOTTA FIGURE OUT WHAT YOU'RE DOING NEXT, GARLAND.
YOU CAN'T JUST SIT THERE WISHING YOU COULD STILL PLAY. YOU'VE GOT TO MOVE ON WITH YO---
LISTEN, MAC.
WAIT... WAS THAT YOU?
HELL YES IT WAS ME! IT'S ALL BACK. ALL OF IT.
HOLY GOD, THAT'S FANTASTIC! BUT HOW?
I DON'T REALLY KNOW. MY HAND JUST STARTED WORKING AGAIN, ALL OF A SUDDEN.
THAT'S AMAZING! WHAT ARE YOU GOING TO DO?
I'M JUST GOING TO SIT HERE AND PLAY. YOU BETTER START THINKING ABOUT THE COMEBACK TOUR.
OF COURSE! CALL ME LATER. THIS IS A GODDAMNED MIRACLE!
MIRACLE. YEAH. SOUNDS ABOUT RIGHT TO ME.

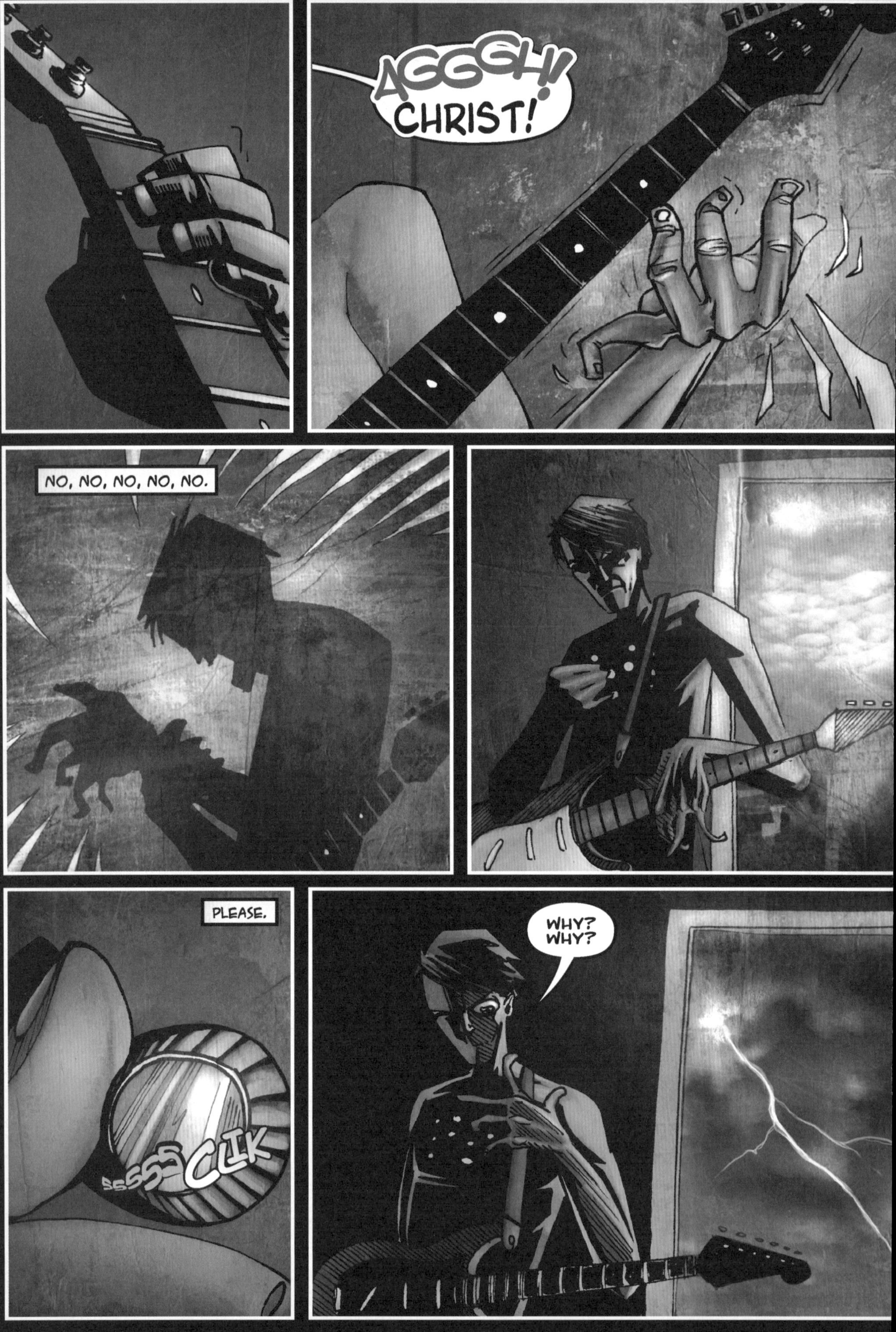
AGGGH! CHRIST!
NO, NO, NO, NO, NO.
PLEASE.
SSSSS CLIK
WHY? WHY?

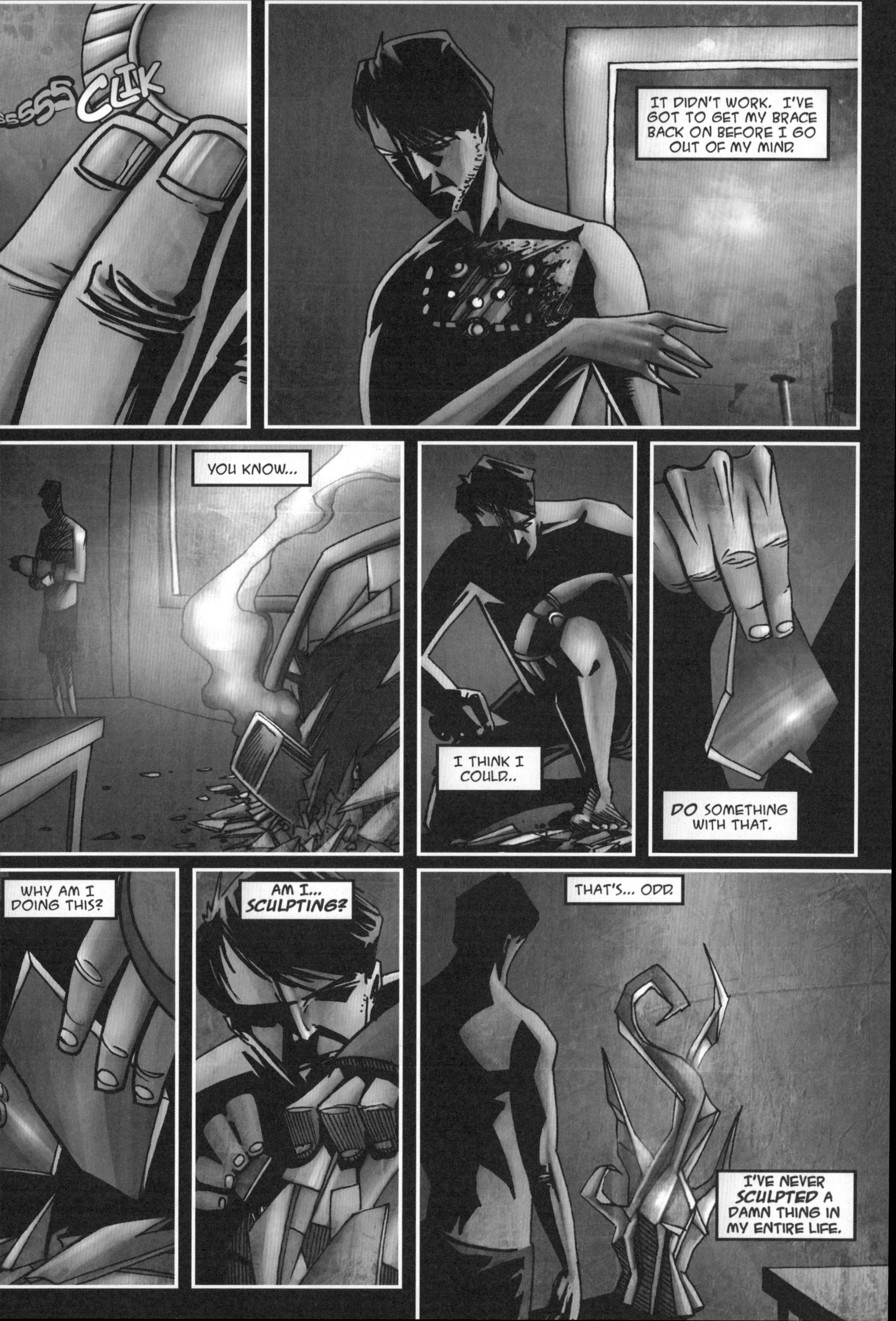
SSSSSS CLIK
IT DIDN'T WORK. I'VE GOT TO GET MY BRACE BACK ON BEFORE I GO OUT OF MY MIND.
YOU KNOW...
I THINK I COULD...
DO SOMETHING WITH THAT.
WHY AM I DOING THIS?
AM I... SCULPTING?
THAT'S... ODD.
I'VE NEVER SCULPTED A DAMN THING IN MY ENTIRE LIFE.

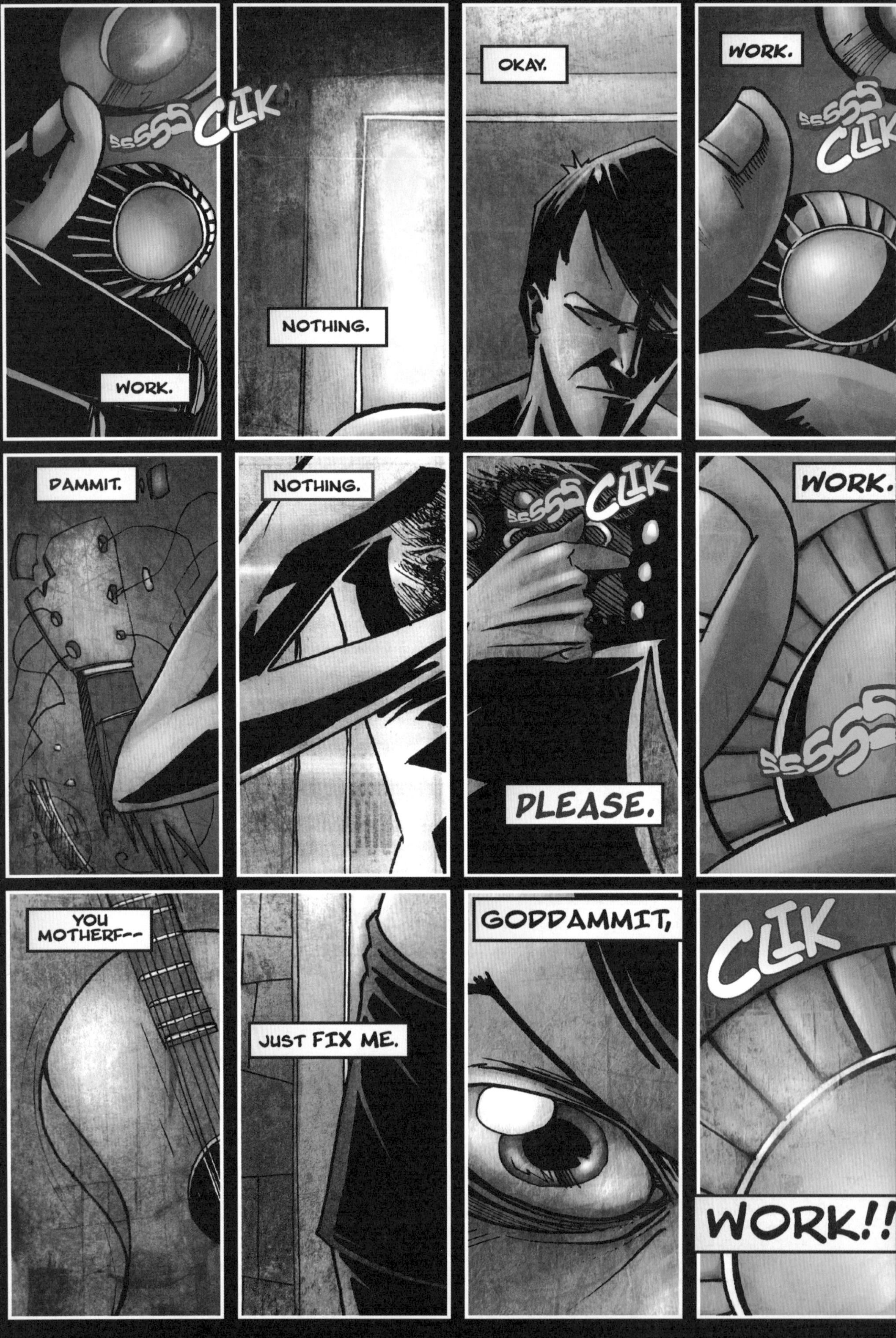

sssss CLIK
WORK.
NOTHING.
OKAY.
WORK.
sssss CLIK
DAMMIT.
NOTHING.
sssss CLIK
PLEASE.
WORK.
sssss
YOU MOTHERF--
JUST FIX ME.
GODDAMMIT,
CLIK
WORK!!

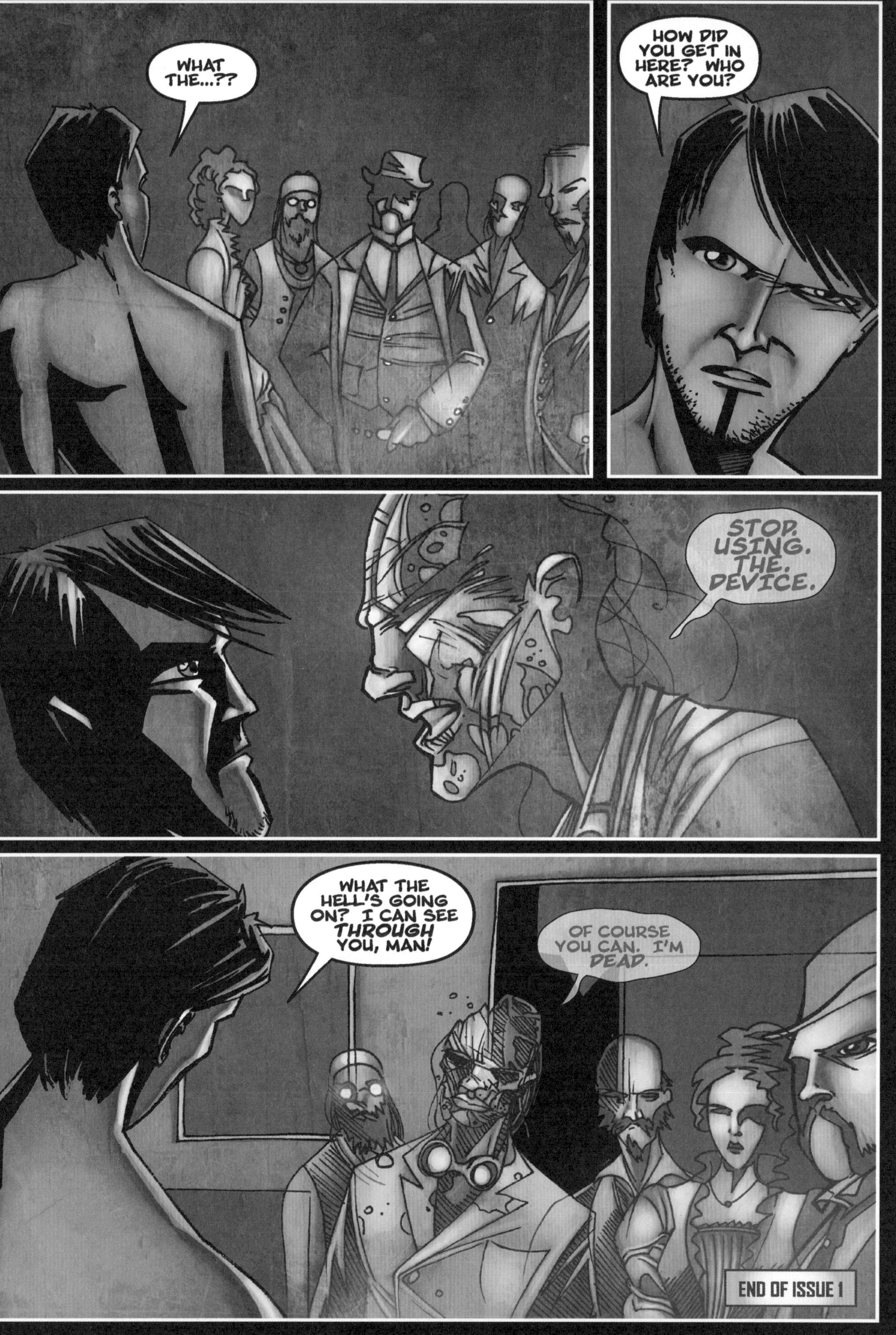
WHAT THE...??
HOW DID YOU GET IN HERE? WHO ARE YOU?
STOP. USING. THE. DEVICE.
WHAT THE HELL'S GOING ON? I CAN SEE *THROUGH* YOU, MAN!
OF COURSE YOU CAN. I'M *DEAD*.
END OF ISSUE 1

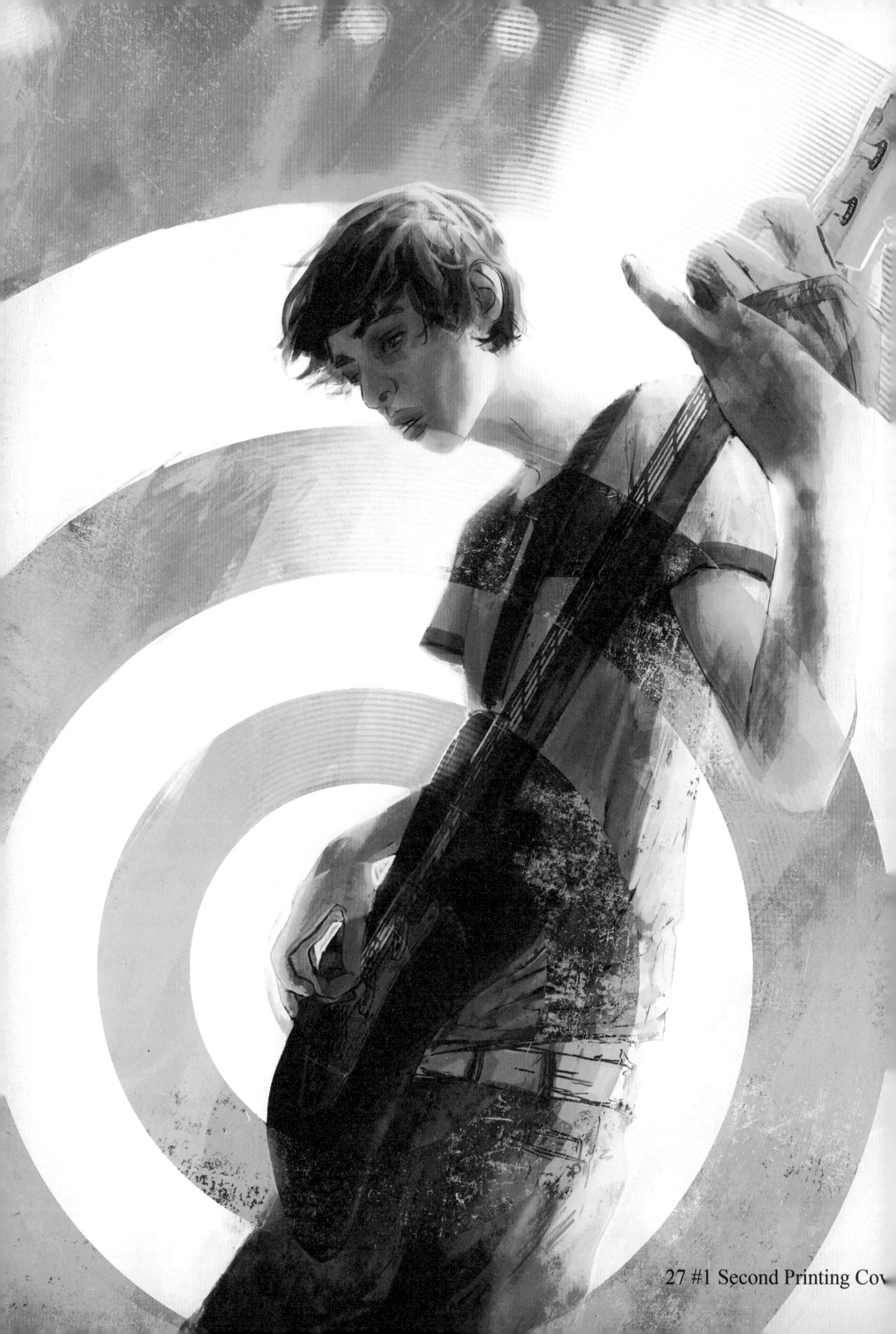

27 #1 Second Printing Cov

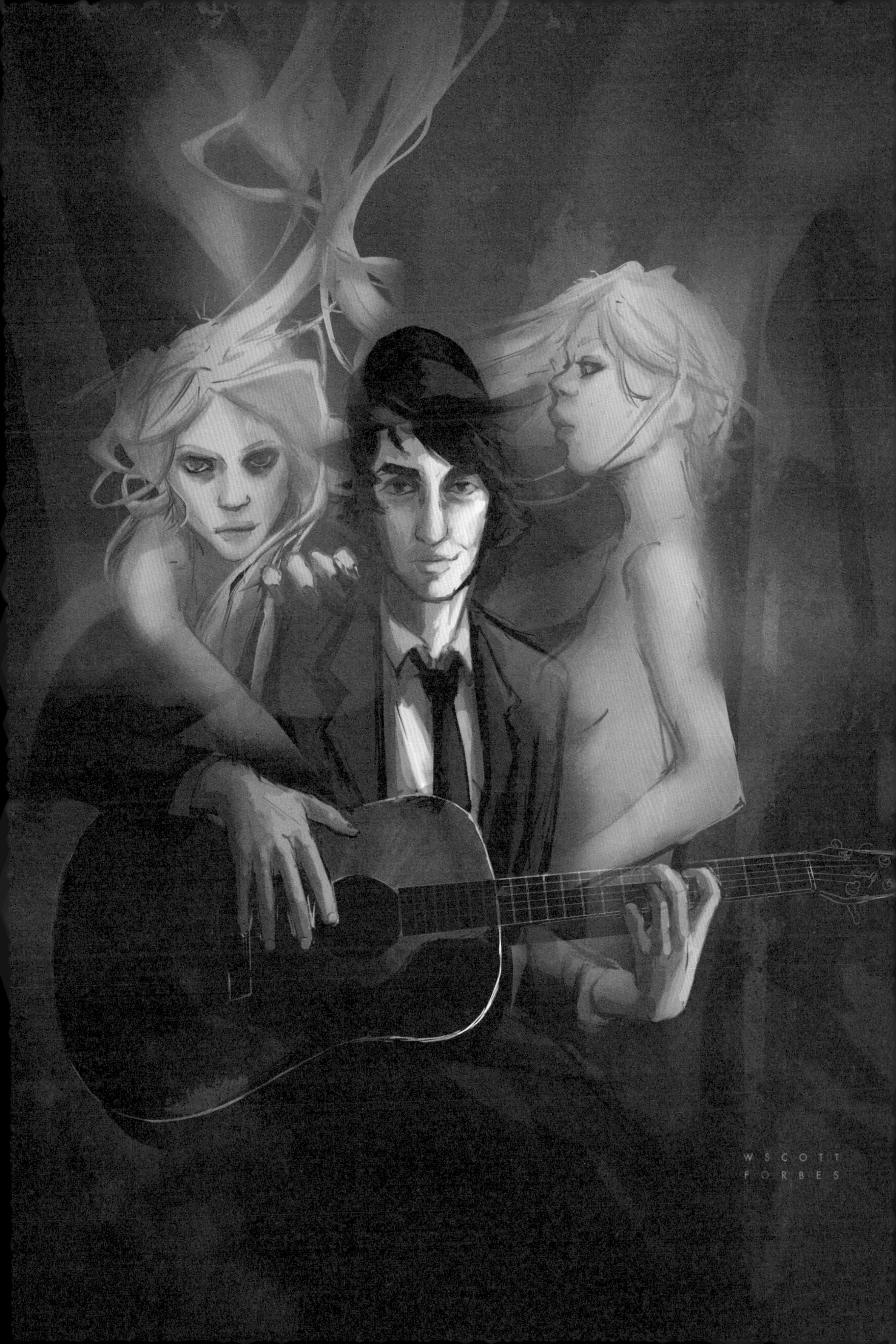
W SCOTT
FORBES

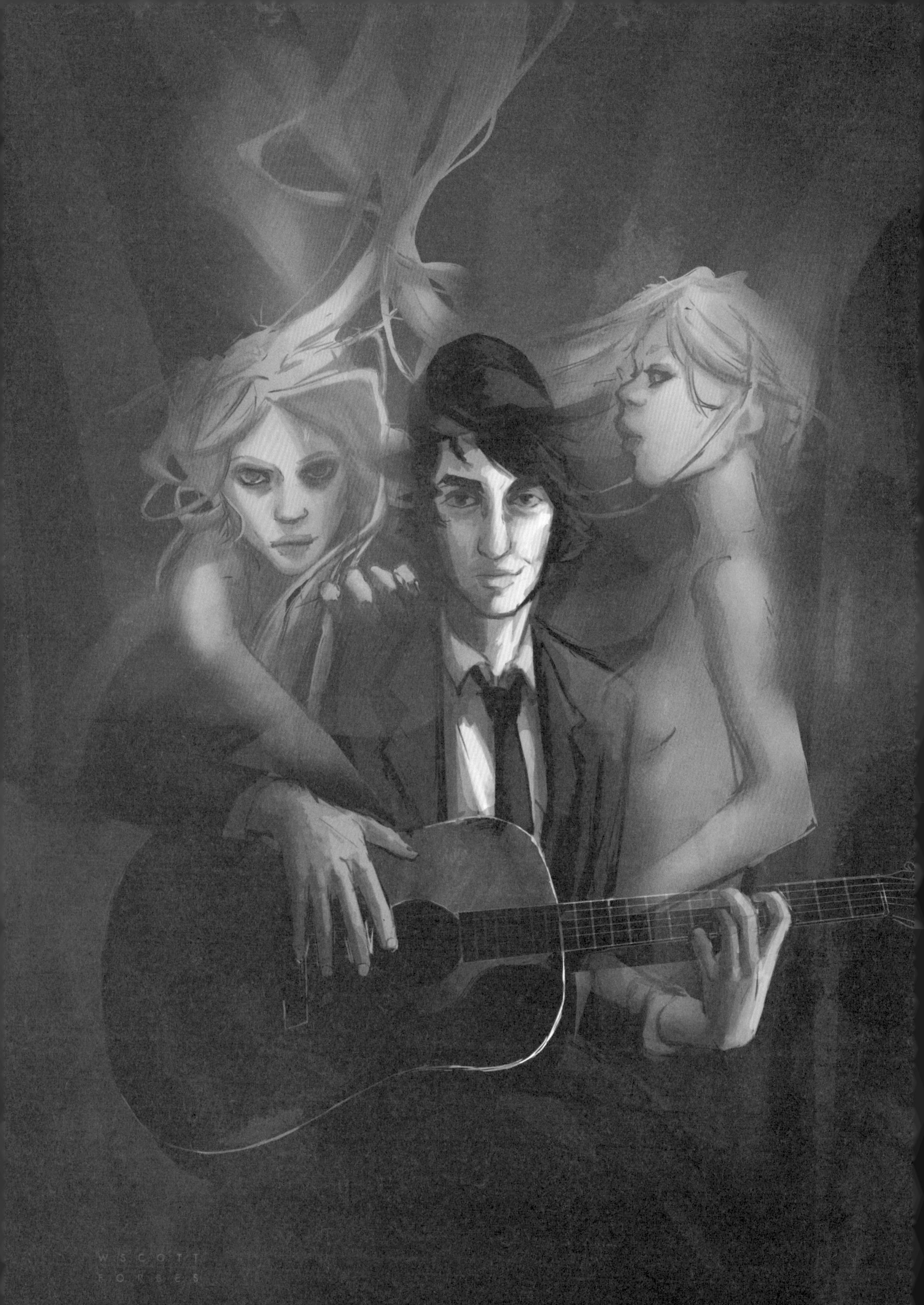
WSCOTT
FORBES

27 #2 Second Printing co

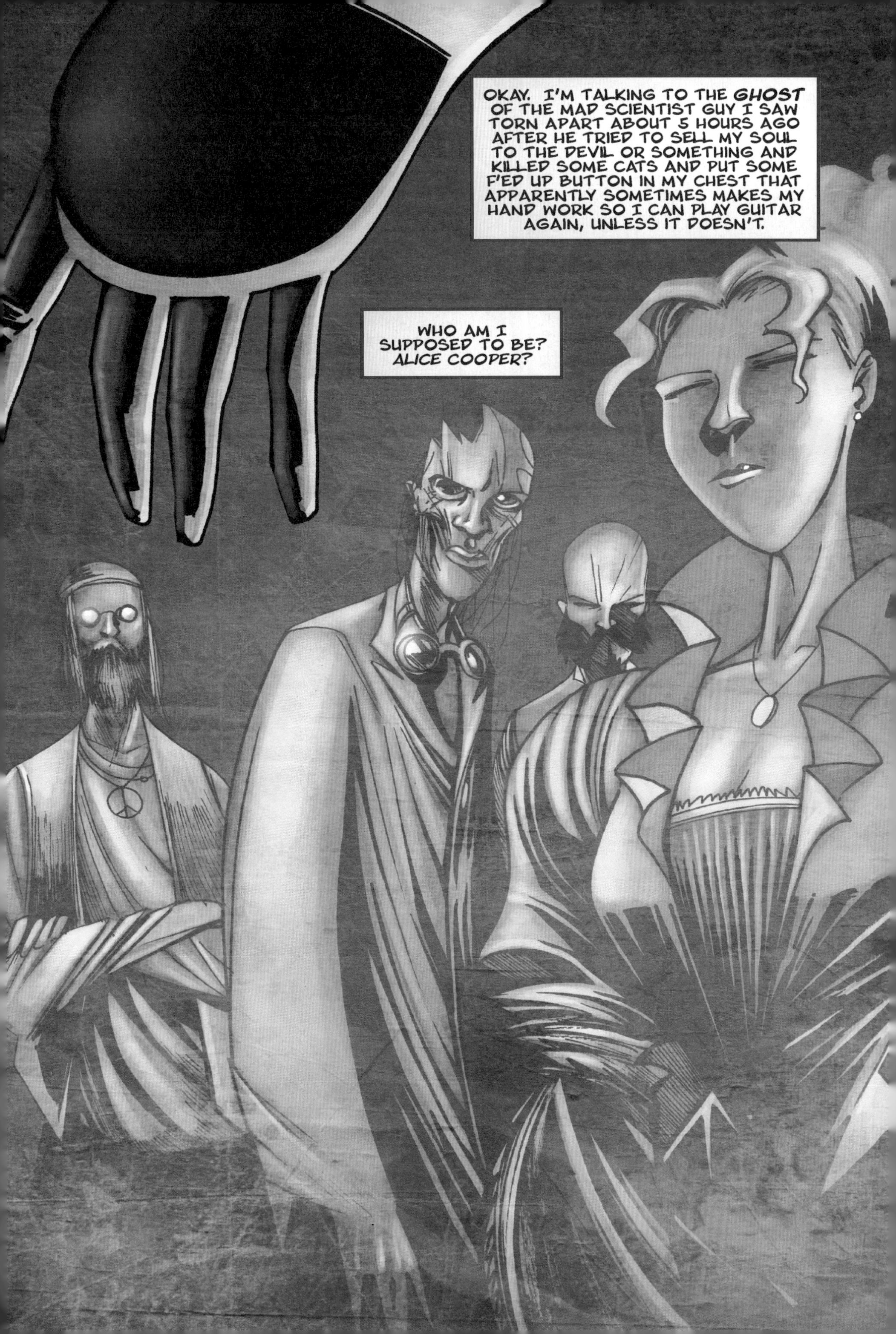

OKAY. I'M TALKING TO THE GHOST OF THE MAD SCIENTIST GUY I SAW TORN APART ABOUT 5 HOURS AGO AFTER HE TRIED TO SELL MY SOUL TO THE DEVIL OR SOMETHING AND KILLED SOME CATS AND PUT SOME F'ED UP BUTTON IN MY CHEST THAT APPARENTLY SOMETIMES MAKES MY HAND WORK SO I CAN PLAY GUITAR AGAIN, UNLESS IT DOESN'T.
WHO AM I SUPPOSED TO BE? ALICE COOPER?

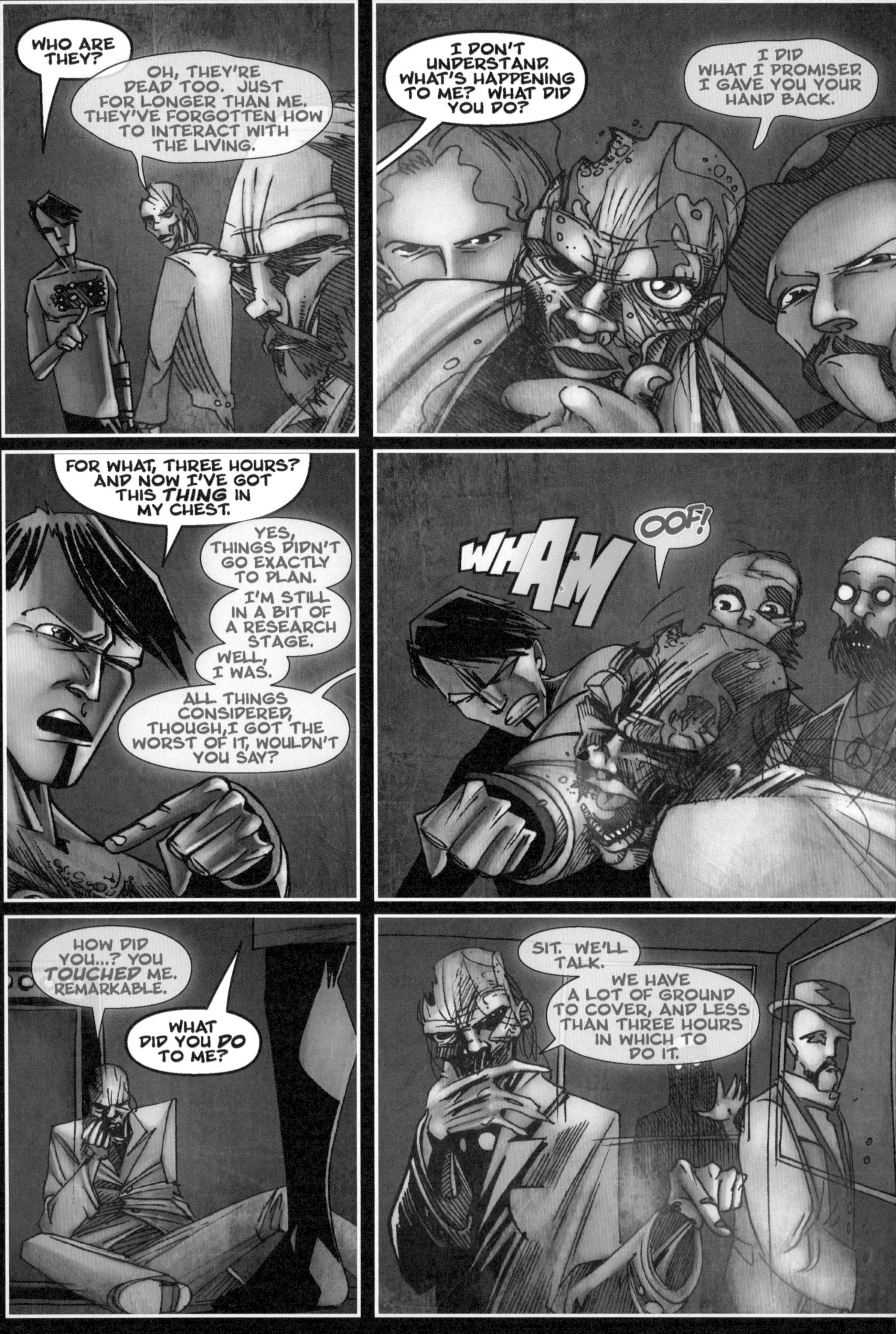
WHO ARE THEY?
OH, THEY'RE DEAD TOO. JUST FOR LONGER THAN ME. THEY'VE FORGOTTEN HOW TO INTERACT WITH THE LIVING.
I DON'T UNDERSTAND. WHAT'S HAPPENING TO ME? WHAT DID YOU DO?
I DID WHAT I PROMISED. I GAVE YOU YOUR HAND BACK.
FOR WHAT, THREE HOURS? AND NOW I'VE GOT THIS *THING* IN MY CHEST.
YES, THINGS DIDN'T GO EXACTLY TO PLAN.
I'M STILL IN A BIT OF A RESEARCH STAGE.
WELL, I WAS.
ALL THINGS CONSIDERED, THOUGH, I GOT THE WORST OF IT, WOULDN'T YOU SAY?
WHAM
OOF!
HOW DID YOU...? YOU *TOUCHED* ME. REMARKABLE.
WHAT DID YOU *DO* TO ME?
SIT. WE'LL TALK.
WE HAVE A LOT OF GROUND TO COVER, AND LESS THAN THREE HOURS IN WHICH TO DO IT.

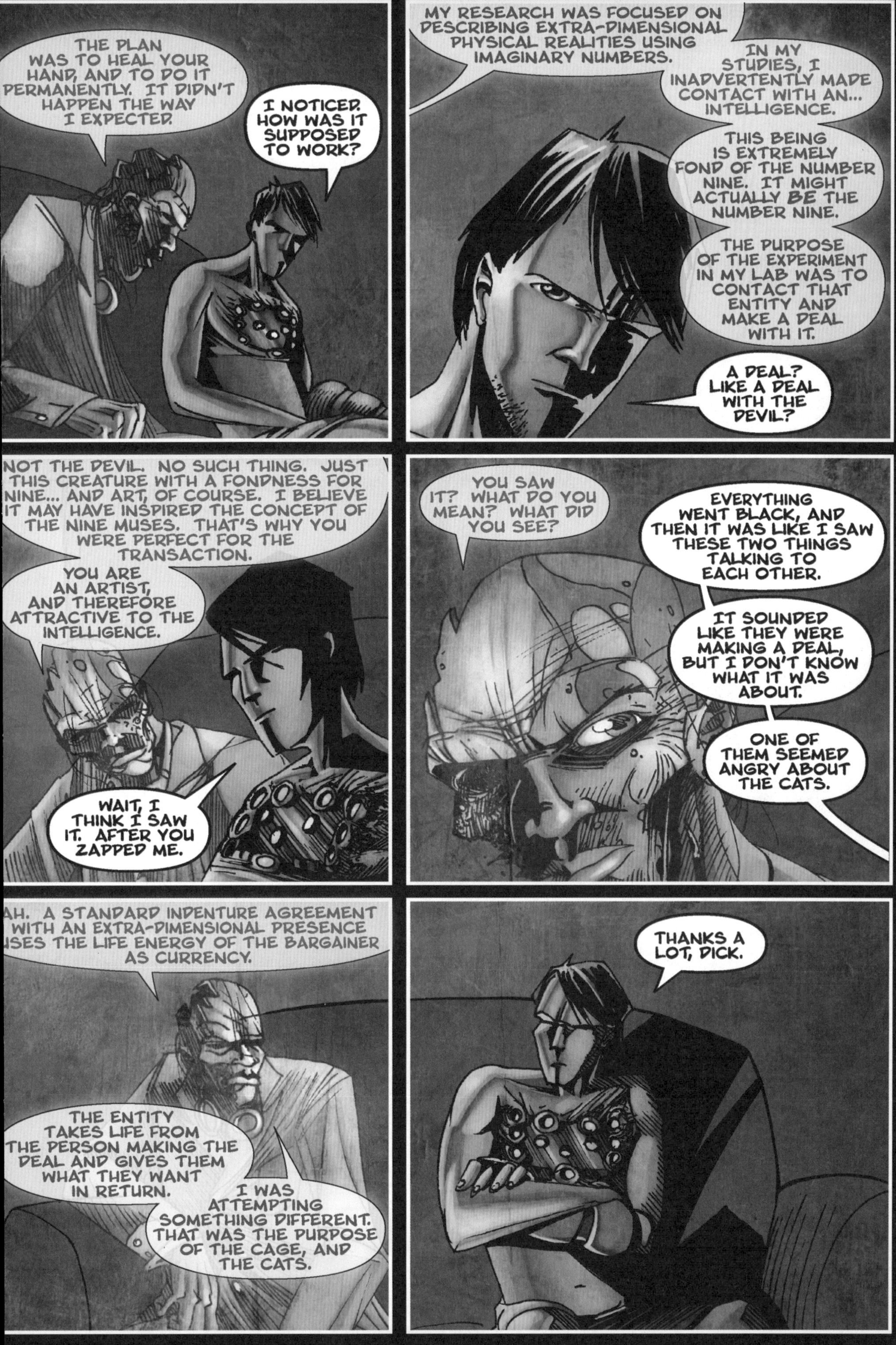

THE PLAN WAS TO HEAL YOUR HAND, AND TO DO IT PERMANENTLY. IT DIDN'T HAPPEN THE WAY I EXPECTED.
I NOTICED. HOW WAS IT SUPPOSED TO WORK?
MY RESEARCH WAS FOCUSED ON DESCRIBING EXTRA-DIMENSIONAL PHYSICAL REALITIES USING IMAGINARY NUMBERS.
IN MY STUDIES, I INADVERTENTLY MADE CONTACT WITH AN... INTELLIGENCE.
THIS BEING IS EXTREMELY FOND OF THE NUMBER NINE. IT MIGHT ACTUALLY *BE* THE NUMBER NINE.
THE PURPOSE OF THE EXPERIMENT IN MY LAB WAS TO CONTACT THAT ENTITY AND MAKE A DEAL WITH IT.
A DEAL? LIKE A DEAL WITH THE DEVIL?
NOT THE DEVIL. NO SUCH THING. JUST THIS CREATURE WITH A FONDNESS FOR NINE... AND ART, OF COURSE. I BELIEVE IT MAY HAVE INSPIRED THE CONCEPT OF THE NINE MUSES. THAT'S WHY YOU WERE PERFECT FOR THE TRANSACTION.
YOU ARE AN ARTIST, AND THEREFORE ATTRACTIVE TO THE INTELLIGENCE.
WAIT, I THINK I SAW IT. AFTER YOU ZAPPED ME.
YOU SAW IT? WHAT DO YOU MEAN? WHAT DID YOU SEE?
EVERYTHING WENT BLACK, AND THEN IT WAS LIKE I SAW THESE TWO THINGS TALKING TO EACH OTHER.
IT SOUNDED LIKE THEY WERE MAKING A DEAL, BUT I DON'T KNOW WHAT IT WAS ABOUT.
ONE OF THEM SEEMED ANGRY ABOUT THE CATS.
AH. A STANDARD INDENTURE AGREEMENT WITH AN EXTRA-DIMENSIONAL PRESENCE USES THE LIFE ENERGY OF THE BARGAINER AS CURRENCY.
THE ENTITY TAKES LIFE FROM THE PERSON MAKING THE DEAL AND GIVES THEM WHAT THEY WANT IN RETURN.
I WAS ATTEMPTING SOMETHING DIFFERENT. THAT WAS THE PURPOSE OF THE CAGE, AND THE CATS.
THANKS A LOT, DICK.

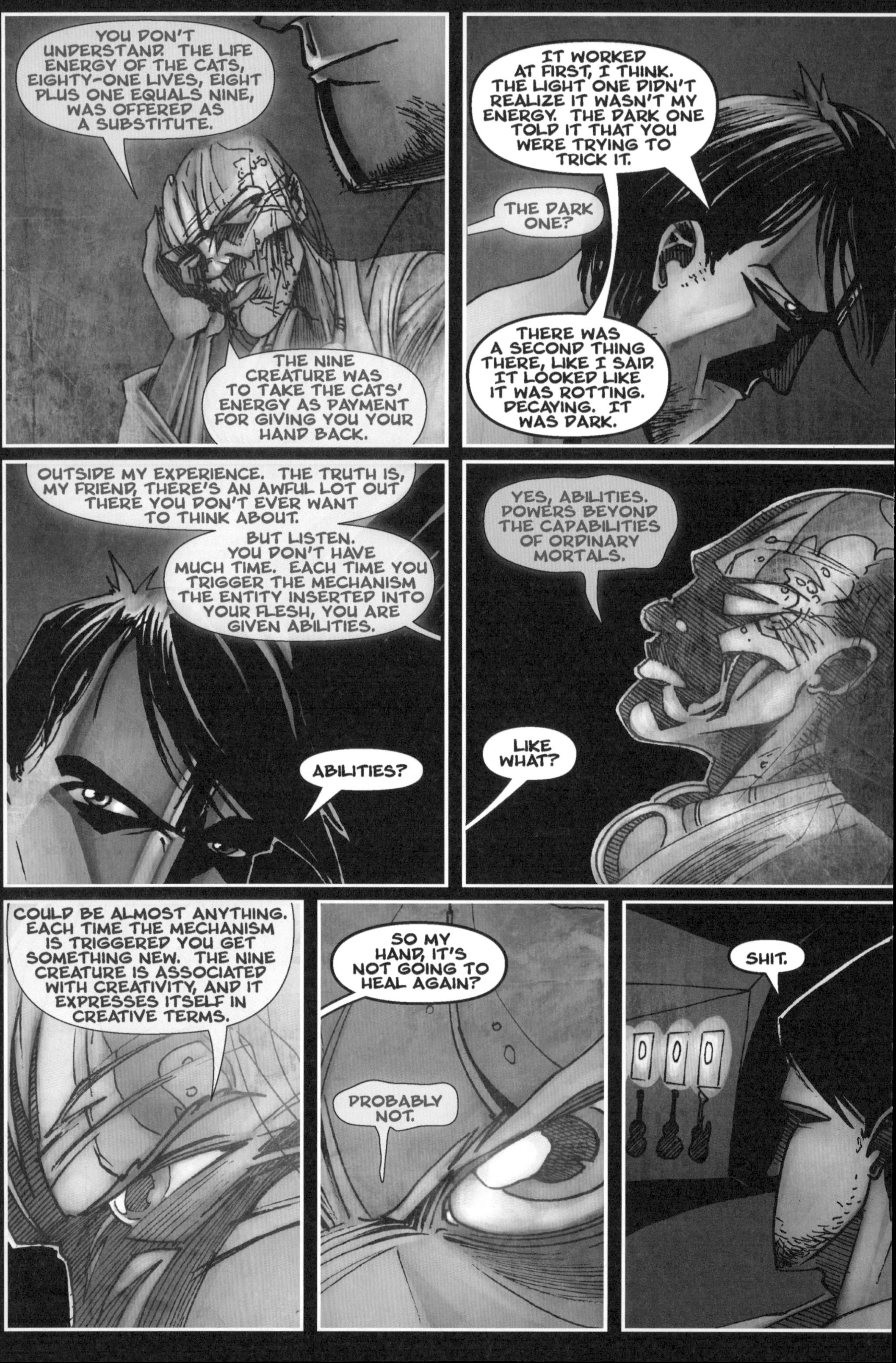
YOU DON'T UNDERSTAND. THE LIFE ENERGY OF THE CATS, EIGHTY-ONE LIVES, EIGHT PLUS ONE EQUALS NINE, WAS OFFERED AS A SUBSTITUTE.
THE NINE CREATURE WAS TO TAKE THE CATS' ENERGY AS PAYMENT FOR GIVING YOU YOUR HAND BACK.
IT WORKED AT FIRST, I THINK. THE LIGHT ONE DIDN'T REALIZE IT WASN'T MY ENERGY. THE DARK ONE TOLD IT THAT YOU WERE TRYING TO TRICK IT.
THE DARK ONE?
THERE WAS A SECOND THING THERE, LIKE I SAID. IT LOOKED LIKE IT WAS ROTTING. DECAYING. IT WAS DARK.
OUTSIDE MY EXPERIENCE. THE TRUTH IS, MY FRIEND, THERE'S AN AWFUL LOT OUT THERE YOU DON'T EVER WANT TO THINK ABOUT.
BUT LISTEN. YOU DON'T HAVE MUCH TIME. EACH TIME YOU TRIGGER THE MECHANISM THE ENTITY INSERTED INTO YOUR FLESH, YOU ARE GIVEN ABILITIES.
ABILITIES?
YES, ABILITIES. POWERS BEYOND THE CAPABILITIES OF ORDINARY MORTALS.
LIKE WHAT?
COULD BE ALMOST ANYTHING. EACH TIME THE MECHANISM IS TRIGGERED YOU GET SOMETHING NEW. THE NINE CREATURE IS ASSOCIATED WITH CREATIVITY, AND IT EXPRESSES ITSELF IN CREATIVE TERMS.
SO MY HAND, IT'S NOT GOING TO HEAL AGAIN?
PROBABLY NOT.
SHIT.

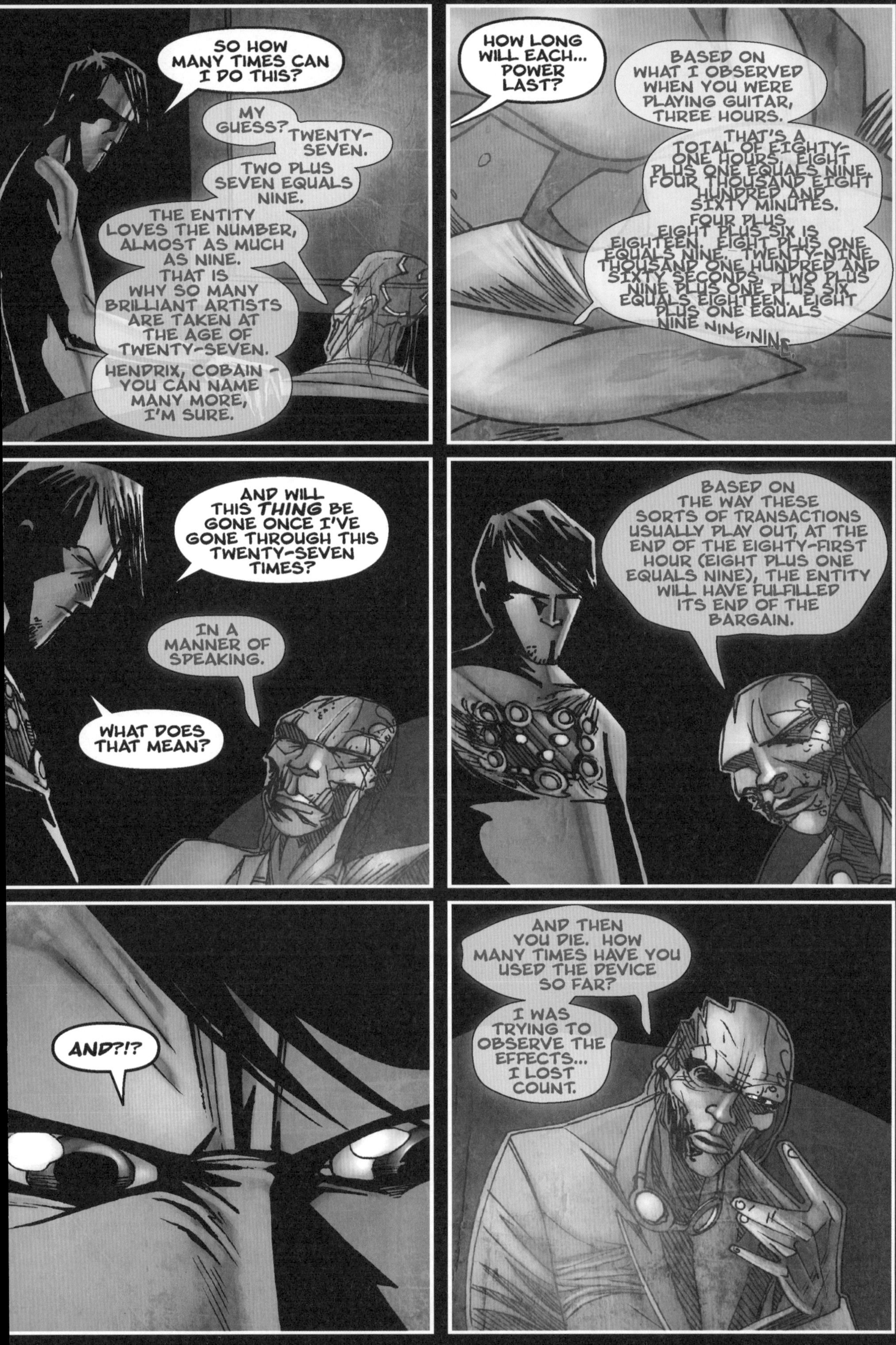
SO HOW MANY TIMES CAN I DO THIS?
MY GUESS? TWENTY-SEVEN.
TWO PLUS SEVEN EQUALS NINE.
THE ENTITY LOVES THE NUMBER, ALMOST AS MUCH AS NINE.
THAT IS WHY SO MANY BRILLIANT ARTISTS ARE TAKEN AT THE AGE OF TWENTY-SEVEN.
HENDRIX, COBAIN - YOU CAN NAME MANY MORE, I'M SURE.
HOW LONG WILL EACH... POWER LAST?
BASED ON WHAT I OBSERVED WHEN YOU WERE PLAYING GUITAR, THREE HOURS.
THAT'S A TOTAL OF EIGHTY-ONE HOURS. EIGHT PLUS ONE EQUALS NINE. FOUR THOUSAND EIGHT HUNDRED AND SIXTY MINUTES.
FOUR PLUS EIGHT PLUS SIX IS EIGHTEEN. EIGHT PLUS ONE EQUALS NINE. TWENTY-NINE THOUSAND ONE HUNDRED AND SIXTY SECONDS. TWO PLUS NINE PLUS ONE PLUS SIX EQUALS EIGHTEEN. EIGHT PLUS ONE EQUALS NINE NINE NINE NINE.
AND WILL THIS *THING* BE GONE ONCE I'VE GONE THROUGH THIS TWENTY-SEVEN TIMES?
IN A MANNER OF SPEAKING.
WHAT DOES THAT MEAN?
BASED ON THE WAY THESE SORTS OF TRANSACTIONS USUALLY PLAY OUT, AT THE END OF THE EIGHTY-FIRST HOUR (EIGHT PLUS ONE EQUALS NINE), THE ENTITY WILL HAVE FULFILLED ITS END OF THE BARGAIN.
AND?!?
AND THEN YOU DIE. HOW MANY TIMES HAVE YOU USED THE DEVICE SO FAR?
I WAS TRYING TO OBSERVE THE EFFECTS... I LOST COUNT.

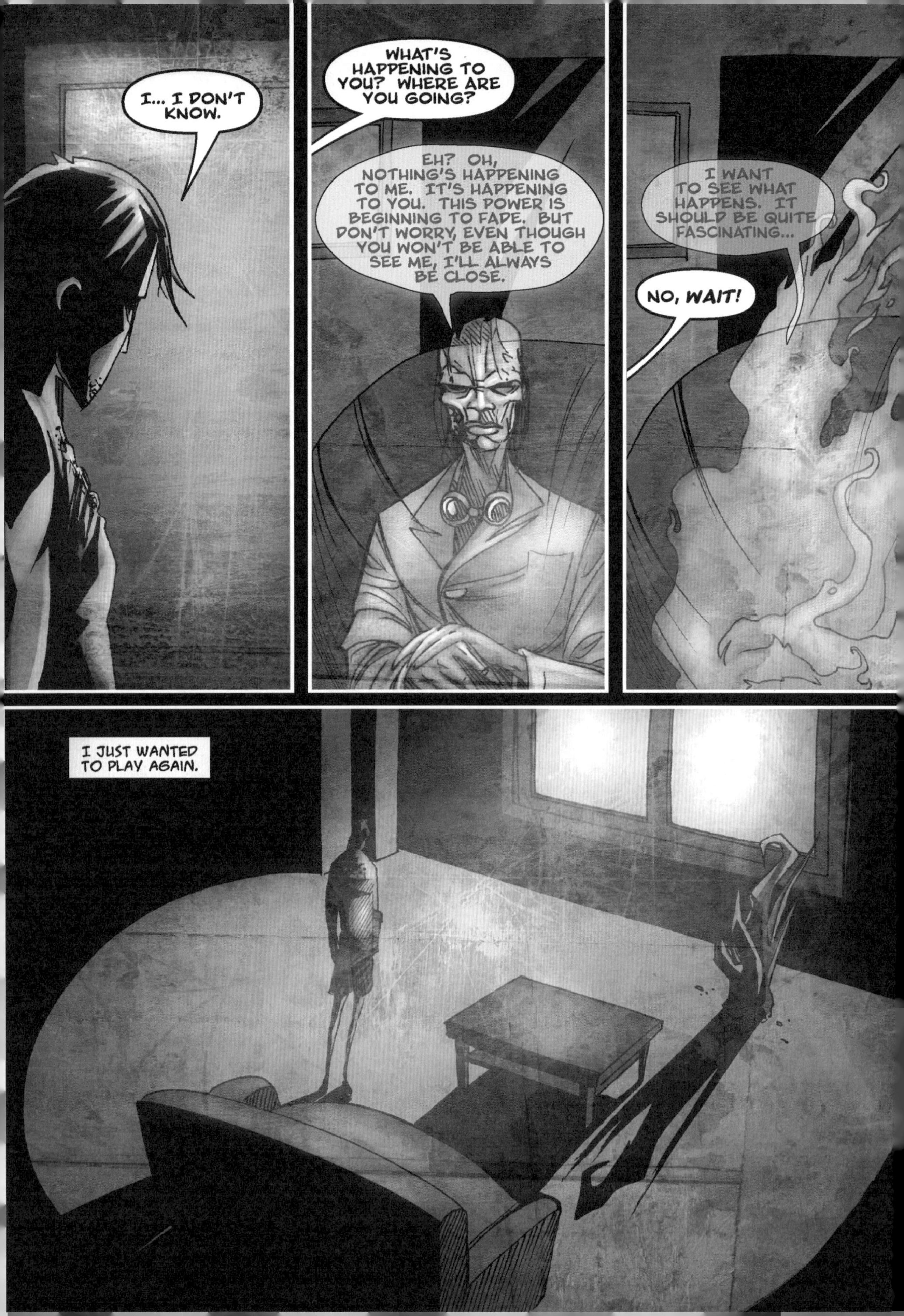

I... I DON'T KNOW.
WHAT'S HAPPENING TO YOU? WHERE ARE YOU GOING?
EH? OH, NOTHING'S HAPPENING TO ME. IT'S HAPPENING TO YOU. THIS POWER IS BEGINNING TO FADE. BUT DON'T WORRY, EVEN THOUGH YOU WON'T BE ABLE TO SEE ME, I'LL ALWAYS BE CLOSE.
I WANT TO SEE WHAT HAPPENS. IT SHOULD BE QUITE FASCINATING...
NO, WAIT!
I JUST WANTED TO PLAY AGAIN.

OKAY.

ONE.

TWO.

THREE.

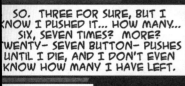

SO. THREE FOR SURE, BUT I KNOW I PUSHED IT... HOW MANY... SIX, SEVEN TIMES? MORE? TWENTY-SEVEN BUTTON-PUSHES UNTIL I DIE, AND I DON'T EVEN KNOW HOW MANY I HAVE LEFT.

NUMBERS... NINE. I'VE GOT TO FIGURE OUT THE NUMBERS.

BUZZ

MR. GARLAND? MAY WE COME UP? WE'D LIKE TO SPEAK WITH YOU FOR A MOMENT.

WHO ARE YOU?

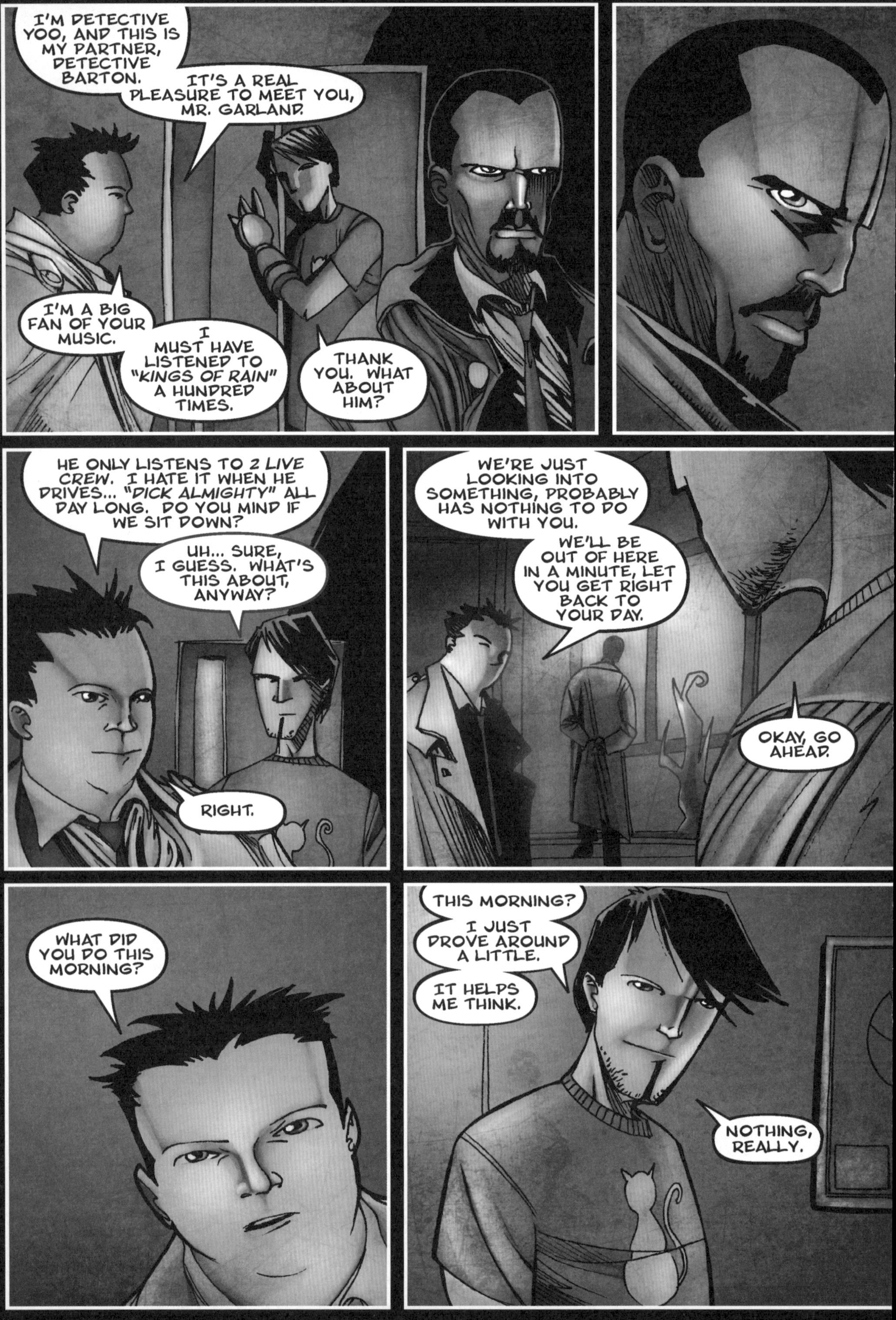
I'M DETECTIVE YOO, AND THIS IS MY PARTNER, DETECTIVE BARTON.
IT'S A REAL PLEASURE TO MEET YOU, MR. GARLAND.
I'M A BIG FAN OF YOUR MUSIC.
I MUST HAVE LISTENED TO "KINGS OF RAIN" A HUNDRED TIMES.
THANK YOU. WHAT ABOUT HIM?
HE ONLY LISTENS TO 2 LIVE CREW. I HATE IT WHEN HE DRIVES... "DICK ALMIGHTY" ALL DAY LONG. DO YOU MIND IF WE SIT DOWN?
UH... SURE, I GUESS. WHAT'S THIS ABOUT, ANYWAY?
RIGHT.
WE'RE JUST LOOKING INTO SOMETHING, PROBABLY HAS NOTHING TO DO WITH YOU.
WE'LL BE OUT OF HERE IN A MINUTE, LET YOU GET RIGHT BACK TO YOUR DAY.
OKAY, GO AHEAD.
WHAT DID YOU DO THIS MORNING?
THIS MORNING?
I JUST DROVE AROUND A LITTLE.
IT HELPS ME THINK.
NOTHING, REALLY.

DRIVING?

THAT'S RIGHT. IN MY CAR.

YOU DIDN'T GET OUT, MAYBE WALK AROUND A LITTLE?

MAYBE, I DON'T KNOW, I MEAN... I MIGHT HAVE STOPPED TO GET A SODA OR SOMETHING.

YEAH, THAT MAKES SENSE. BECAUSE IT WOULD BE PRETTY WEIRD, YOU KNOW –

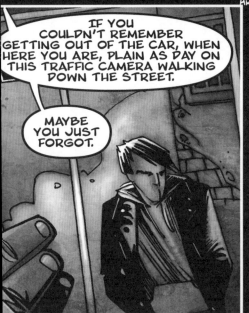

IF YOU COULDN'T REMEMBER GETTING OUT OF THE CAR, WHEN HERE YOU ARE, PLAIN AS DAY ON THIS TRAFFIC CAMERA WALKING DOWN THE STREET.

MAYBE YOU JUST FORGOT.

IS THERE SOME SORT OF PROBLEM? I DIDN'T REALIZE TAKING A WALK WAS...

OH, NO, NO PROBLEM. I'M NOT TRYING TO PUT YOU ON THE SPOT!

YOU JUST SAID YOU WERE DRIVING, BUT HERE YOU ARE WALKING – JUST WANT TO BE CLEAR.

LET ME GET TO THE POINT HERE.

SOMETHING HAPPENED DOWN IN THAT NEIGHBORHOOD EARLIER TODAY. IT'S MOSTLY EMPTY WAREHOUSES, JUST STORAGE.

DURING THE TIME OF THE INCIDENT, PRETTY MUCH THE ONLY PERSON WHO SHOWS UP ON ANY CAMS IN THE AREA IS YOU.

WHAT IS THAT GUY'S DEAL? JESUS.

DO YOU MIND, MAN? THAT'S MY BEDROOM.

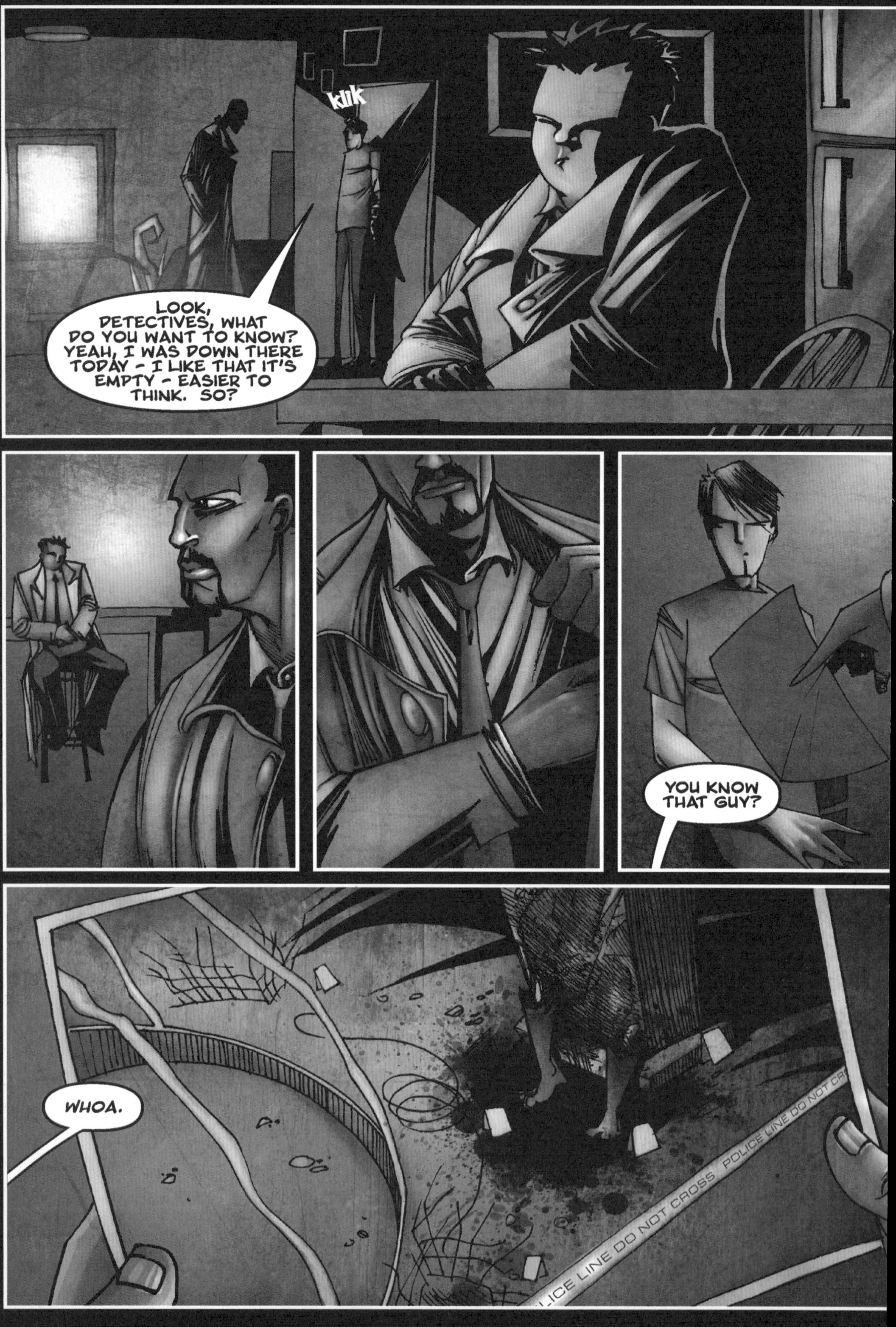
klik
LOOK, DETECTIVES, WHAT DO YOU WANT TO KNOW? YEAH, I WAS DOWN THERE TODAY - I LIKE THAT IT'S EMPTY - EASIER TO THINK. SO?
YOU KNOW THAT GUY?
WHOA.
POLICE LINE DO NOT CROSS

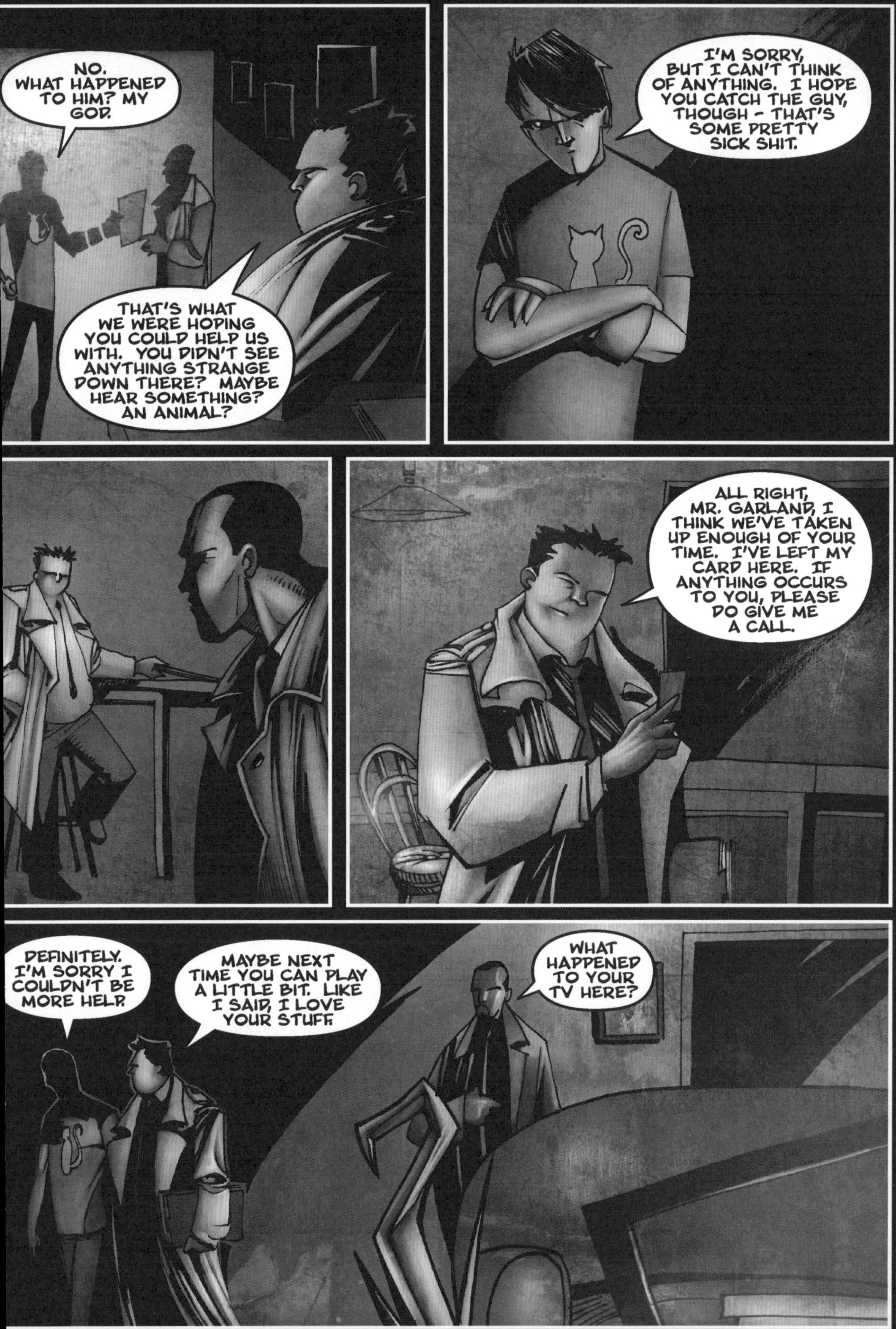
NO. WHAT HAPPENED TO HIM? MY GOD.
THAT'S WHAT WE WERE HOPING YOU COULD HELP US WITH. YOU DIDN'T SEE ANYTHING STRANGE DOWN THERE? MAYBE HEAR SOMETHING? AN ANIMAL?
I'M SORRY, BUT I CAN'T THINK OF ANYTHING. I HOPE YOU CATCH THE GUY, THOUGH - THAT'S SOME PRETTY SICK SHIT.
ALL RIGHT, MR. GARLAND, I THINK WE'VE TAKEN UP ENOUGH OF YOUR TIME. I'VE LEFT MY CARD HERE. IF ANYTHING OCCURS TO YOU, PLEASE DO GIVE ME A CALL.
DEFINITELY. I'M SORRY I COULDN'T BE MORE HELP.
MAYBE NEXT TIME YOU CAN PLAY A LITTLE BIT. LIKE I SAID, I LOVE YOUR STUFF.
WHAT HAPPENED TO YOUR TV HERE?

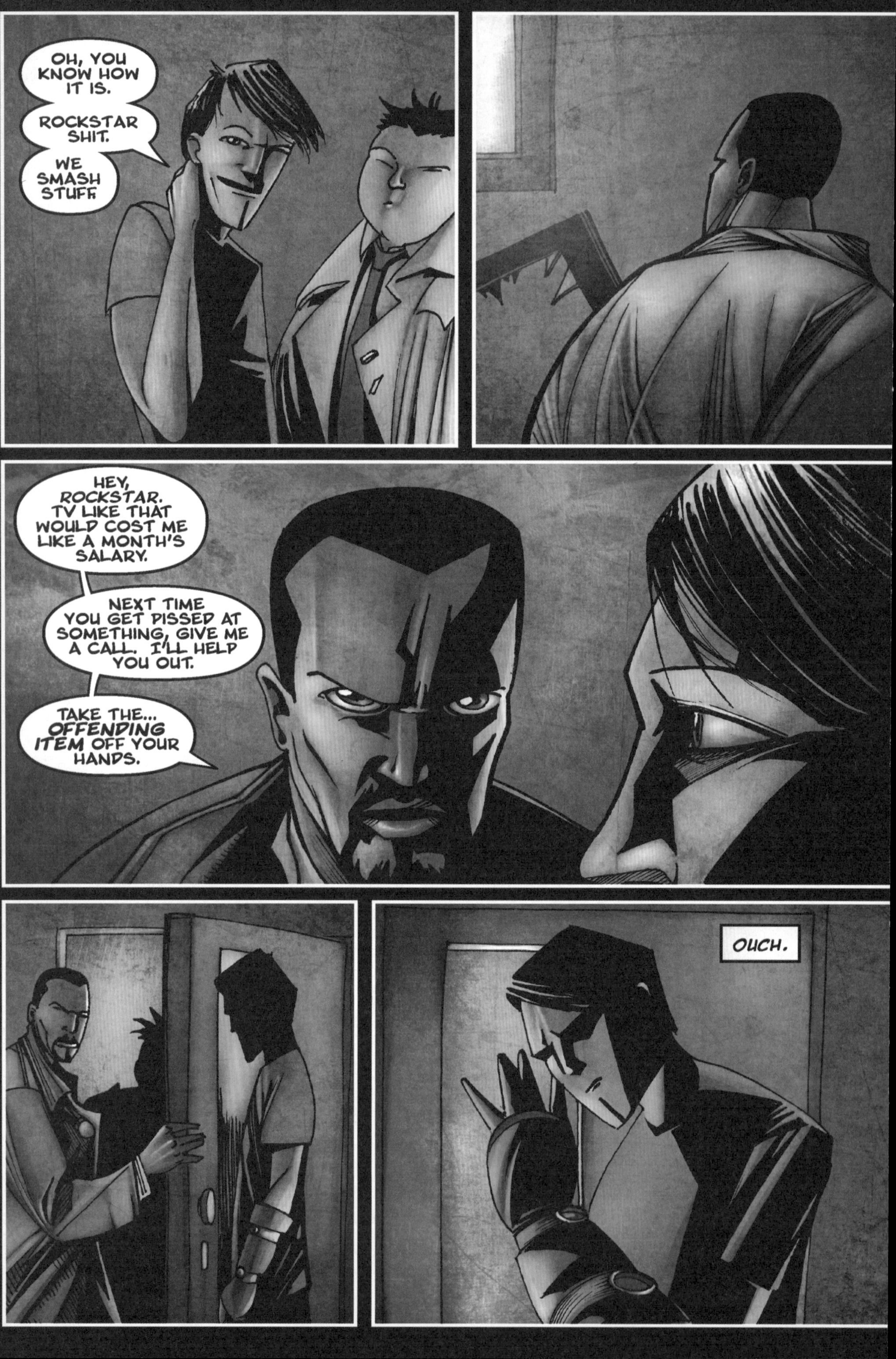
OH, YOU KNOW HOW IT IS.
ROCKSTAR SHIT.
WE SMASH STUFF.
HEY, ROCKSTAR. TV LIKE THAT WOULD COST ME LIKE A MONTH'S SALARY.
NEXT TIME YOU GET PISSED AT SOMETHING, GIVE ME A CALL. I'LL HELP YOU OUT.
TAKE THE... OFFENDING ITEM OFF YOUR HANDS.
OUCH.

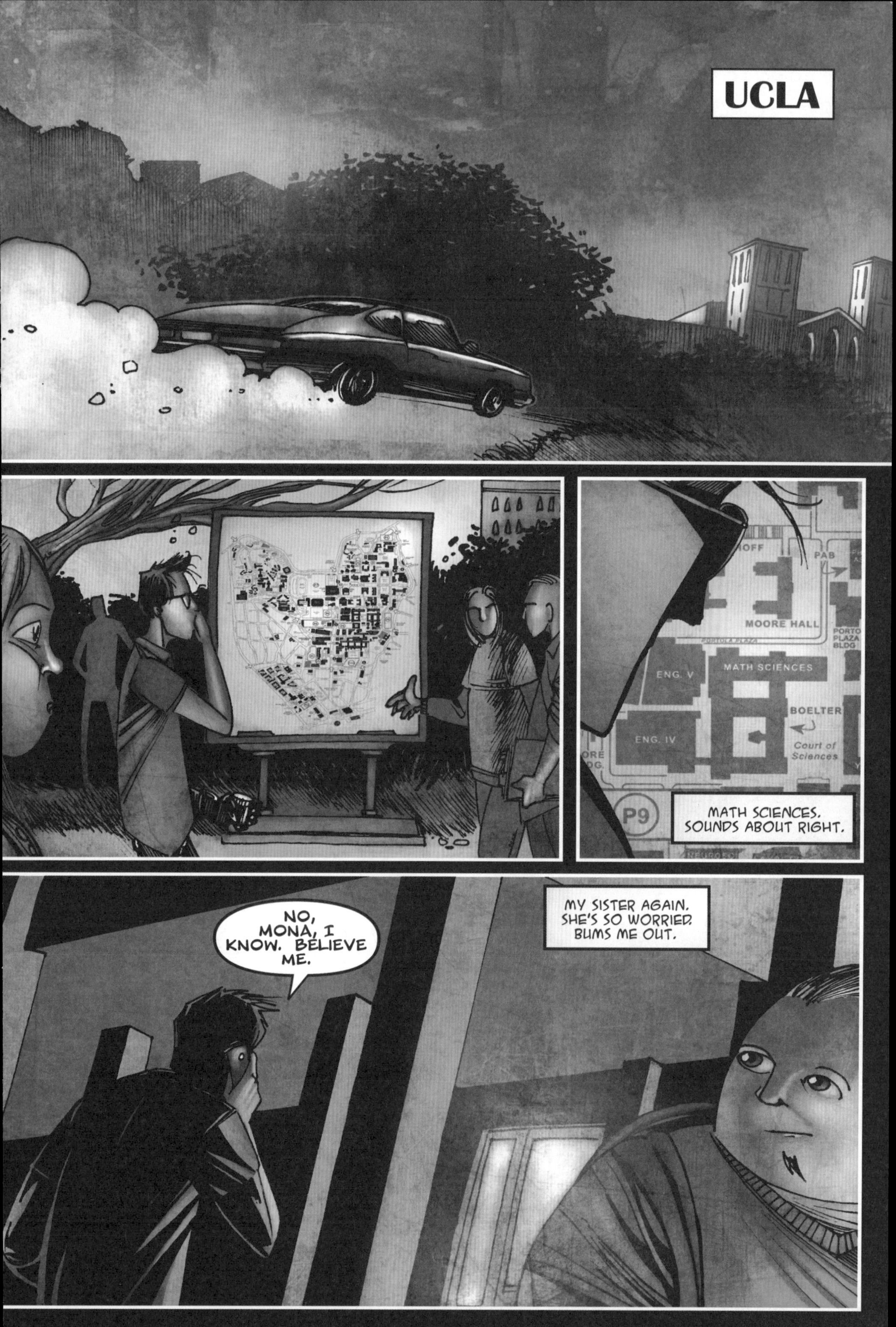
UCLA
PAB
MOORE HALL
PORTO PLAZA BLDG
ENG. V
MATH SCIENCES
BOELTER
ENG. IV
Court of Sciences
P9
MATH SCIENCES. SOUNDS ABOUT RIGHT.
NO, MONA, I KNOW. BELIEVE ME.
MY SISTER AGAIN. SHE'S SO WORRIED. BUMS ME OUT.

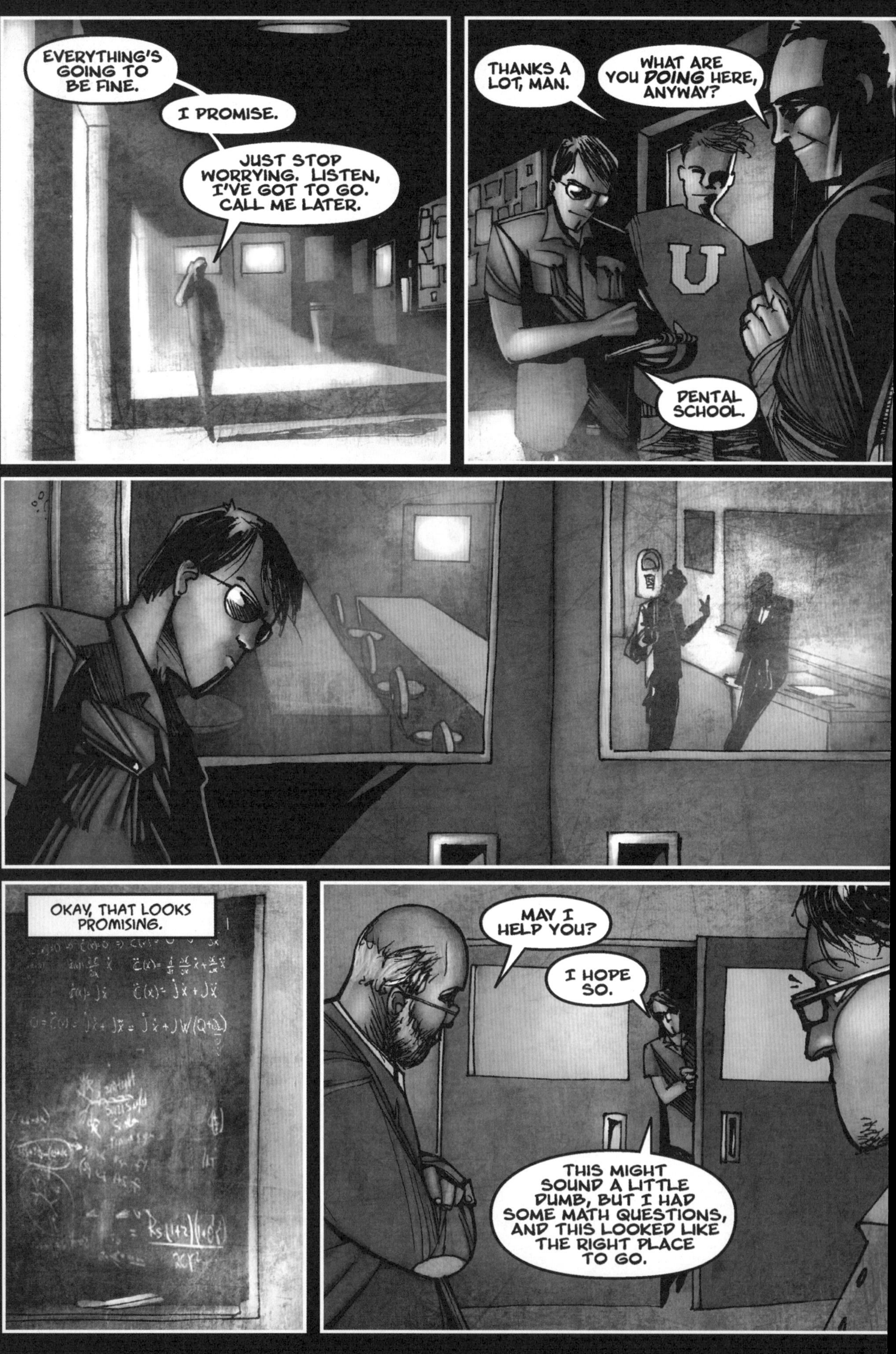
EVERYTHING'S GOING TO BE FINE.
I PROMISE.
JUST STOP WORRYING. LISTEN, I'VE GOT TO GO. CALL ME LATER.
THANKS A LOT, MAN.
WHAT ARE YOU DOING HERE, ANYWAY?
DENTAL SCHOOL.
U
OKAY, THAT LOOKS PROMISING.
MAY I HELP YOU?
I HOPE SO.
THIS MIGHT SOUND A LITTLE DUMB, BUT I HAD SOME MATH QUESTIONS, AND THIS LOOKED LIKE THE RIGHT PLACE TO GO.

ACTUALLY, THAT SOUNDED EXCEEDINGLY DUMB. ARE YOU A STUDENT HERE?

UH, PROFESSOR, THIS IS...

I'M NOT A STUDENT. I'M A MUSICIAN. BUT SOMETHING ODD HAPPENED TO ME, AND I THINK IT HAS TO DO WITH NUMBERS, AND SO I—

AH, I SEE. WELL, THIS ISN'T SOME SORT OF MATHEMATICAL SOUP KITCHEN, MY FRIEND.

MY ADVICE, MR. MUSICIAN — APPLY FOR ADMISSION TO UCLA.

IF YOU ARE SOMEHOW ACCEPTED, TAKE SIX SEMESTERS OF UNDERGRADUATE MATHEMATICS.

THEN, SHOW EXTRAORDINARY PROMISE IN THE FIELD OF QUANTUM DISSIPATIVE SYSTEMS, AND PERHAPS YOU WILL BE ACCEPTED AS A STUDENT FOR MY COURSE.

AT THAT POINT, YOU MAY ASK AS MANY QUESTIONS AS YOU WISH.

GOOD DAY.

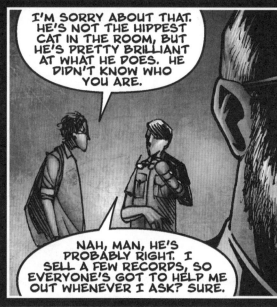

I'M SORRY ABOUT THAT. HE'S NOT THE HIPPEST CAT IN THE ROOM, BUT HE'S PRETTY BRILLIANT AT WHAT HE DOES. HE DIDN'T KNOW WHO YOU ARE.

NAH, MAN, HE'S PROBABLY RIGHT. I SELL A FEW RECORDS, SO EVERYONE'S GOT TO HELP ME OUT WHENEVER I ASK? SURE.

CAN I HELP YOU OUT, MAYBE? I'M A GRAD STUDENT — I'M NOT AS GOOD AS THE PROFESSOR, BUT I'VE SPENT ABOUT HALF A MILLION BUCKS ON CLASSES HERE. I SHOULD HAVE PICKED SOMETHING UP, RIGHT?

WHATEVER, SURE. LET'S SIT DOWN. I'LL TELL YOU ALL ABOUT IT.

UH, WHAT IF WE GO OUTSIDE, YOU KNOW, WALK AND TALK?

YOU WANT A LITTLE RIDE-ALONG CRED. THAT'S COOL. HELP ME OUT AND YOU'RE WELCOME TO AS MUCH GASH AS IT'LL GET YOU.

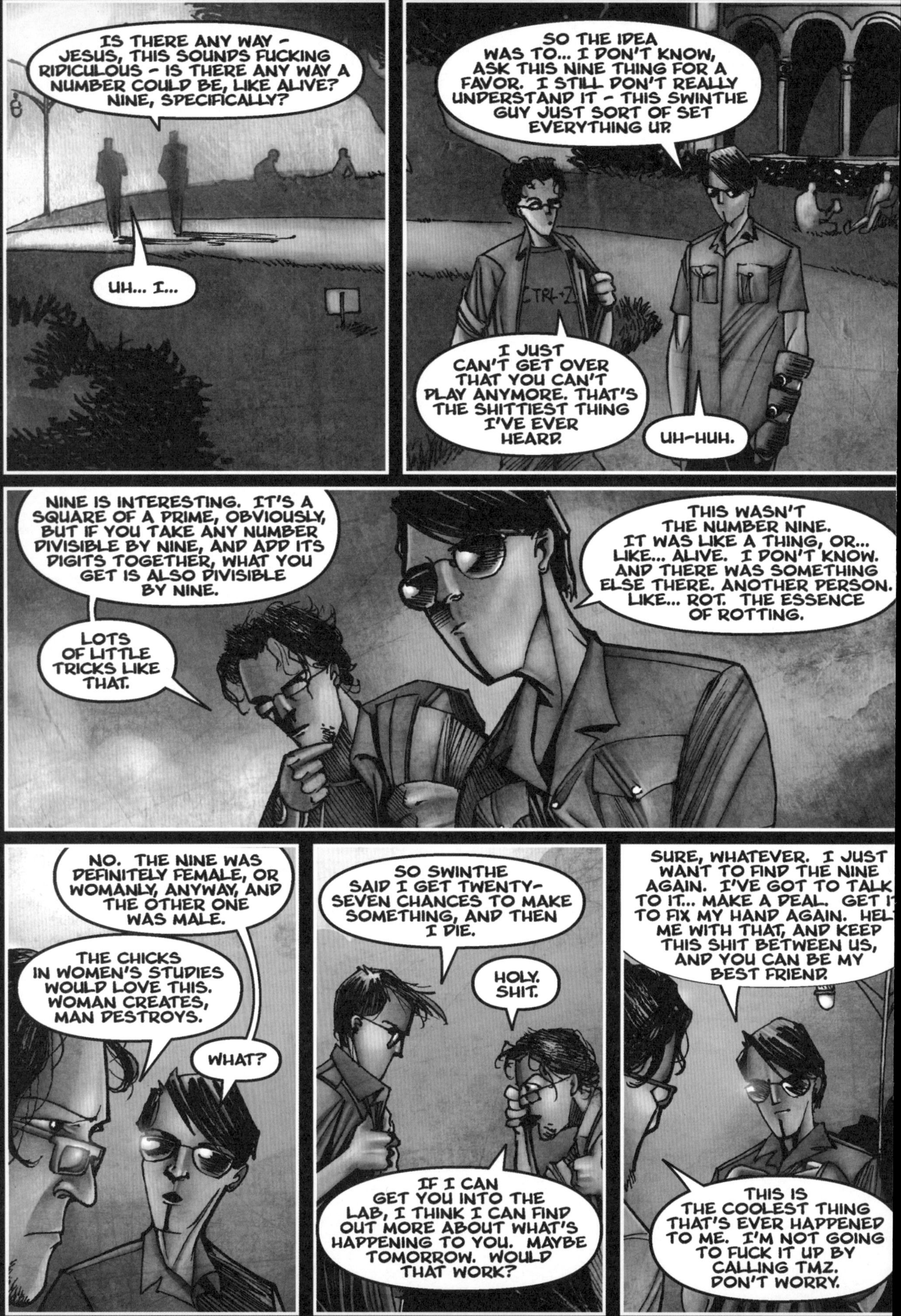
IS THERE ANY WAY - JESUS, THIS SOUNDS FUCKING RIDICULOUS - IS THERE ANY WAY A NUMBER COULD BE, LIKE ALIVE? NINE, SPECIFICALLY?
UH... I...
SO THE IDEA WAS TO... I DON'T KNOW, ASK THIS NINE THING FOR A FAVOR. I STILL DON'T REALLY UNDERSTAND IT - THIS SWINTHE GUY JUST SORT OF SET EVERYTHING UP.
CTRL+Z
I JUST CAN'T GET OVER THAT YOU CAN'T PLAY ANYMORE. THAT'S THE SHITTIEST THING I'VE EVER HEARD.
UH-HUH.
NINE IS INTERESTING. IT'S A SQUARE OF A PRIME, OBVIOUSLY, BUT IF YOU TAKE ANY NUMBER DIVISIBLE BY NINE, AND ADD ITS DIGITS TOGETHER, WHAT YOU GET IS ALSO DIVISIBLE BY NINE.
LOTS OF LITTLE TRICKS LIKE THAT.
THIS WASN'T THE NUMBER NINE. IT WAS LIKE A THING, OR... LIKE... ALIVE. I DON'T KNOW. AND THERE WAS SOMETHING ELSE THERE. ANOTHER PERSON. LIKE... ROT. THE ESSENCE OF ROTTING.
NO. THE NINE WAS DEFINITELY FEMALE, OR WOMANLY, ANYWAY, AND THE OTHER ONE WAS MALE.
THE CHICKS IN WOMEN'S STUDIES WOULD LOVE THIS. WOMAN CREATES, MAN DESTROYS.
WHAT?
SO SWINTHE SAID I GET TWENTY-SEVEN CHANCES TO MAKE SOMETHING, AND THEN I DIE.
HOLY. SHIT.
IF I CAN GET YOU INTO THE LAB, I THINK I CAN FIND OUT MORE ABOUT WHAT'S HAPPENING TO YOU. MAYBE TOMORROW. WOULD THAT WORK?
SURE, WHATEVER. I JUST WANT TO FIND THE NINE AGAIN. I'VE GOT TO TALK TO IT... MAKE A DEAL. GET IT TO FIX MY HAND AGAIN. HELP ME WITH THAT, AND KEEP THIS SHIT BETWEEN US, AND YOU CAN BE MY BEST FRIEND.
THIS IS THE COOLEST THING THAT'S EVER HAPPENED TO ME. I'M NOT GOING TO FUCK IT UP BY CALLING TMZ. DON'T WORRY.

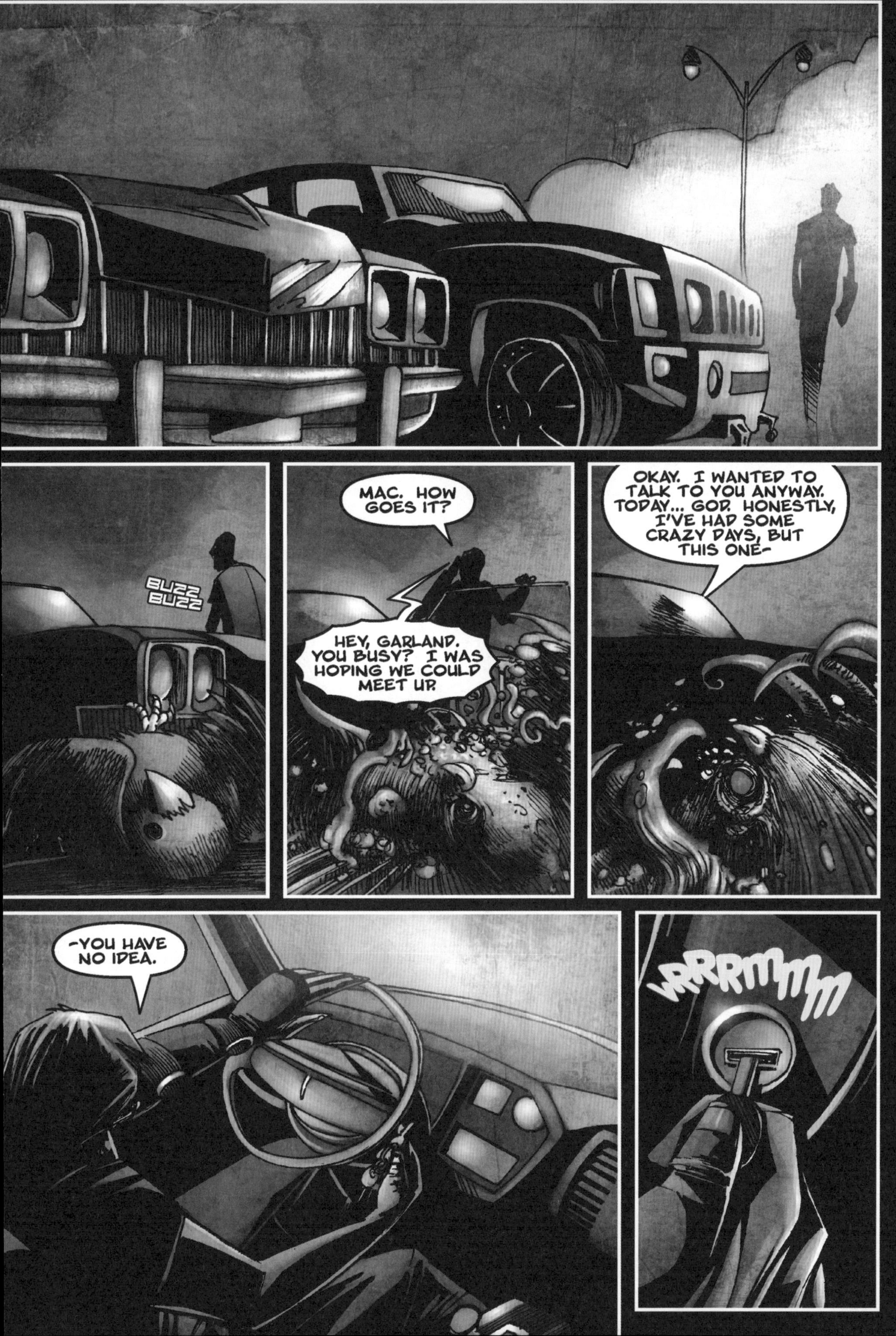
BUZZ BUZZ
MAC. HOW GOES IT?
HEY, GARLAND. YOU BUSY? I WAS HOPING WE COULD MEET UP.
OKAY. I WANTED TO TALK TO YOU ANYWAY. TODAY... GOD. HONESTLY, I'VE HAD SOME CRAZY DAYS, BUT THIS ONE-
-YOU HAVE NO IDEA.
VRRRMMMM

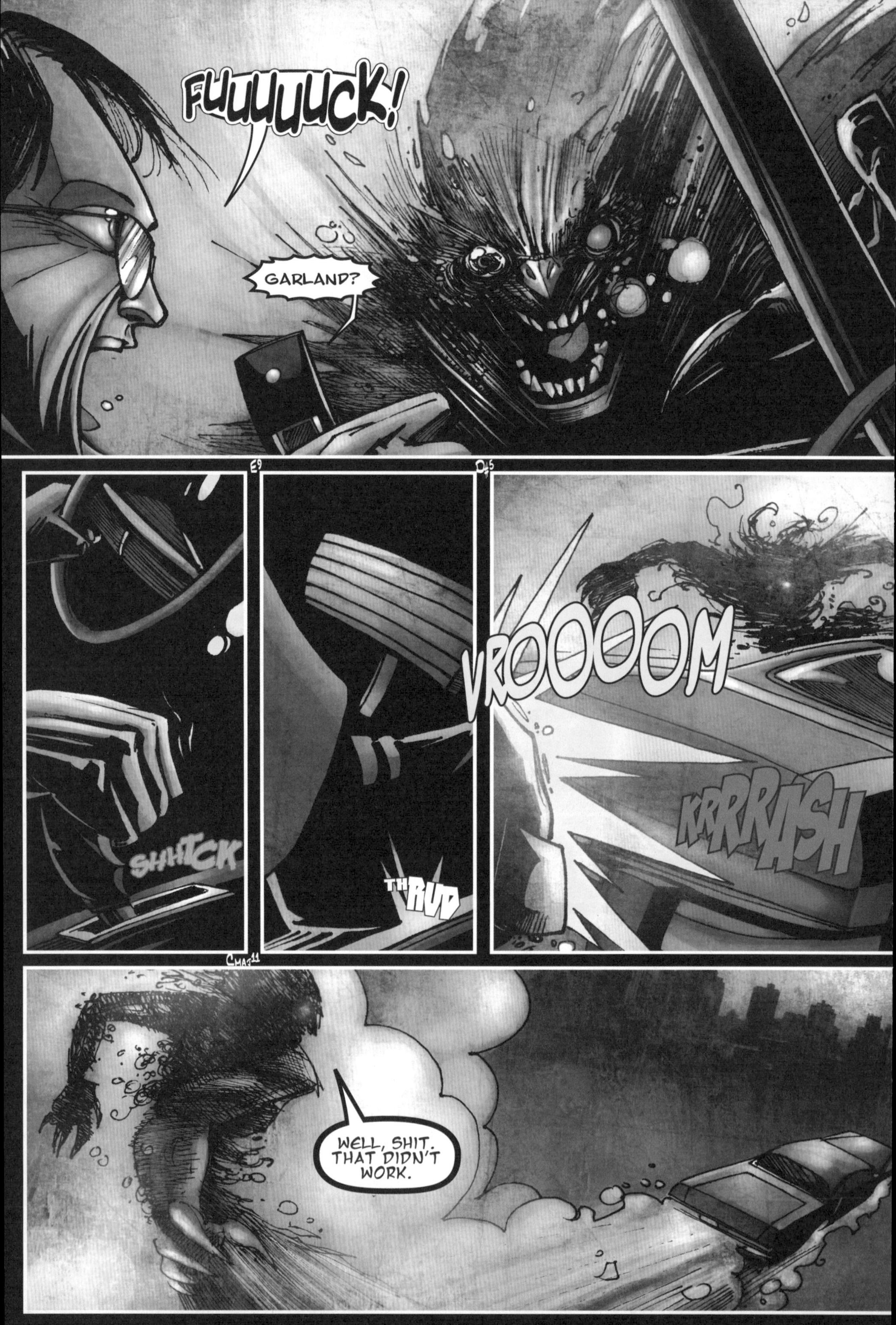
FUUUUUCK!
GARLAND?
SHHTCK
THRUD
VROOOOM
KRRRASH
WELL, SHIT. THAT DIDN'T WORK.

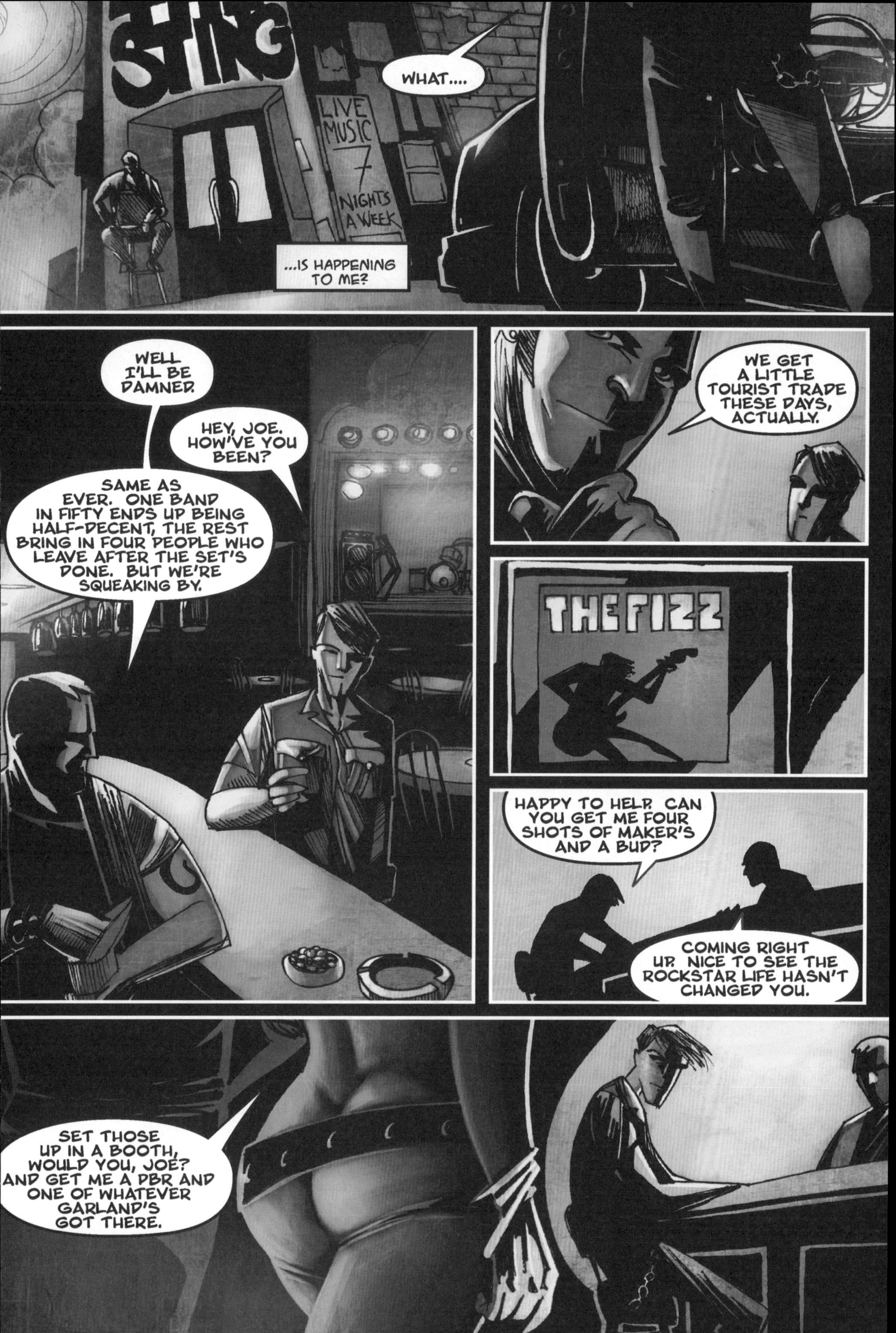

STING
LIVE MUSIC 7 NIGHTS A WEEK
WHAT....
...IS HAPPENING TO ME?
WELL I'LL BE DAMNED.
HEY, JOE. HOW'VE YOU BEEN?
SAME AS EVER. ONE BAND IN FIFTY ENDS UP BEING HALF-DECENT, THE REST BRING IN FOUR PEOPLE WHO LEAVE AFTER THE SET'S DONE. BUT WE'RE SQUEAKING BY.
WE GET A LITTLE TOURIST TRADE THESE DAYS, ACTUALLY.
THE FIZZ
HAPPY TO HELP. CAN YOU GET ME FOUR SHOTS OF MAKER'S AND A BUD?
COMING RIGHT UP. NICE TO SEE THE ROCKSTAR LIFE HASN'T CHANGED YOU.
SET THOSE UP IN A BOOTH, WOULD YOU, JOE? AND GET ME A PBR AND ONE OF WHATEVER GARLAND'S GOT THERE.

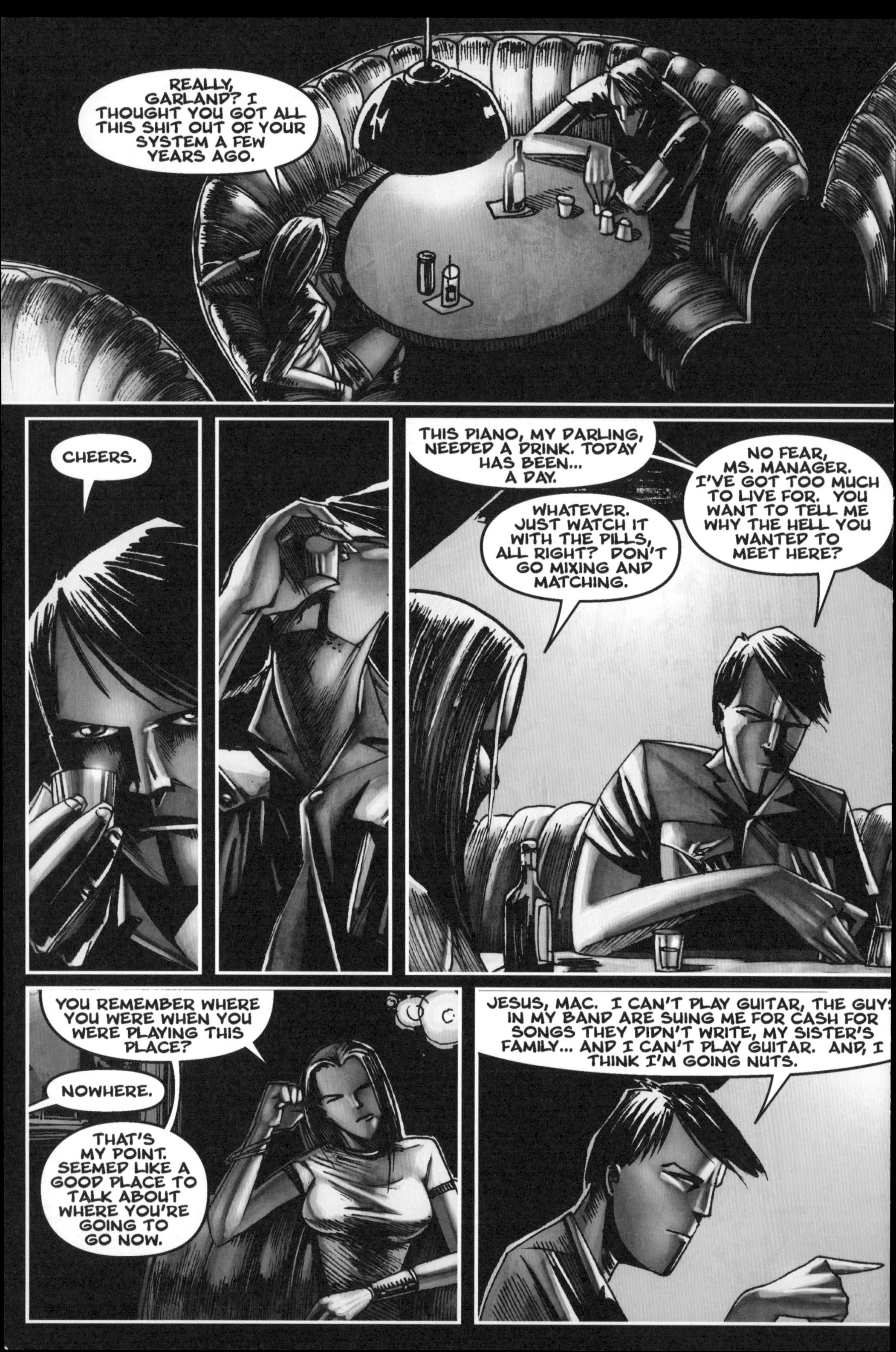
REALLY, GARLAND? I THOUGHT YOU GOT ALL THIS SHIT OUT OF YOUR SYSTEM A FEW YEARS AGO.
CHEERS.
THIS PIANO, MY DARLING, NEEDED A DRINK. TODAY HAS BEEN... A DAY.
WHATEVER. JUST WATCH IT WITH THE PILLS, ALL RIGHT? DON'T GO MIXING AND MATCHING.
NO FEAR, MS. MANAGER. I'VE GOT TOO MUCH TO LIVE FOR. YOU WANT TO TELL ME WHY THE HELL YOU WANTED TO MEET HERE?
YOU REMEMBER WHERE YOU WERE WHEN YOU WERE PLAYING THIS PLACE?
NOWHERE.
THAT'S MY POINT. SEEMED LIKE A GOOD PLACE TO TALK ABOUT WHERE YOU'RE GOING TO GO NOW.
JESUS, MAC. I CAN'T PLAY GUITAR, THE GUYS IN MY BAND ARE SUING ME FOR CASH FOR SONGS THEY DIDN'T WRITE, MY SISTER'S FAMILY... AND I CAN'T PLAY GUITAR. AND, I THINK I'M GOING NUTS.

I'VE BEEN DOING SOME READING, AND I THOUGHT MAYBE...

DON'T.

HAPPY BIRTHDAY.

JUST LISTEN - THIS GUY KOTTKE WAS A BRILLIANT PLAYER, UNTIL HE GOT THIS TENDON PROBLEM IN HIS RIGHT HAND. HE REINVENTED HIS ENTIRE APPROACH TO THE INSTRUMENT. REVERSED IT.

MAC, YOU KNOW THE WAY I PLAY - USED TO PLAY. YOU WANT ME TO GO LEFTY, LIKE HENDRIX?

EVEN IF I DID, I CAN'T EVEN HOLD A PEN IN MY LEFT HAND - HOW AM I SUPPOSED TO HOLD A PICK?

LEO KOTTKE

THAT'S NOT WHAT I'M SAYING. KOTTKE ADAPTED. LOTS OF PLAYERS DID IT - DJANGO REINHARDT HAD HALF HIS FINGERS FUSED TOGETHER IN A FIRE, FOR GOD'S SAKE. HE STILL PLAYED.

AND TONY IOMMI LOST THREE FINGERTIPS IN A STEEL PRESS, AND LES PAUL GOT HIS HAND SLASHED UP IN A CAR ACCIDENT.

SO WHAT? THEY AREN'T ME. NONE OF THIS WILL HELP.

AT LEAST CALL THIS GUY. HE'S A SPECIALIST - HE DESIGNS BRACES. HE CAN MAKE YOU SOMETHING THAT'S A HUNDRED TIMES LIGHTER AND MORE FLEXIBLE THAN WHAT YOU'VE GOT. YOU'D NEVER BE ABLE TO FRET WITH IT, BUT IF YOU DID GO LEFTY, I BET YOU COULD USE IT TO PICK.

EVEN IF I DID, MAC, I'D HAVE TO COMPLETELY RELEARN HOW TO PLAY. YOU THINK PEOPLE WOULD BUY MY RECORDS IF I CAN'T DO THE SAME SHIT LEFTY THAT I COULD DO RIGHTY? IT'S NOT WORTH IT.

THAT'S NOT TRUE, GARLAND. YOUR PLAYING ISN'T JUST IN YOUR HANDS. ALL THE KNOWLEDGE, ALL THOSE YEARS OF PRACTICE. IT'S STILL IN YOUR HEAD. YOUR SOUL. YOU JUST HAVE TO FIND A NEW WAY TO BRING IT OUT.

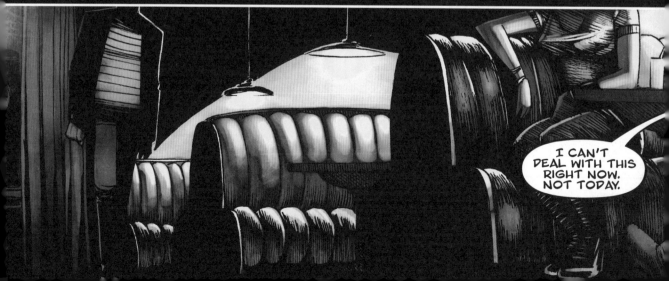

I CAN'T DEAL WITH THIS RIGHT NOW. NOT TODAY.

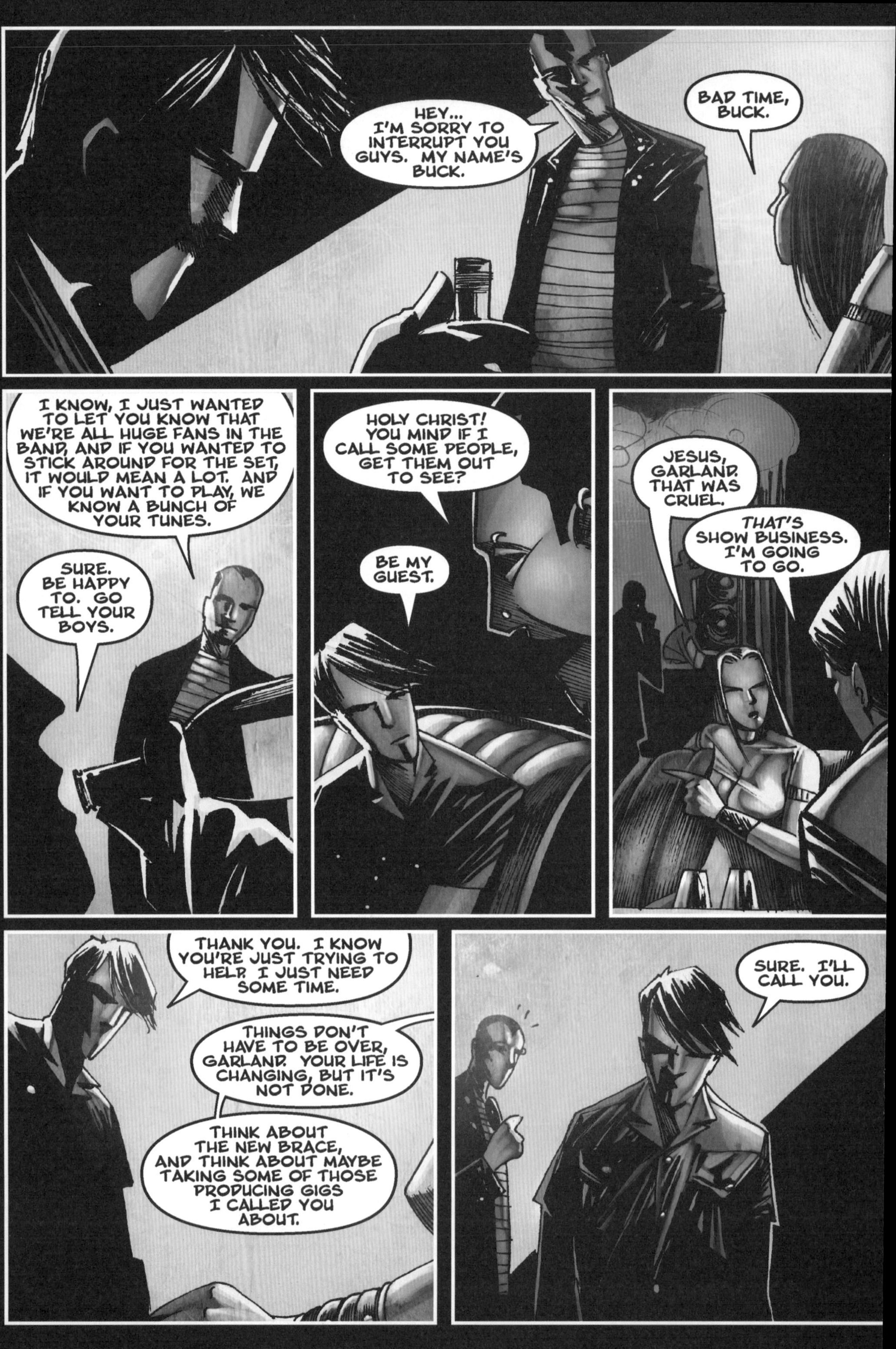
HEY... I'M SORRY TO INTERRUPT YOU GUYS. MY NAME'S BUCK.
BAD TIME, BUCK.
I KNOW, I JUST WANTED TO LET YOU KNOW THAT WE'RE ALL HUGE FANS IN THE BAND, AND IF YOU WANTED TO STICK AROUND FOR THE SET, IT WOULD MEAN A LOT. AND IF YOU WANT TO PLAY, WE KNOW A BUNCH OF YOUR TUNES.
SURE. BE HAPPY TO. GO TELL YOUR BOYS.
HOLY CHRIST! YOU MIND IF I CALL SOME PEOPLE, GET THEM OUT TO SEE?
BE MY GUEST.
JESUS, GARLAND. THAT WAS CRUEL.
THAT'S SHOW BUSINESS. I'M GOING TO GO.
THANK YOU. I KNOW YOU'RE JUST TRYING TO HELP. I JUST NEED SOME TIME.
THINGS DON'T HAVE TO BE OVER, GARLAND. YOUR LIFE IS CHANGING, BUT IT'S NOT DONE.
THINK ABOUT THE NEW BRACE, AND THINK ABOUT MAYBE TAKING SOME OF THOSE PRODUCING GIGS I CALLED YOU ABOUT.
SURE. I'LL CALL YOU.

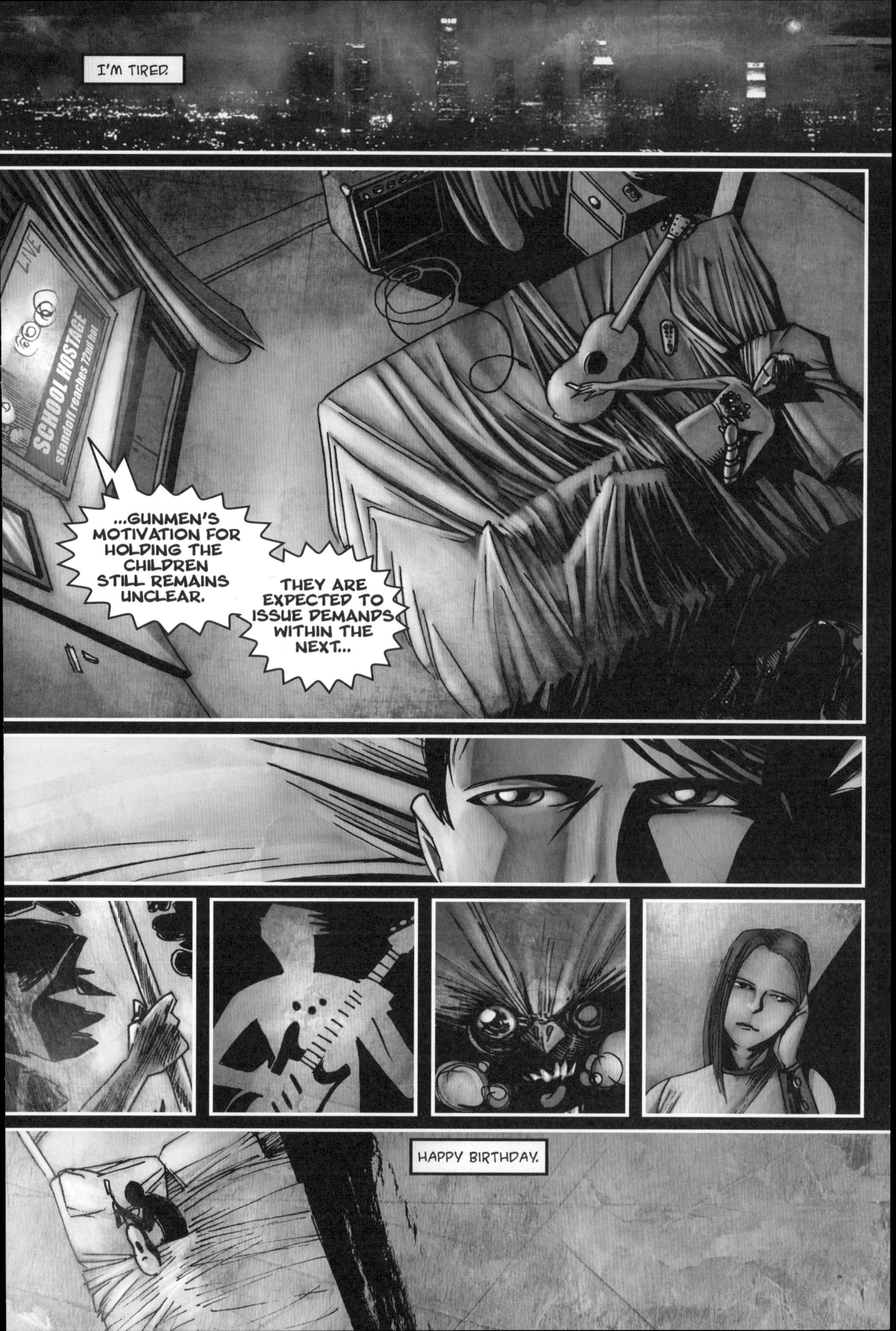

I'M TIRED.
LIVE
SCHOOL HOSTAGE
standoff reaches 72nd ho
...GUNMEN'S MOTIVATION FOR HOLDING THE CHILDREN STILL REMAINS UNCLEAR.
THEY ARE EXPECTED TO ISSUE DEMANDS WITHIN THE NEXT...
HAPPY BIRTHDAY.

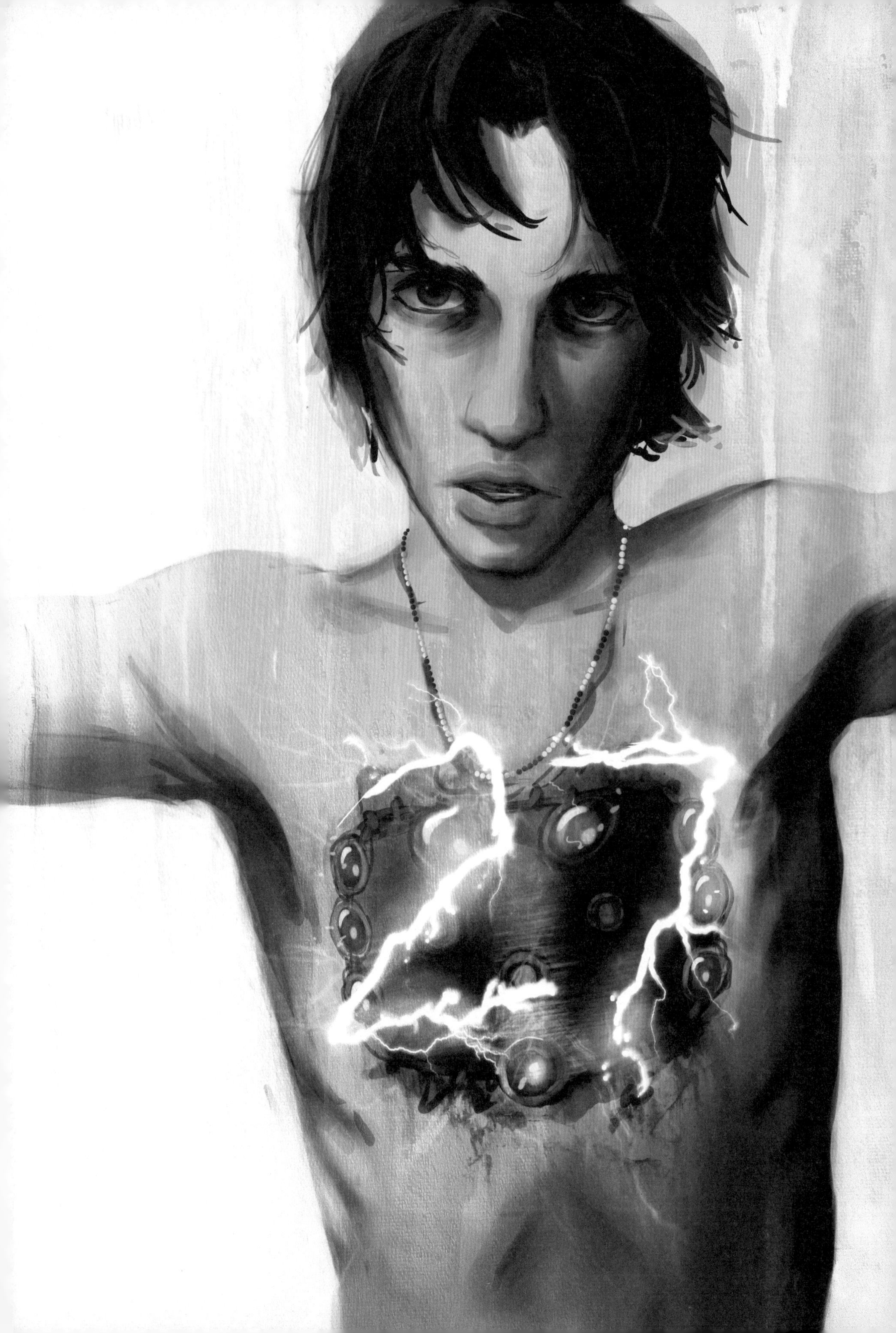

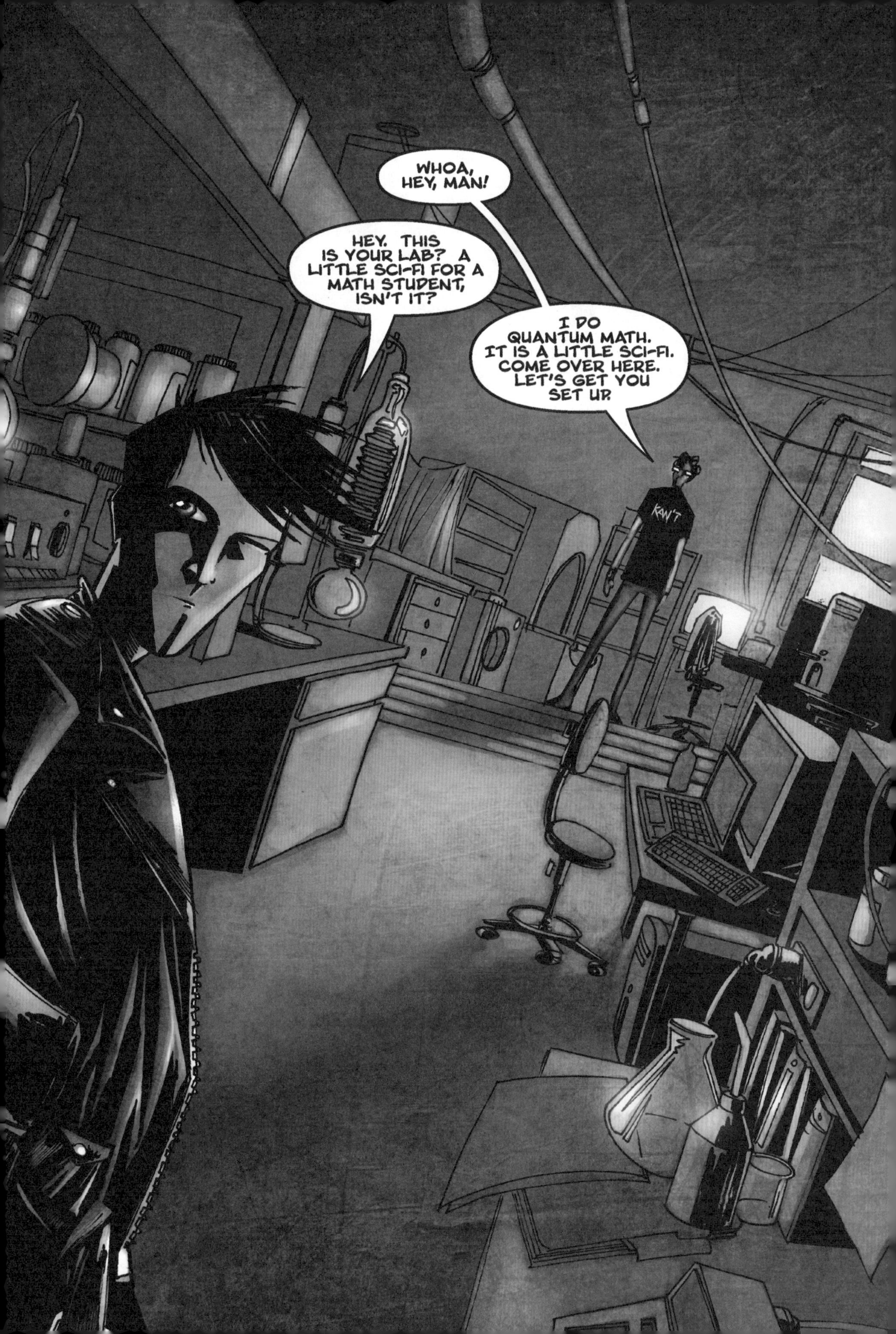
WHOA, HEY, MAN!
HEY. THIS IS YOUR LAB? A LITTLE SCI-FI FOR A MATH STUDENT, ISN'T IT?
I DO QUANTUM MATH. IT IS A LITTLE SCI-FI. COME OVER HERE. LET'S GET YOU SET UP.
KAN'T

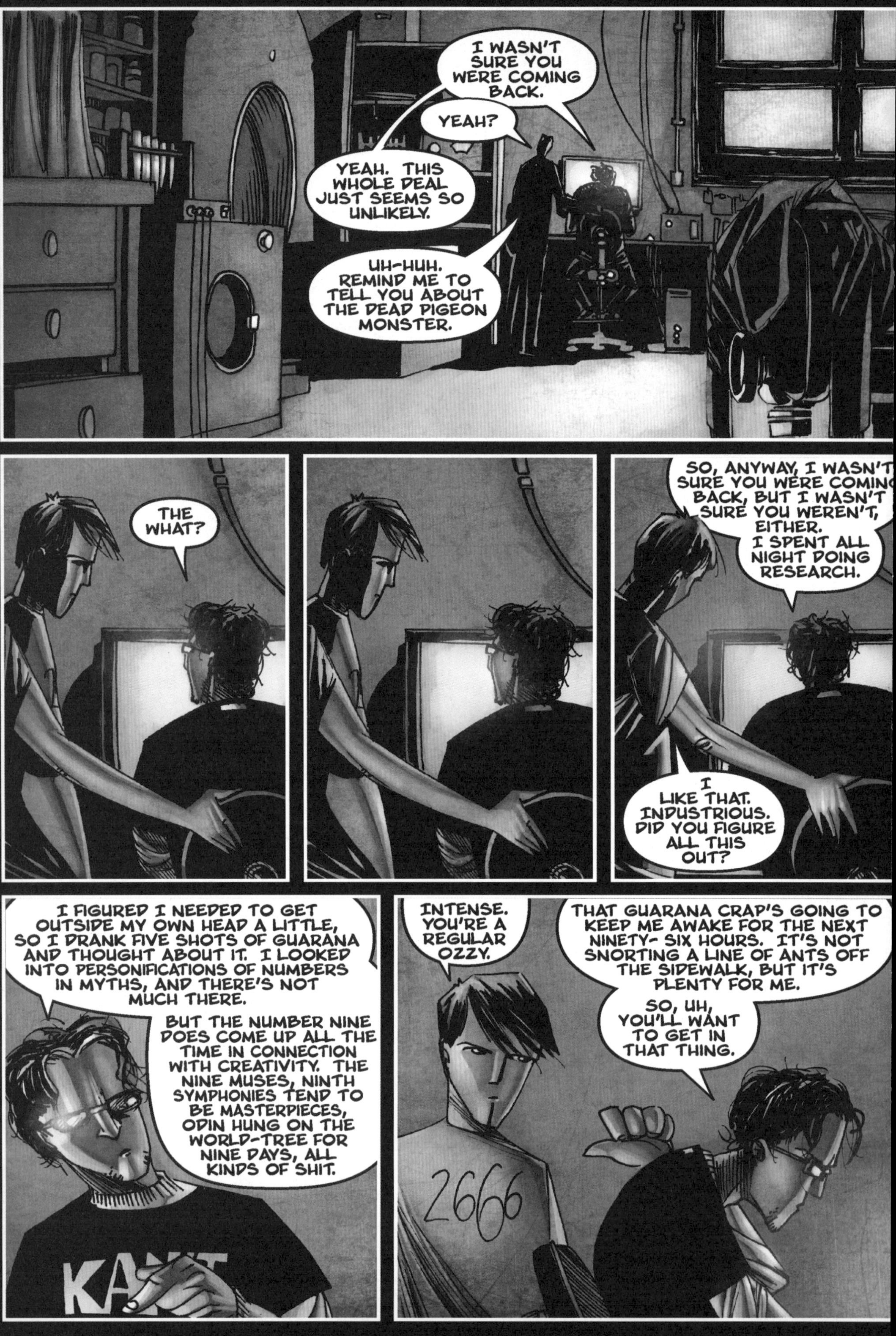
I WASN'T SURE YOU WERE COMING BACK.
YEAH?
YEAH. THIS WHOLE DEAL JUST SEEMS SO UNLIKELY.
UH-HUH. REMIND ME TO TELL YOU ABOUT THE DEAD PIGEON MONSTER.
THE WHAT?
SO, ANYWAY, I WASN'T SURE YOU WERE COMING BACK, BUT I WASN'T SURE YOU WEREN'T, EITHER. I SPENT ALL NIGHT DOING RESEARCH.
I LIKE THAT. INDUSTRIOUS. DID YOU FIGURE ALL THIS OUT?
I FIGURED I NEEDED TO GET OUTSIDE MY OWN HEAD A LITTLE, SO I DRANK FIVE SHOTS OF GUARANA AND THOUGHT ABOUT IT. I LOOKED INTO PERSONIFICATIONS OF NUMBERS IN MYTHS, AND THERE'S NOT MUCH THERE.
BUT THE NUMBER NINE DOES COME UP ALL THE TIME IN CONNECTION WITH CREATIVITY. THE NINE MUSES, NINTH SYMPHONIES TEND TO BE MASTERPIECES, ODIN HUNG ON THE WORLD-TREE FOR NINE DAYS, ALL KINDS OF SHIT.
INTENSE. YOU'RE A REGULAR OZZY.
THAT GUARANA CRAP'S GOING TO KEEP ME AWAKE FOR THE NEXT NINETY- SIX HOURS. IT'S NOT SNORTING A LINE OF ANTS OFF THE SIDEWALK, BUT IT'S PLENTY FOR ME.
SO, UH, YOU'LL WANT TO GET IN THAT THING.
2666

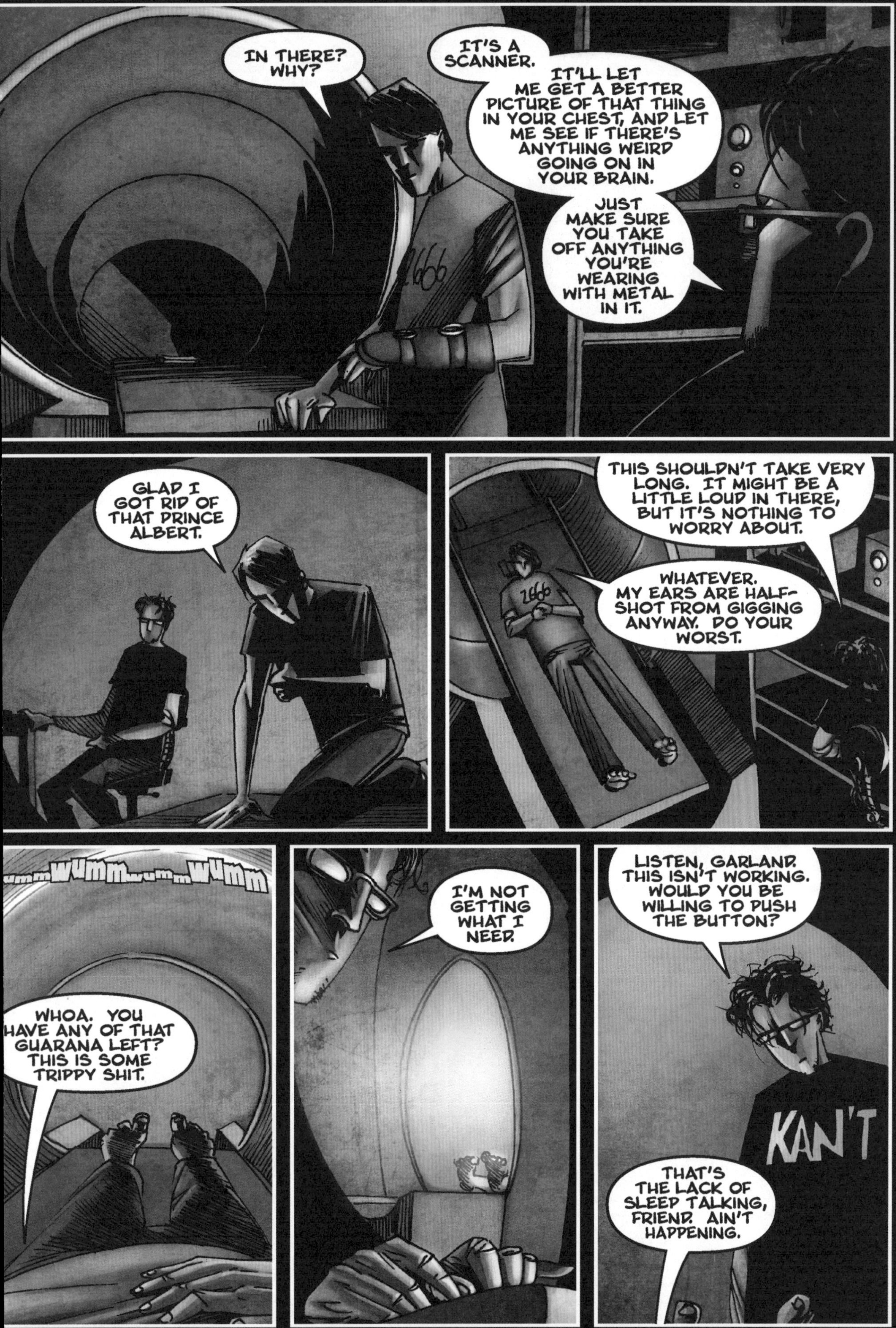
IN THERE? WHY?
IT'S A SCANNER.
IT'LL LET ME GET A BETTER PICTURE OF THAT THING IN YOUR CHEST, AND LET ME SEE IF THERE'S ANYTHING WEIRD GOING ON IN YOUR BRAIN.
JUST MAKE SURE YOU TAKE OFF ANYTHING YOU'RE WEARING WITH METAL IN IT.
2666
GLAD I GOT RID OF THAT PRINCE ALBERT.
THIS SHOULDN'T TAKE VERY LONG. IT MIGHT BE A LITTLE LOUD IN THERE, BUT IT'S NOTHING TO WORRY ABOUT.
WHATEVER. MY EARS ARE HALF-SHOT FROM GIGGING ANYWAY. DO YOUR WORST.
wummWUMMwummWUMM
WHOA. YOU HAVE ANY OF THAT GUARANA LEFT? THIS IS SOME TRIPPY SHIT.
I'M NOT GETTING WHAT I NEED.
LISTEN, GARLAND. THIS ISN'T WORKING. WOULD YOU BE WILLING TO PUSH THE BUTTON?
KAN'T
THAT'S THE LACK OF SLEEP TALKING, FRIEND. AIN'T HAPPENING.

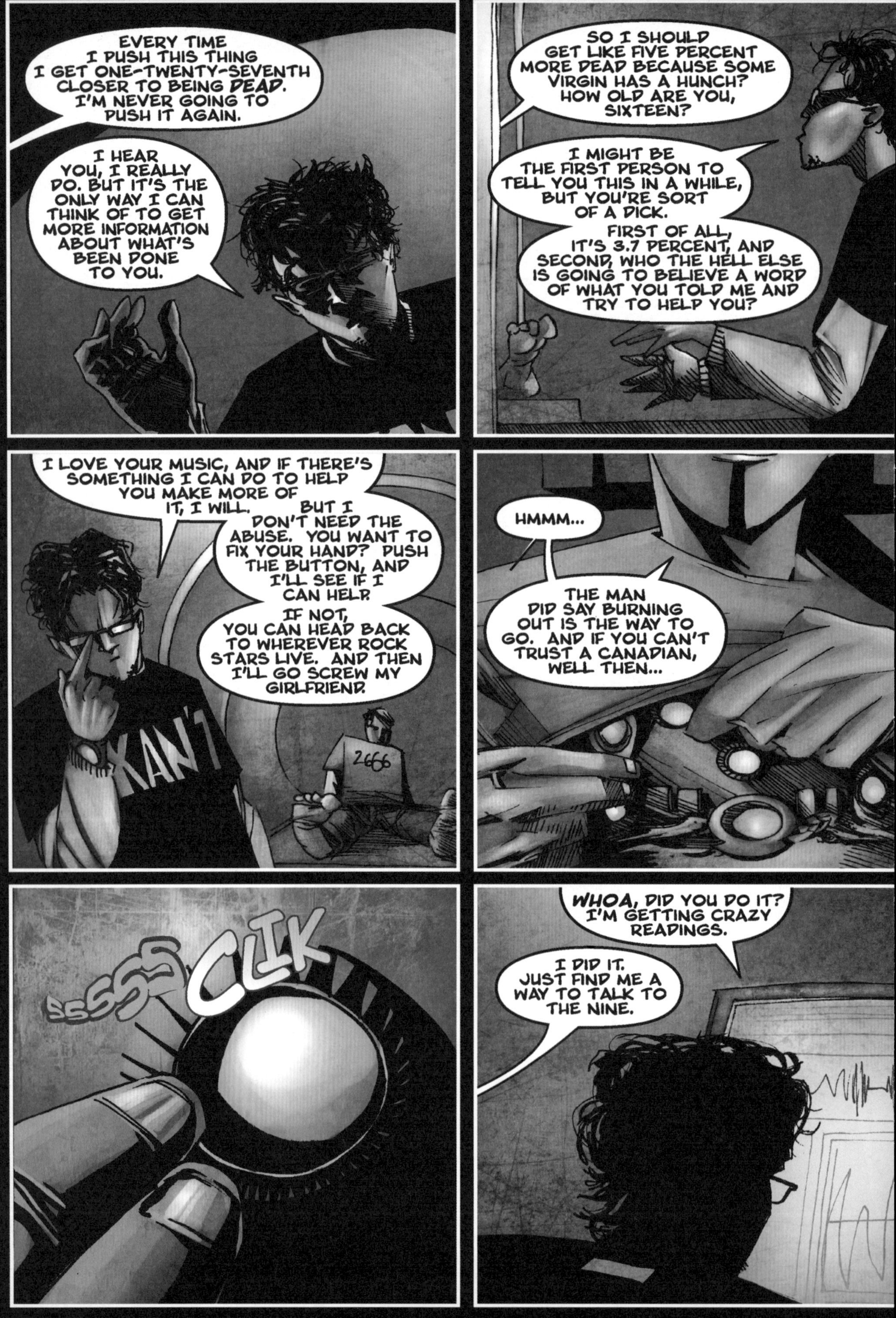
EVERY TIME I PUSH THIS THING I GET ONE-TWENTY-SEVENTH CLOSER TO BEING DEAD. I'M NEVER GOING TO PUSH IT AGAIN.
I HEAR YOU, I REALLY DO. BUT IT'S THE ONLY WAY I CAN THINK OF TO GET MORE INFORMATION ABOUT WHAT'S BEEN DONE TO YOU.
SO I SHOULD GET LIKE FIVE PERCENT MORE DEAD BECAUSE SOME VIRGIN HAS A HUNCH? HOW OLD ARE YOU, SIXTEEN?
I MIGHT BE THE FIRST PERSON TO TELL YOU THIS IN A WHILE, BUT YOU'RE SORT OF A DICK.
FIRST OF ALL, IT'S 3.7 PERCENT, AND SECOND, WHO THE HELL ELSE IS GOING TO BELIEVE A WORD OF WHAT YOU TOLD ME AND TRY TO HELP YOU?
I LOVE YOUR MUSIC, AND IF THERE'S SOMETHING I CAN DO TO HELP YOU MAKE MORE OF IT, I WILL.
BUT I DON'T NEED THE ABUSE. YOU WANT TO FIX YOUR HAND? PUSH THE BUTTON, AND I'LL SEE IF I CAN HELP.
IF NOT, YOU CAN HEAD BACK TO WHEREVER ROCK STARS LIVE. AND THEN I'LL GO SCREW MY GIRLFRIEND.
KANT
2666
HMMM...
THE MAN DID SAY BURNING OUT IS THE WAY TO GO. AND IF YOU CAN'T TRUST A CANADIAN, WELL THEN...
SSSSS
CLIK
WHOA, DID YOU DO IT? I'M GETTING CRAZY READINGS.
I DID IT. JUST FIND ME A WAY TO TALK TO THE NINE.

JESUS, MAN, HOW LONG HAVE I BEEN IN HERE?
ALMOST AN HOUR. LISTEN, I'M GETTING AMAZING STUFF. IT'S LIKE THERE'S SOMETHING FUNNELING ENERGY INTO YOU. I'VE ALMOST GOT IT TRACED BACK TO ITS SOURCE. JUST A LITTLE LONGER.
HURRY IT UP. THESE LIGHTS ARE STARTING TO DRIVE ME A LITTLE BUGGY.
CLOSE YOUR EYES. DO SOMETHING TO DISTRACT YOU.
SING A SONG OR SOMETHING. IT WON'T BOTHER ME.
SHRRRMMM
WHAT THE? GARLAND, DID YOU GET OUT OF THE SCANNER?
GARLAND?

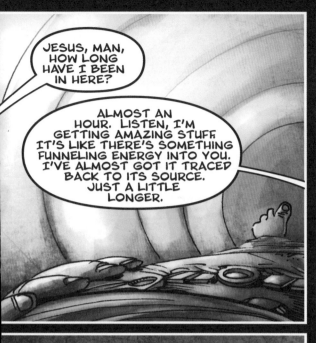

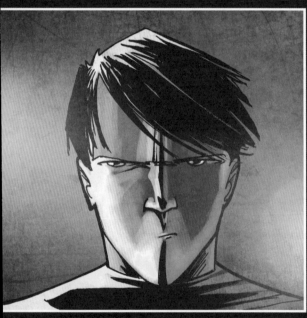

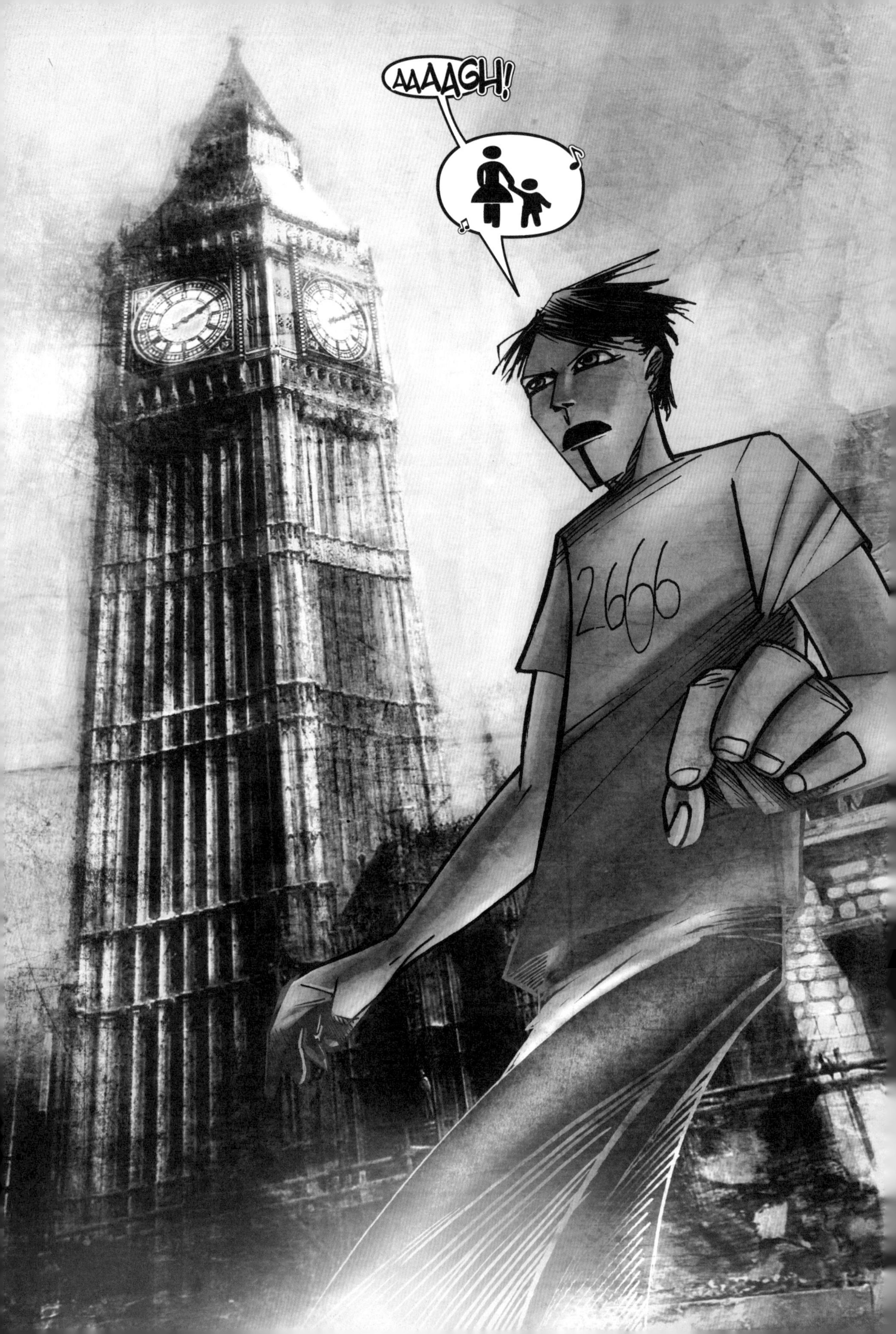
AAAAGH!
2666

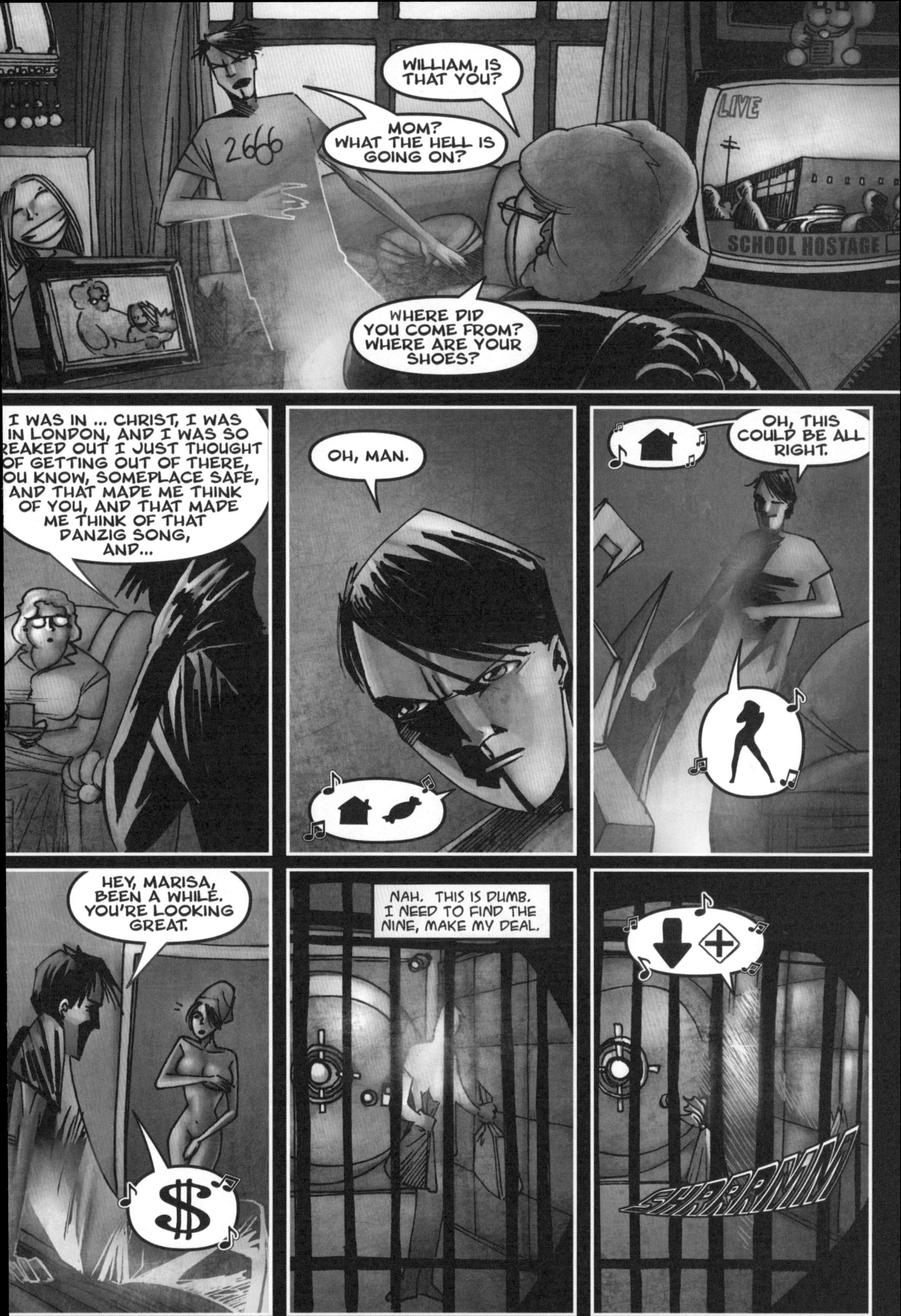

LIVE
SCHOOL HOSTAGE
WILLIAM, IS THAT YOU?
MOM? WHAT THE HELL IS GOING ON?
WHERE DID YOU COME FROM? WHERE ARE YOUR SHOES?
I WAS IN ... CHRIST, I WAS IN LONDON, AND I WAS SO FREAKED OUT I JUST THOUGHT OF GETTING OUT OF THERE, YOU KNOW, SOMEPLACE SAFE, AND THAT MADE ME THINK OF YOU, AND THAT MADE ME THINK OF THAT DANZIG SONG, AND...
OH, MAN.
OH, THIS COULD BE ALL RIGHT.
HEY, MARISA, BEEN A WHILE. YOU'RE LOOKING GREAT.
$
NAH. THIS IS DUMB. I NEED TO FIND THE NINE, MAKE MY DEAL.
SHRRRMM

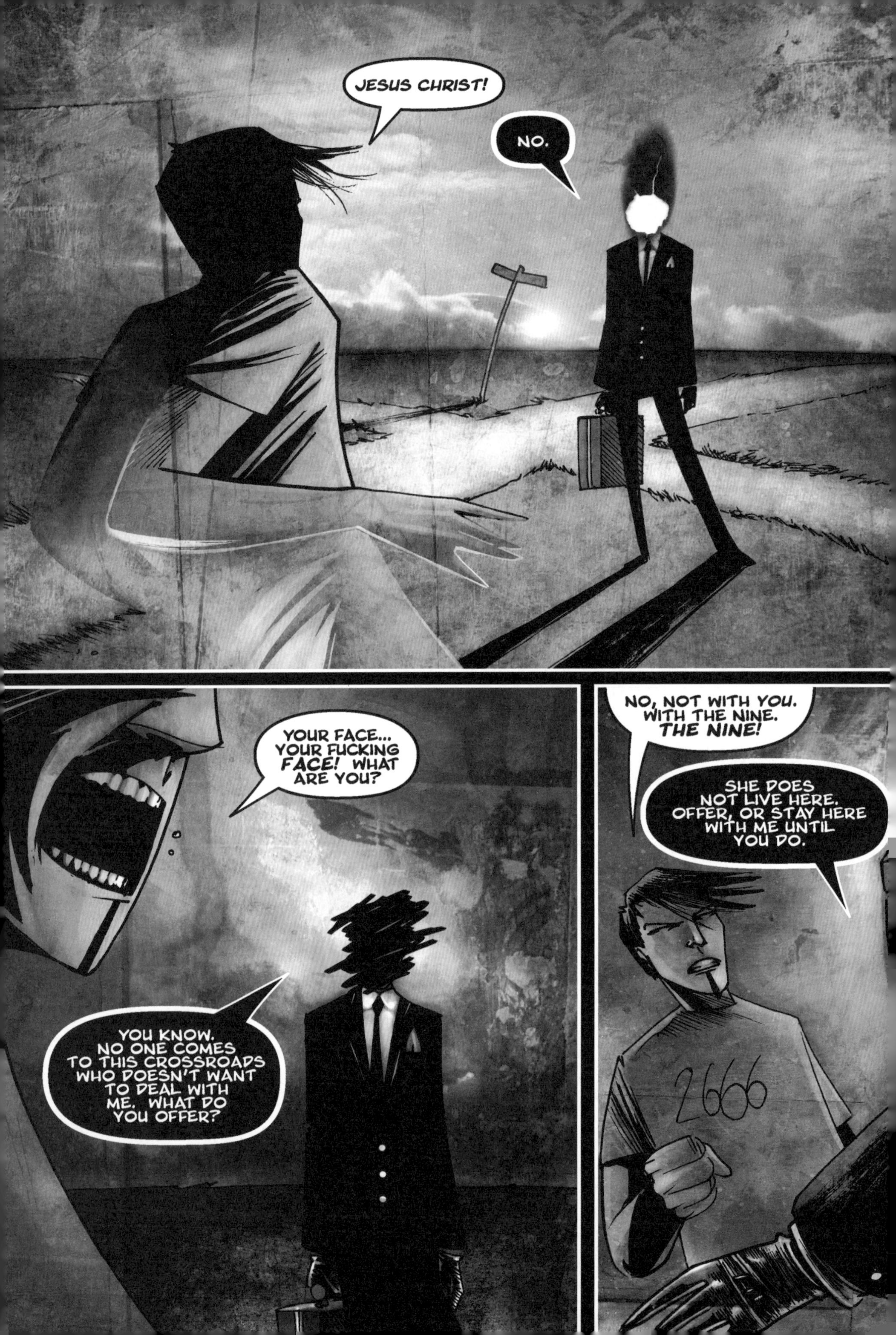
JESUS CHRIST!
NO.
YOUR FACE... YOUR FUCKING FACE! WHAT ARE YOU?
YOU KNOW. NO ONE COMES TO THIS CROSSROADS WHO DOESN'T WANT TO DEAL WITH ME. WHAT DO YOU OFFER?
NO, NOT WITH YOU. WITH THE NINE. THE NINE!
SHE DOES NOT LIVE HERE. OFFER, OR STAY HERE WITH ME UNTIL YOU DO.
2666

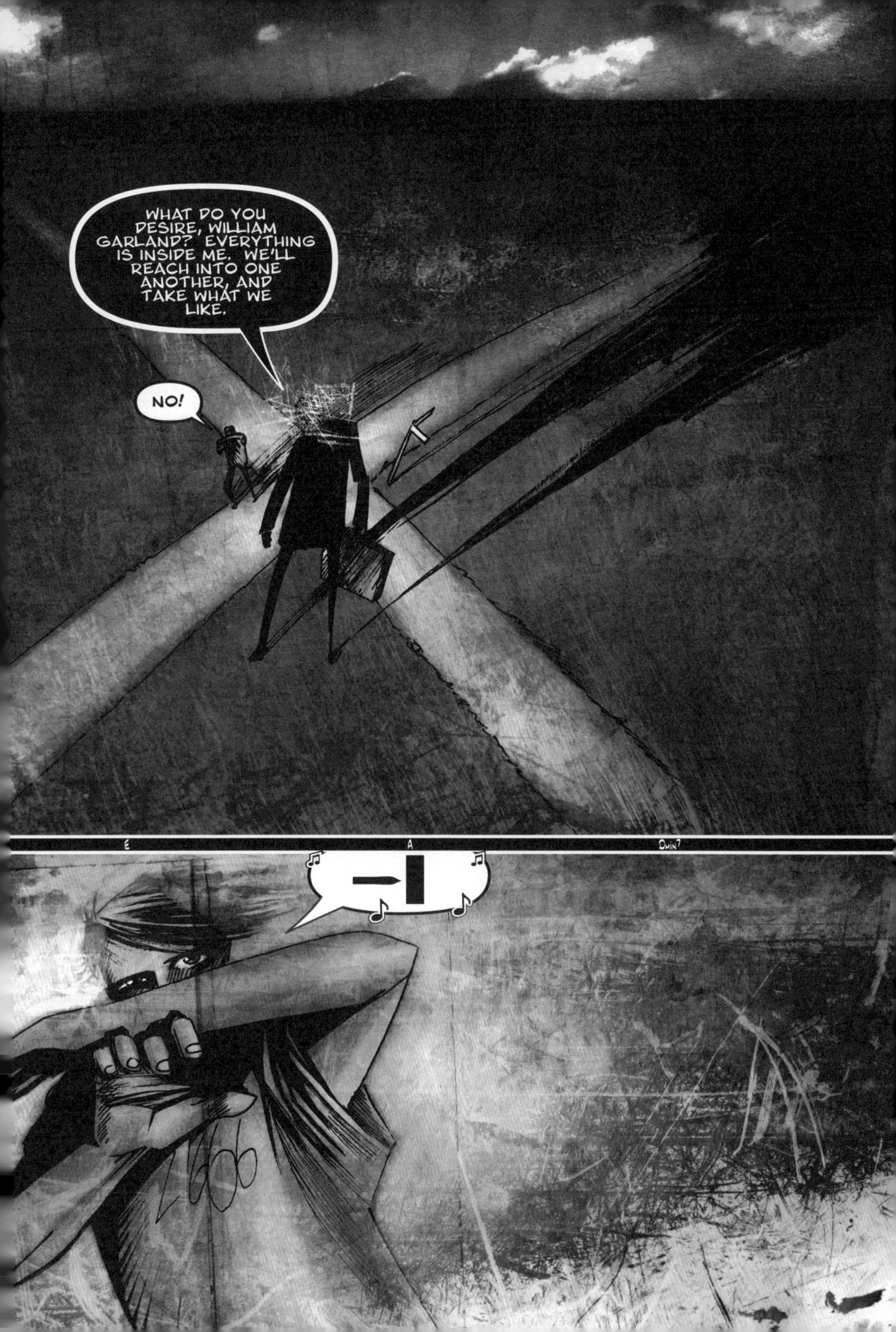
WHAT DO YOU DESIRE, WILLIAM GARLAND? EVERYTHING IS INSIDE ME. WE'LL REACH INTO ONE ANOTHER, AND TAKE WHAT WE LIKE.
NO!
E
A
Dmin7

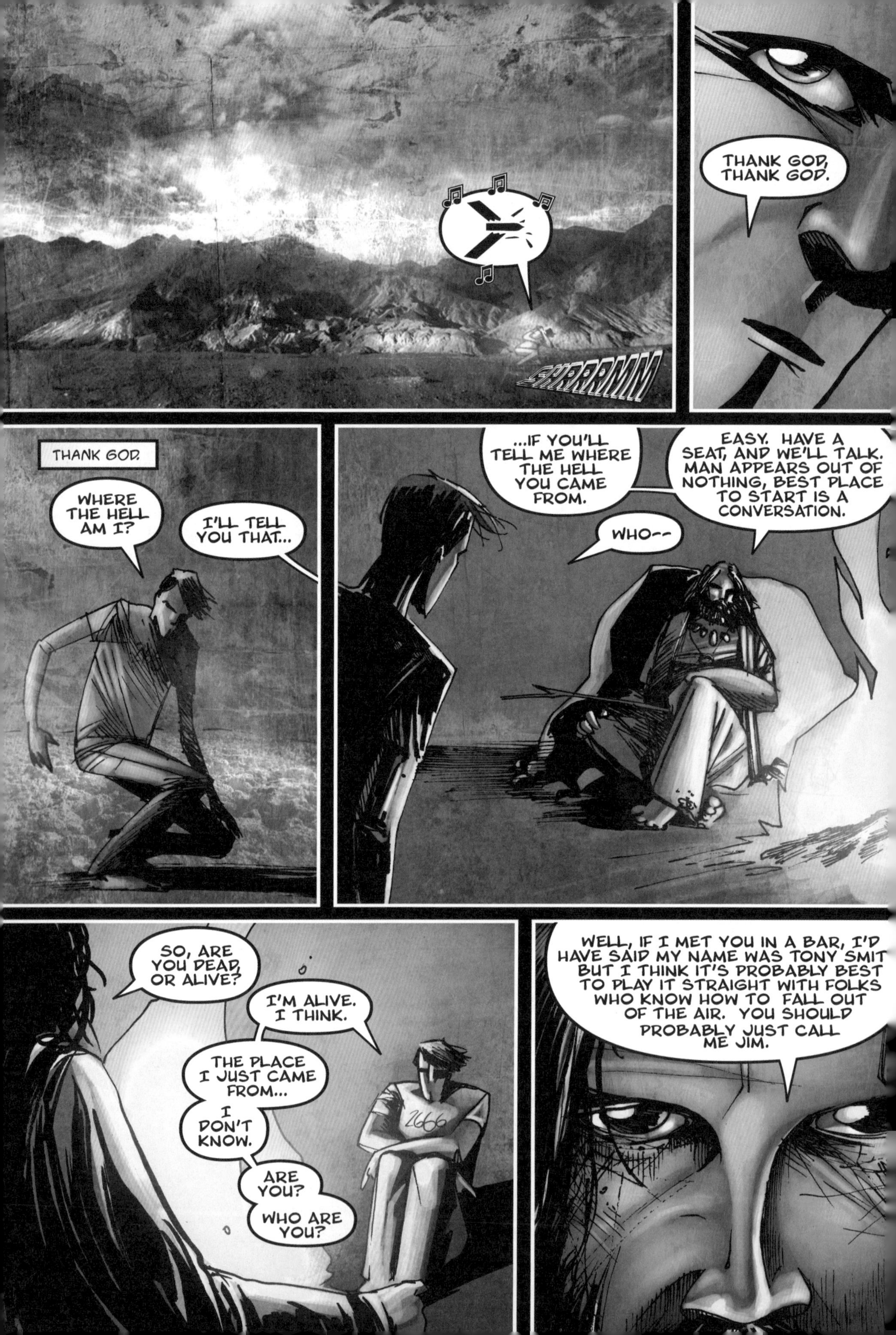
SHRRRMM
THANK GOD, THANK GOD.
THANK GOD.
WHERE THE HELL AM I?
I'LL TELL YOU THAT...
...IF YOU'LL TELL ME WHERE THE HELL YOU CAME FROM.
WHO--
EASY. HAVE A SEAT, AND WE'LL TALK. MAN APPEARS OUT OF NOTHING, BEST PLACE TO START IS A CONVERSATION.
SO, ARE YOU DEAD, OR ALIVE?
I'M ALIVE. I THINK.
THE PLACE I JUST CAME FROM...
I DON'T KNOW.
ARE YOU?
WHO ARE YOU?
2666
WELL, IF I MET YOU IN A BAR, I'D HAVE SAID MY NAME WAS TONY SMIT BUT I THINK IT'S PROBABLY BEST TO PLAY IT STRAIGHT WITH FOLKS WHO KNOW HOW TO FALL OUT OF THE AIR. YOU SHOULD PROBABLY JUST CALL ME JIM.

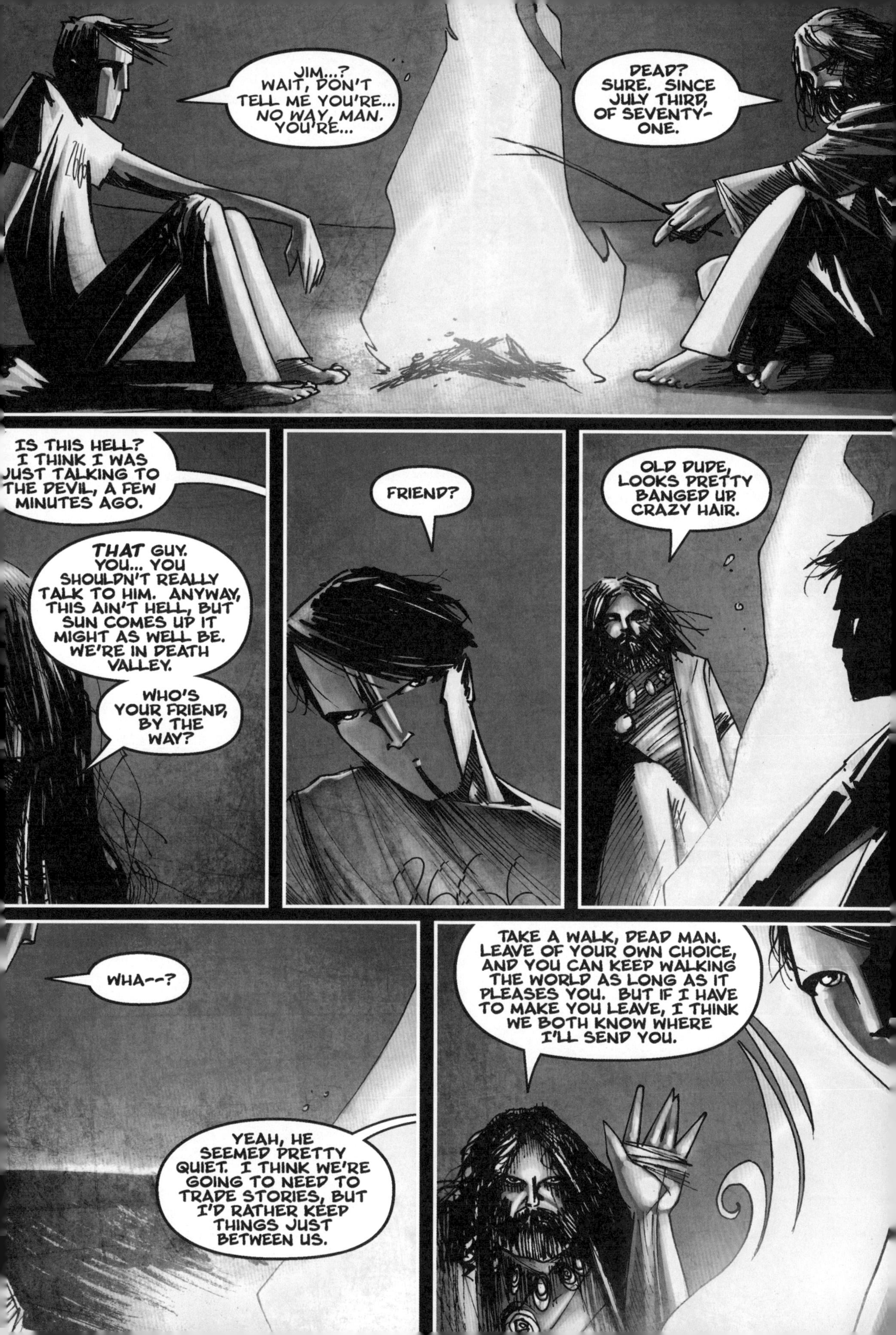
JIM...? WAIT, DON'T TELL ME YOU'RE... NO WAY, MAN. YOU'RE...
DEAD? SURE. SINCE JULY THIRD, OF SEVENTY-ONE.
IS THIS HELL? I THINK I WAS JUST TALKING TO THE DEVIL, A FEW MINUTES AGO.
THAT GUY. YOU... YOU SHOULDN'T REALLY TALK TO HIM. ANYWAY, THIS AIN'T HELL, BUT SUN COMES UP IT MIGHT AS WELL BE. WE'RE IN DEATH VALLEY.
WHO'S YOUR FRIEND, BY THE WAY?
FRIEND?
OLD DUDE, LOOKS PRETTY BANGED UP. CRAZY HAIR.
WHA--?
YEAH, HE SEEMED PRETTY QUIET. I THINK WE'RE GOING TO NEED TO TRADE STORIES, BUT I'D RATHER KEEP THINGS JUST BETWEEN US.
TAKE A WALK, DEAD MAN. LEAVE OF YOUR OWN CHOICE, AND YOU CAN KEEP WALKING THE WORLD AS LONG AS IT PLEASES YOU. BUT IF I HAVE TO MAKE YOU LEAVE, I THINK WE BOTH KNOW WHERE I'LL SEND YOU.

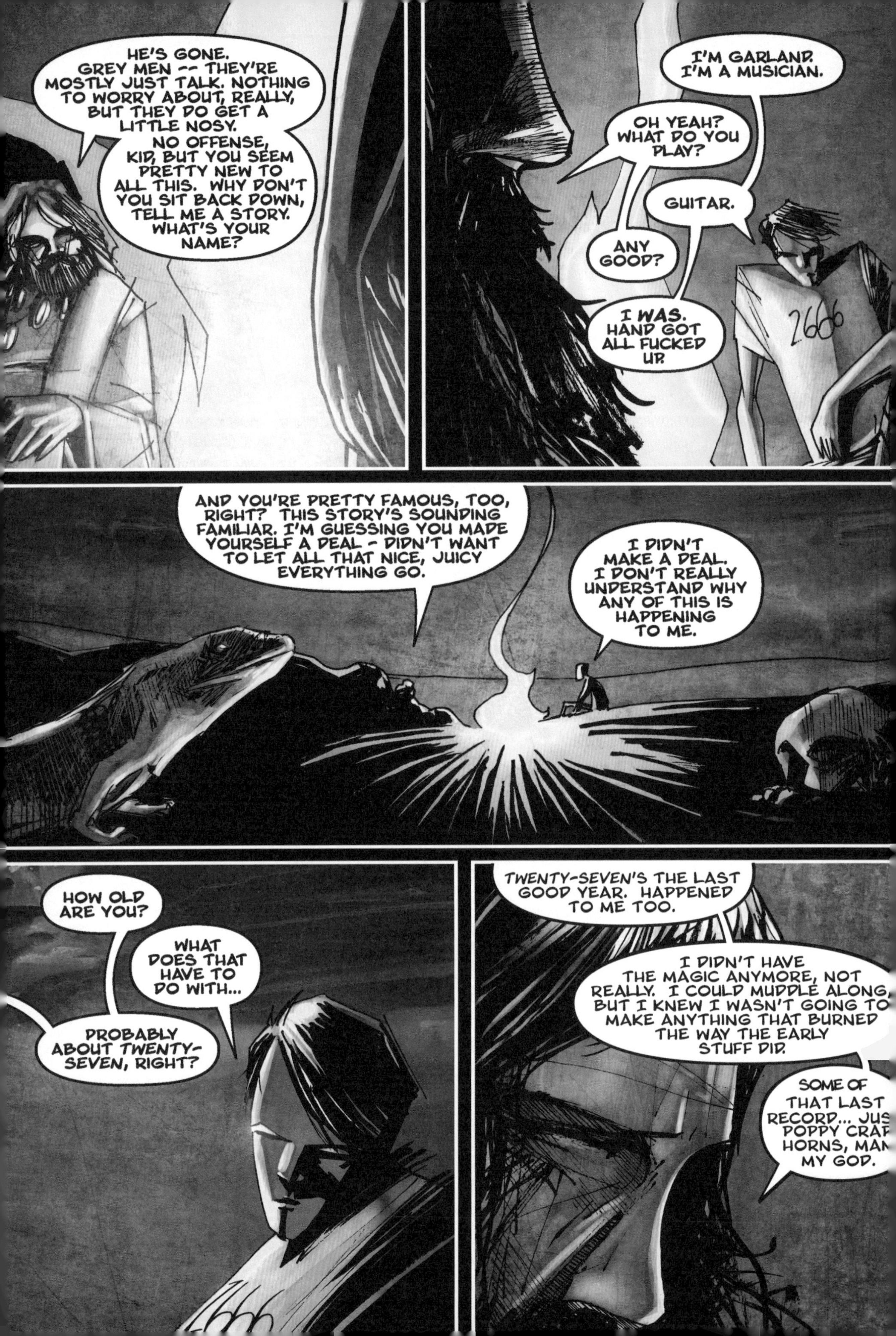
HE'S GONE. GREY MEN -- THEY'RE MOSTLY JUST TALK. NOTHING TO WORRY ABOUT, REALLY, BUT THEY DO GET A LITTLE NOSY.
NO OFFENSE, KID, BUT YOU SEEM PRETTY NEW TO ALL THIS. WHY DON'T YOU SIT BACK DOWN, TELL ME A STORY. WHAT'S YOUR NAME?
I'M GARLAND. I'M A MUSICIAN.
OH YEAH? WHAT DO YOU PLAY?
GUITAR.
ANY GOOD?
I WAS. HAND GOT ALL FUCKED UP.
2666
AND YOU'RE PRETTY FAMOUS, TOO, RIGHT? THIS STORY'S SOUNDING FAMILIAR. I'M GUESSING YOU MADE YOURSELF A DEAL - DIDN'T WANT TO LET ALL THAT NICE, JUICY EVERYTHING GO.
I DIDN'T MAKE A DEAL. I DON'T REALLY UNDERSTAND WHY ANY OF THIS IS HAPPENING TO ME.
HOW OLD ARE YOU?
WHAT DOES THAT HAVE TO DO WITH...
PROBABLY ABOUT TWENTY-SEVEN, RIGHT?
TWENTY-SEVEN'S THE LAST GOOD YEAR. HAPPENED TO ME TOO.
I DIDN'T HAVE THE MAGIC ANYMORE, NOT REALLY. I COULD MUDDLE ALONG, BUT I KNEW I WASN'T GOING TO MAKE ANYTHING THAT BURNED THE WAY THE EARLY STUFF DID.
SOME OF THAT LAST RECORD... JUS POPPY CRAP HORNS, MAN MY GOD.

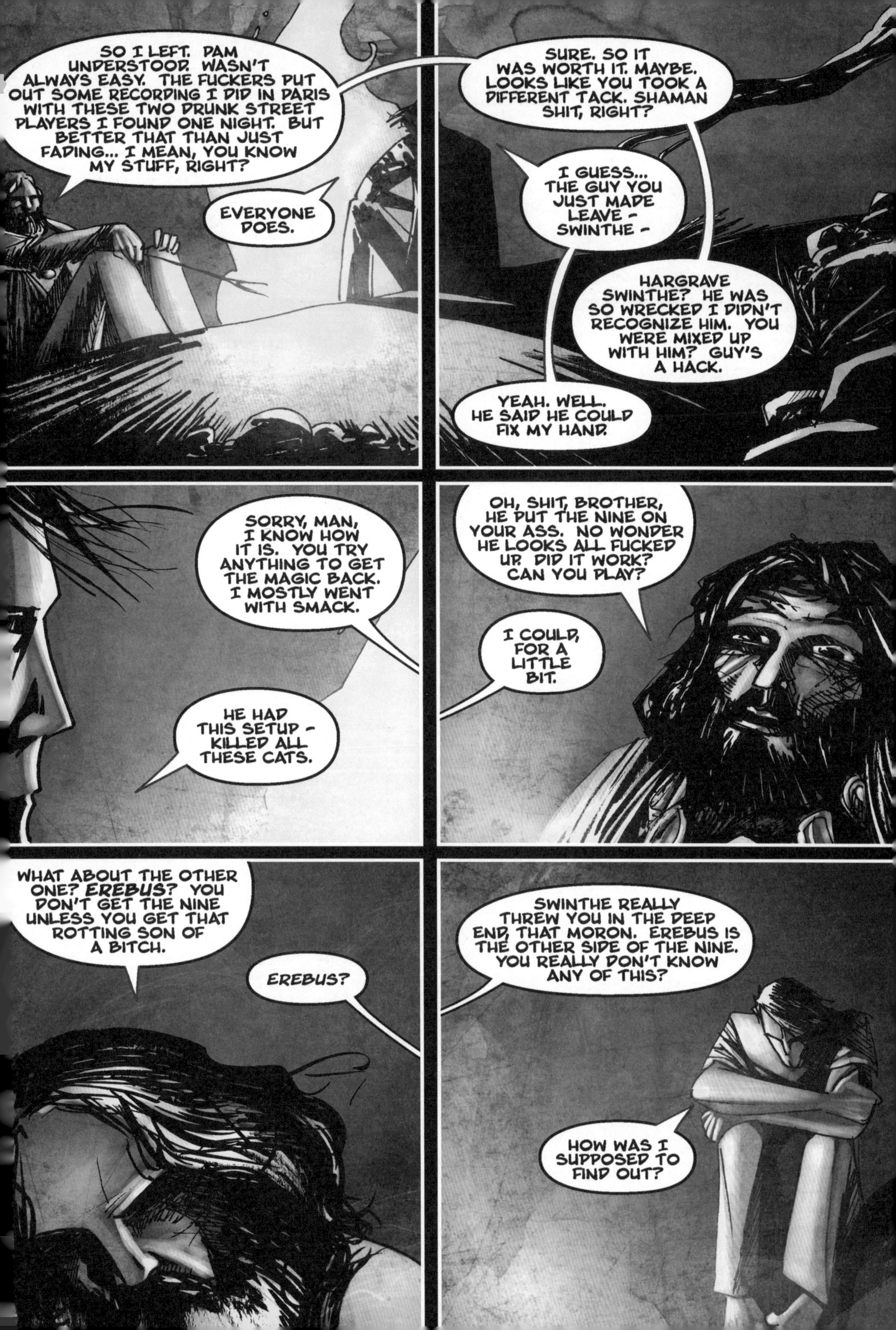
SO I LEFT. DAM UNDERSTOOD. WASN'T ALWAYS EASY. THE FUCKERS PUT OUT SOME RECORDING I DID IN PARIS WITH THESE TWO DRUNK STREET PLAYERS I FOUND ONE NIGHT. BUT BETTER THAT THAN JUST FADING... I MEAN, YOU KNOW MY STUFF, RIGHT?
EVERYONE DOES.
SURE. SO IT WAS WORTH IT. MAYBE. LOOKS LIKE YOU TOOK A DIFFERENT TACK. SHAMAN SHIT, RIGHT?
I GUESS... THE GUY YOU JUST MADE LEAVE - SWINTHE -
HARGRAVE SWINTHE? HE WAS SO WRECKED I DIDN'T RECOGNIZE HIM. YOU WERE MIXED UP WITH HIM? GUY'S A HACK.
YEAH. WELL. HE SAID HE COULD FIX MY HAND.
SORRY, MAN, I KNOW HOW IT IS. YOU TRY ANYTHING TO GET THE MAGIC BACK. I MOSTLY WENT WITH SMACK.
HE HAD THIS SETUP - KILLED ALL THESE CATS.
OH, SHIT, BROTHER, HE PUT THE NINE ON YOUR ASS. NO WONDER HE LOOKS ALL FUCKED UP. DID IT WORK? CAN YOU PLAY?
I COULD, FOR A LITTLE BIT.
WHAT ABOUT THE OTHER ONE? EREBUS? YOU DON'T GET THE NINE UNLESS YOU GET THAT ROTTING SON OF A BITCH.
EREBUS?
SWINTHE REALLY THREW YOU IN THE DEEP END, THAT MORON. EREBUS IS THE OTHER SIDE OF THE NINE. YOU REALLY DON'T KNOW ANY OF THIS?
HOW WAS I SUPPOSED TO FIND OUT?

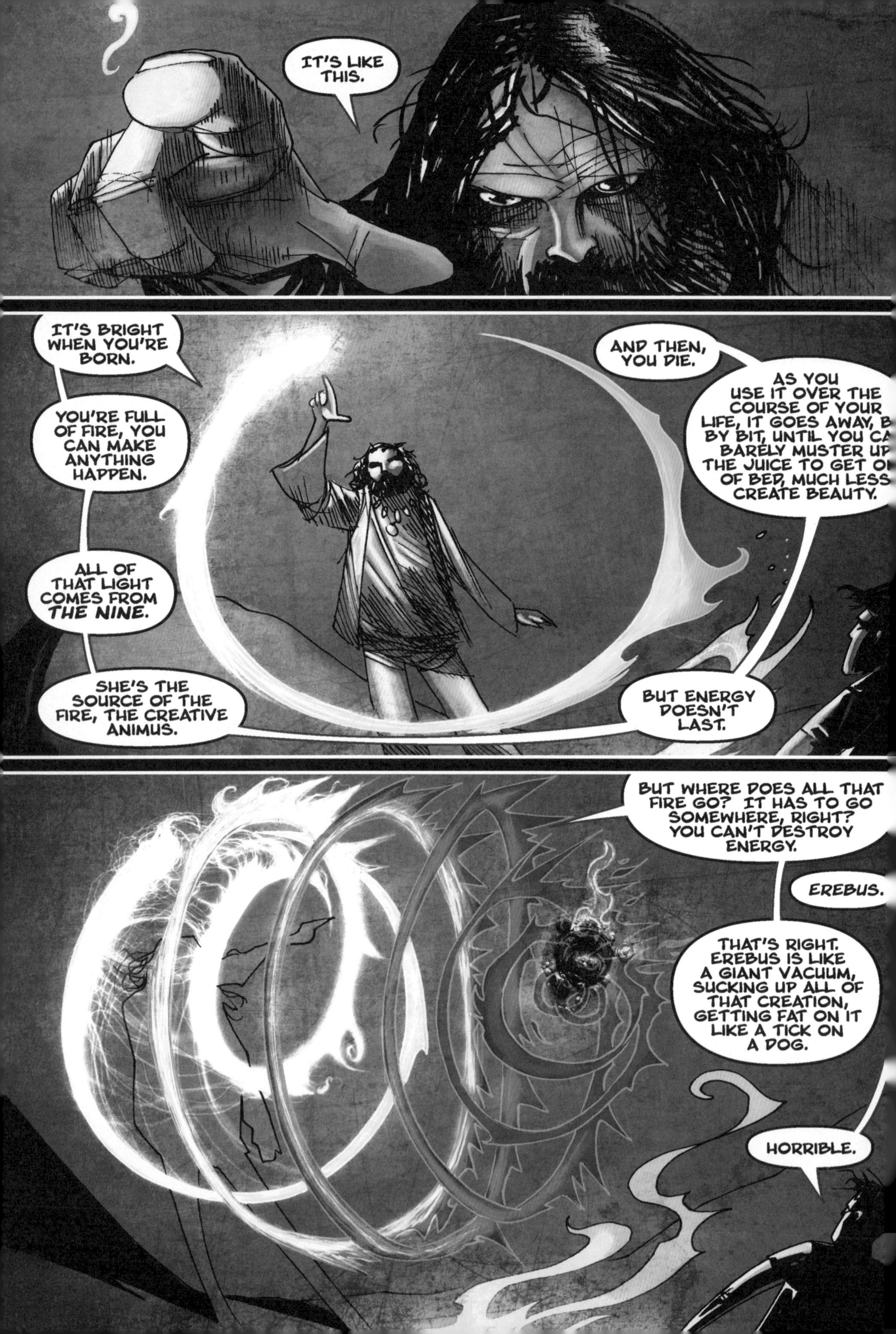
IT'S LIKE THIS.
IT'S BRIGHT WHEN YOU'RE BORN.
YOU'RE FULL OF FIRE, YOU CAN MAKE ANYTHING HAPPEN.
ALL OF THAT LIGHT COMES FROM *THE NINE*.
SHE'S THE SOURCE OF THE FIRE, THE CREATIVE ANIMUS.
BUT ENERGY DOESN'T LAST.
AS YOU USE IT OVER THE COURSE OF YOUR LIFE, IT GOES AWAY, B BY BIT, UNTIL YOU CA BARELY MUSTER UP THE JUICE TO GET O OF BED, MUCH LESS CREATE BEAUTY.
AND THEN, YOU DIE.
BUT WHERE DOES ALL THAT FIRE GO? IT HAS TO GO SOMEWHERE, RIGHT? YOU CAN'T DESTROY ENERGY.
EREBUS.
THAT'S RIGHT. EREBUS IS LIKE A GIANT VACUUM, SUCKING UP ALL OF THAT CREATION, GETTING FAT ON IT LIKE A TICK ON A DOG.
HORRIBLE.

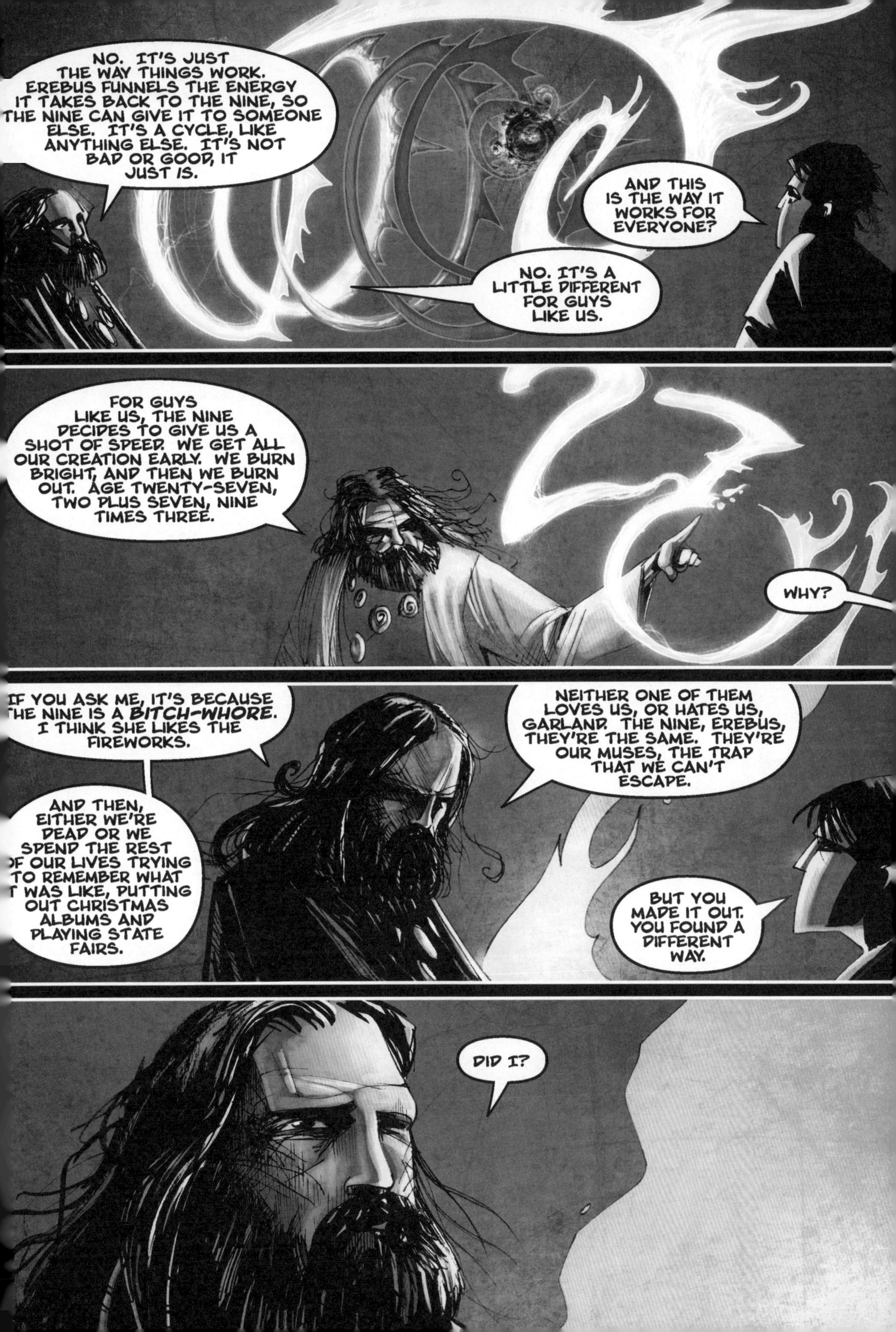
NO. IT'S JUST THE WAY THINGS WORK. EREBUS FUNNELS THE ENERGY IT TAKES BACK TO THE NINE, SO THE NINE CAN GIVE IT TO SOMEONE ELSE. IT'S A CYCLE, LIKE ANYTHING ELSE. IT'S NOT BAD OR GOOD, IT JUST IS.
AND THIS IS THE WAY IT WORKS FOR EVERYONE?
NO. IT'S A LITTLE DIFFERENT FOR GUYS LIKE US.
FOR GUYS LIKE US, THE NINE DECIDES TO GIVE US A SHOT OF SPEED. WE GET ALL OUR CREATION EARLY. WE BURN BRIGHT, AND THEN WE BURN OUT. AGE TWENTY-SEVEN, TWO PLUS SEVEN, NINE TIMES THREE.
WHY?
IF YOU ASK ME, IT'S BECAUSE THE NINE IS A *BITCH-WHORE*. I THINK SHE LIKES THE FIREWORKS.
AND THEN, EITHER WE'RE DEAD OR WE SPEND THE REST OF OUR LIVES TRYING TO REMEMBER WHAT IT WAS LIKE, PUTTING OUT CHRISTMAS ALBUMS AND PLAYING STATE FAIRS.
NEITHER ONE OF THEM LOVES US, OR HATES US, GARLAND. THE NINE, EREBUS, THEY'RE THE SAME. THEY'RE OUR MUSES, THE TRAP THAT WE CAN'T ESCAPE.
BUT YOU MADE IT OUT. YOU FOUND A DIFFERENT WAY.
DID I?

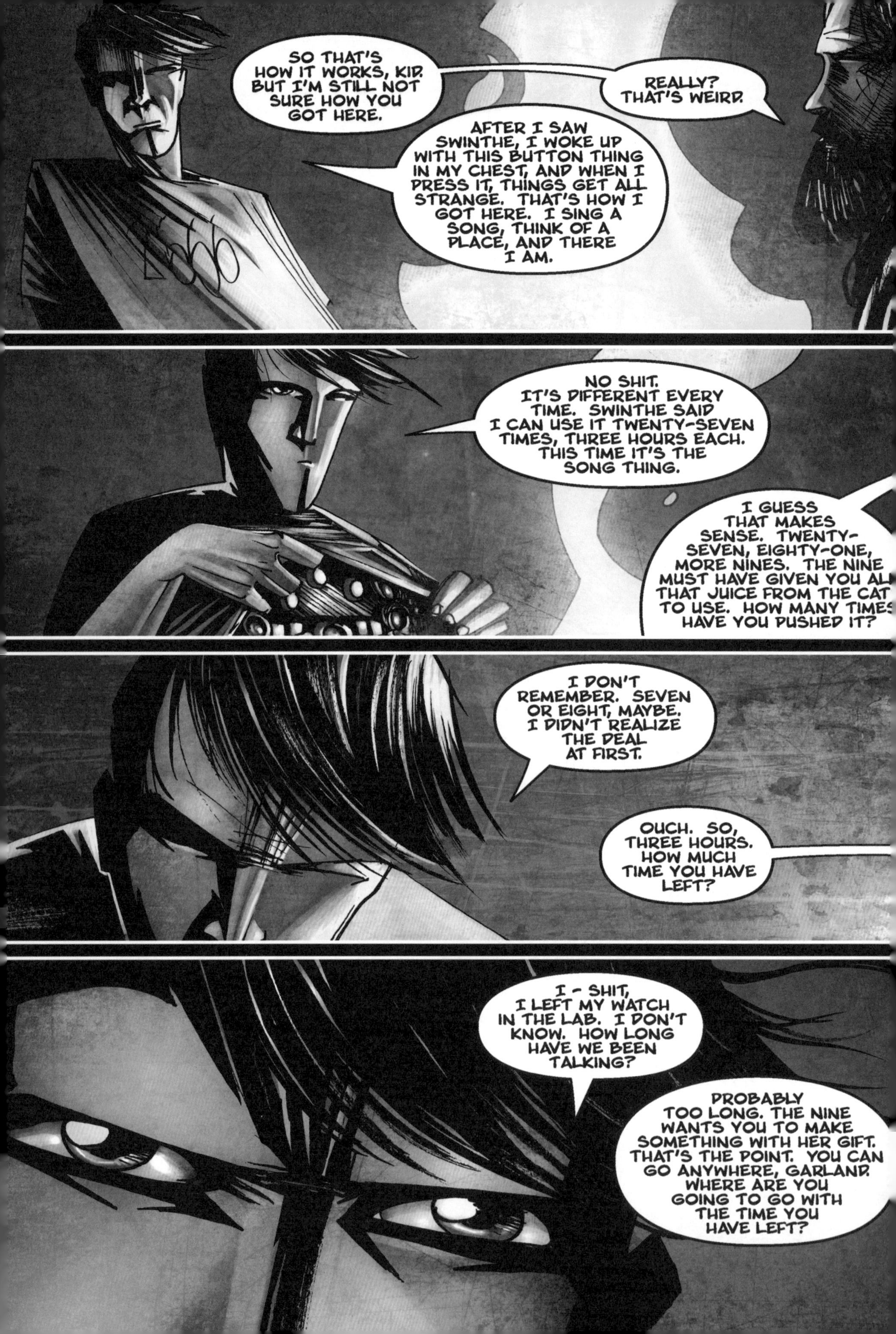
SO THAT'S HOW IT WORKS, KID. BUT I'M STILL NOT SURE HOW YOU GOT HERE.
REALLY? THAT'S WEIRD.
AFTER I SAW SWINTHE, I WOKE UP WITH THIS BUTTON THING IN MY CHEST, AND WHEN I PRESS IT, THINGS GET ALL STRANGE. THAT'S HOW I GOT HERE. I SING A SONG, THINK OF A PLACE, AND THERE I AM.
NO SHIT. IT'S DIFFERENT EVERY TIME. SWINTHE SAID I CAN USE IT TWENTY-SEVEN TIMES, THREE HOURS EACH. THIS TIME IT'S THE SONG THING.
I GUESS THAT MAKES SENSE. TWENTY-SEVEN, EIGHTY-ONE, MORE NINES. THE NINE MUST HAVE GIVEN YOU ALL THAT JUICE FROM THE CAT TO USE. HOW MANY TIMES HAVE YOU PUSHED IT?
I DON'T REMEMBER. SEVEN OR EIGHT, MAYBE. I DIDN'T REALIZE THE DEAL AT FIRST.
OUCH. SO, THREE HOURS. HOW MUCH TIME YOU HAVE LEFT?
I - SHIT, I LEFT MY WATCH IN THE LAB. I DON'T KNOW. HOW LONG HAVE WE BEEN TALKING?
PROBABLY TOO LONG. THE NINE WANTS YOU TO MAKE SOMETHING WITH HER GIFT. THAT'S THE POINT. YOU CAN GO ANYWHERE, GARLAND. WHERE ARE YOU GOING TO GO WITH THE TIME YOU HAVE LEFT?

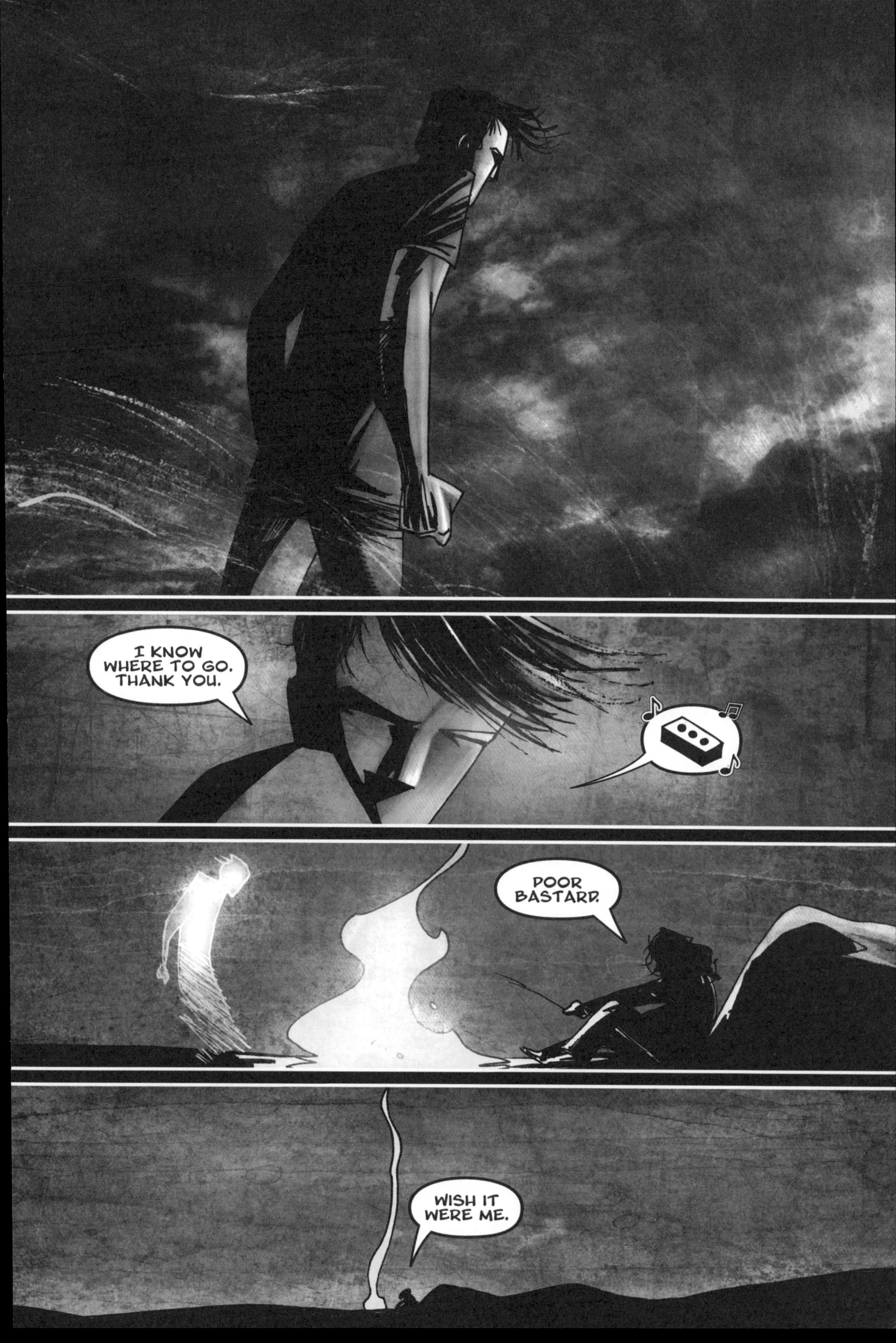
I KNOW WHERE TO GO. THANK YOU.
POOR BASTARD.
WISH IT WERE ME.

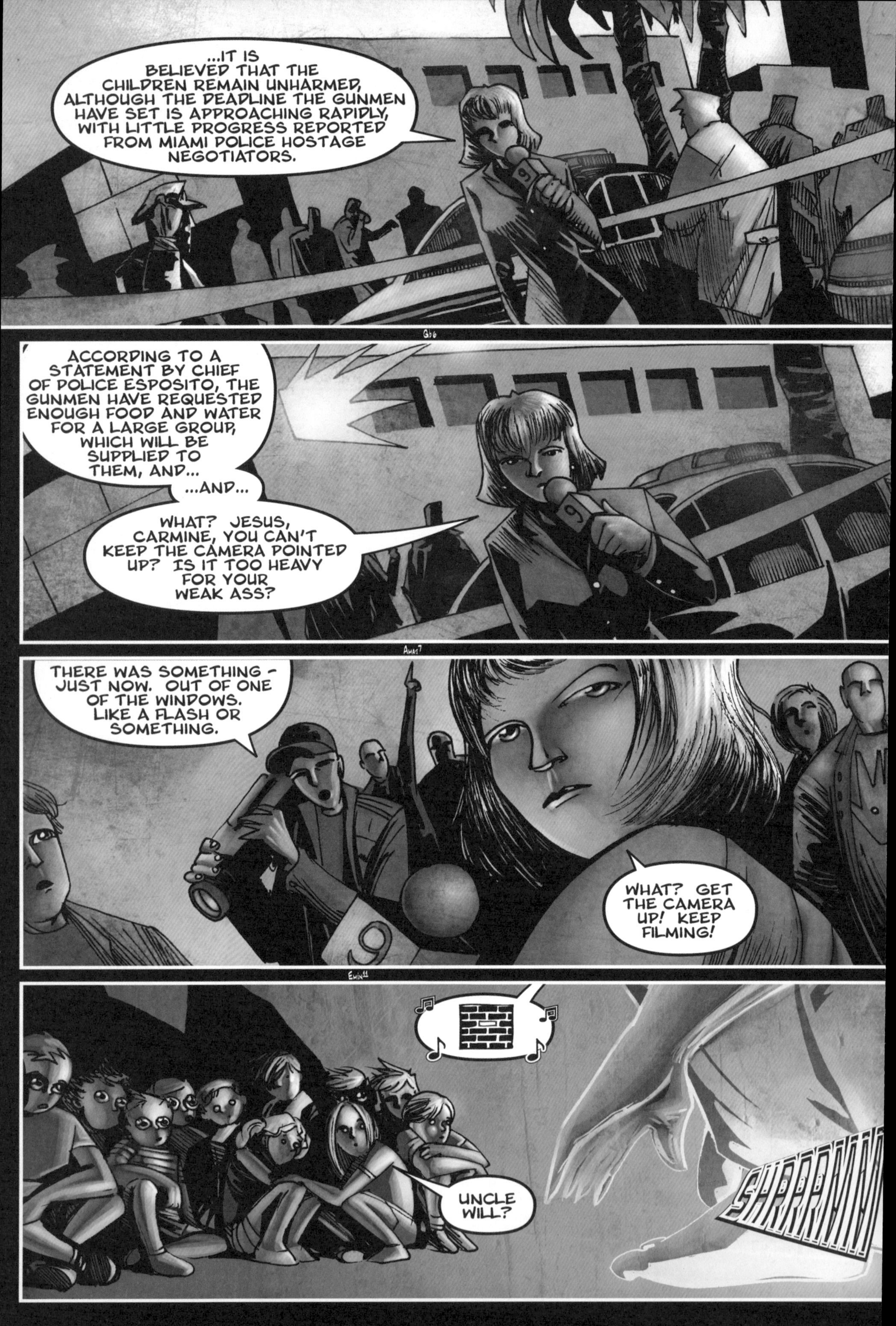
...IT IS BELIEVED THAT THE CHILDREN REMAIN UNHARMED, ALTHOUGH THE DEADLINE THE GUNMEN HAVE SET IS APPROACHING RAPIDLY, WITH LITTLE PROGRESS REPORTED FROM MIAMI POLICE HOSTAGE NEGOTIATORS.
ACCORDING TO A STATEMENT BY CHIEF OF POLICE ESPOSITO, THE GUNMEN HAVE REQUESTED ENOUGH FOOD AND WATER FOR A LARGE GROUP, WHICH WILL BE SUPPLIED TO THEM, AND...
...AND...
WHAT? JESUS, CARMINE, YOU CAN'T KEEP THE CAMERA POINTED UP? IS IT TOO HEAVY FOR YOUR WEAK ASS?
THERE WAS SOMETHING - JUST NOW. OUT OF ONE OF THE WINDOWS. LIKE A FLASH OR SOMETHING.
WHAT? GET THE CAMERA UP! KEEP FILMING!
UNCLE WILL?
SHRRRMMM

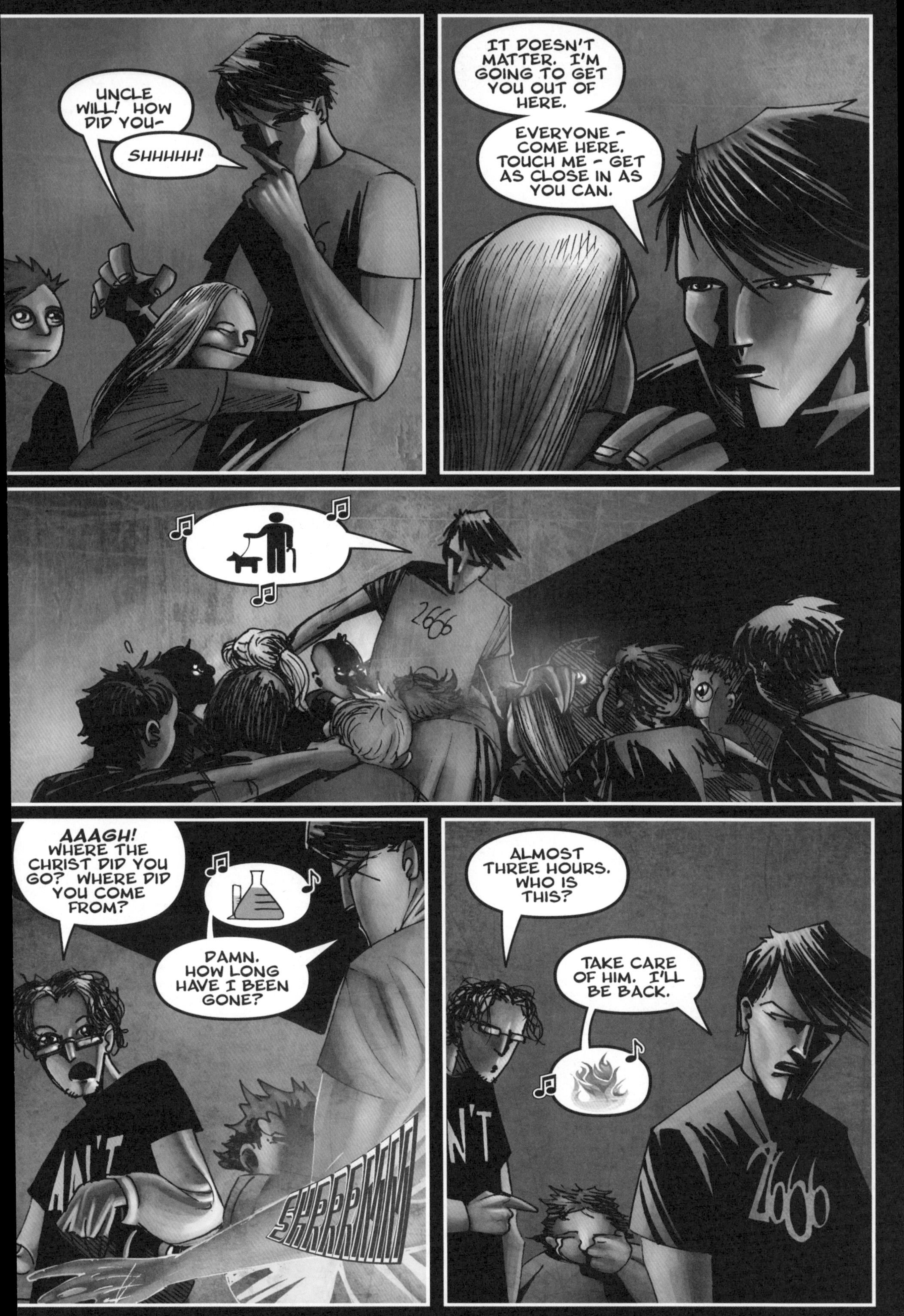
UNCLE WILL! HOW DID YOU-
SHHHHH!
IT DOESN'T MATTER. I'M GOING TO GET YOU OUT OF HERE.
EVERYONE - COME HERE. TOUCH ME - GET AS CLOSE IN AS YOU CAN.
2666
AAAGH! WHERE THE CHRIST DID YOU GO? WHERE DID YOU COME FROM?
DAMN. HOW LONG HAVE I BEEN GONE?
SKRRRIIIIII
ALMOST THREE HOURS. WHO IS THIS?
TAKE CARE OF HIM. I'LL BE BACK.
2666

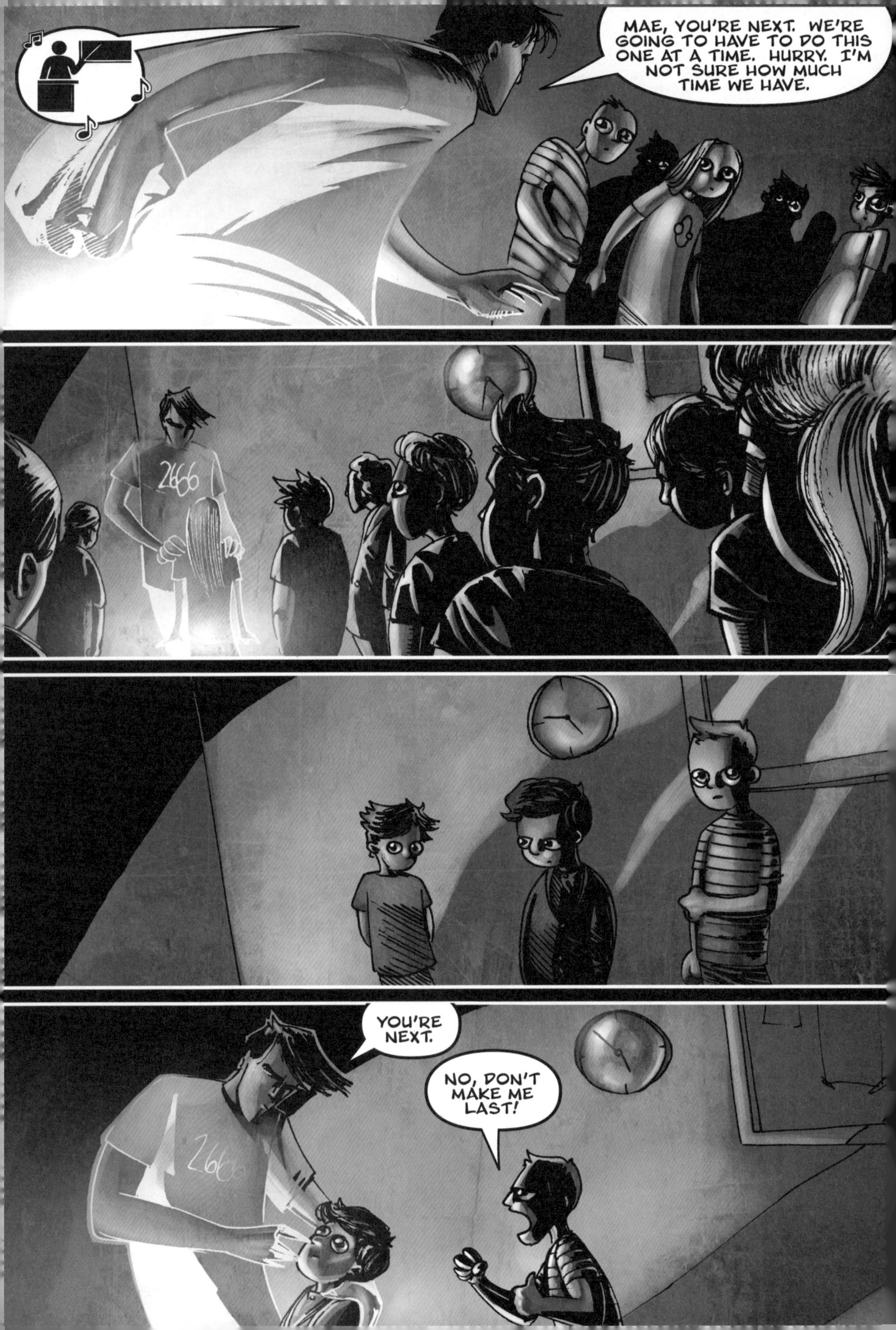
MAE, YOU'RE NEXT. WE'RE GOING TO HAVE TO DO THIS ONE AT A TIME. HURRY. I'M NOT SURE HOW MUCH TIME WE HAVE.
2666
YOU'RE NEXT.
NO, DON'T MAKE ME LAST!

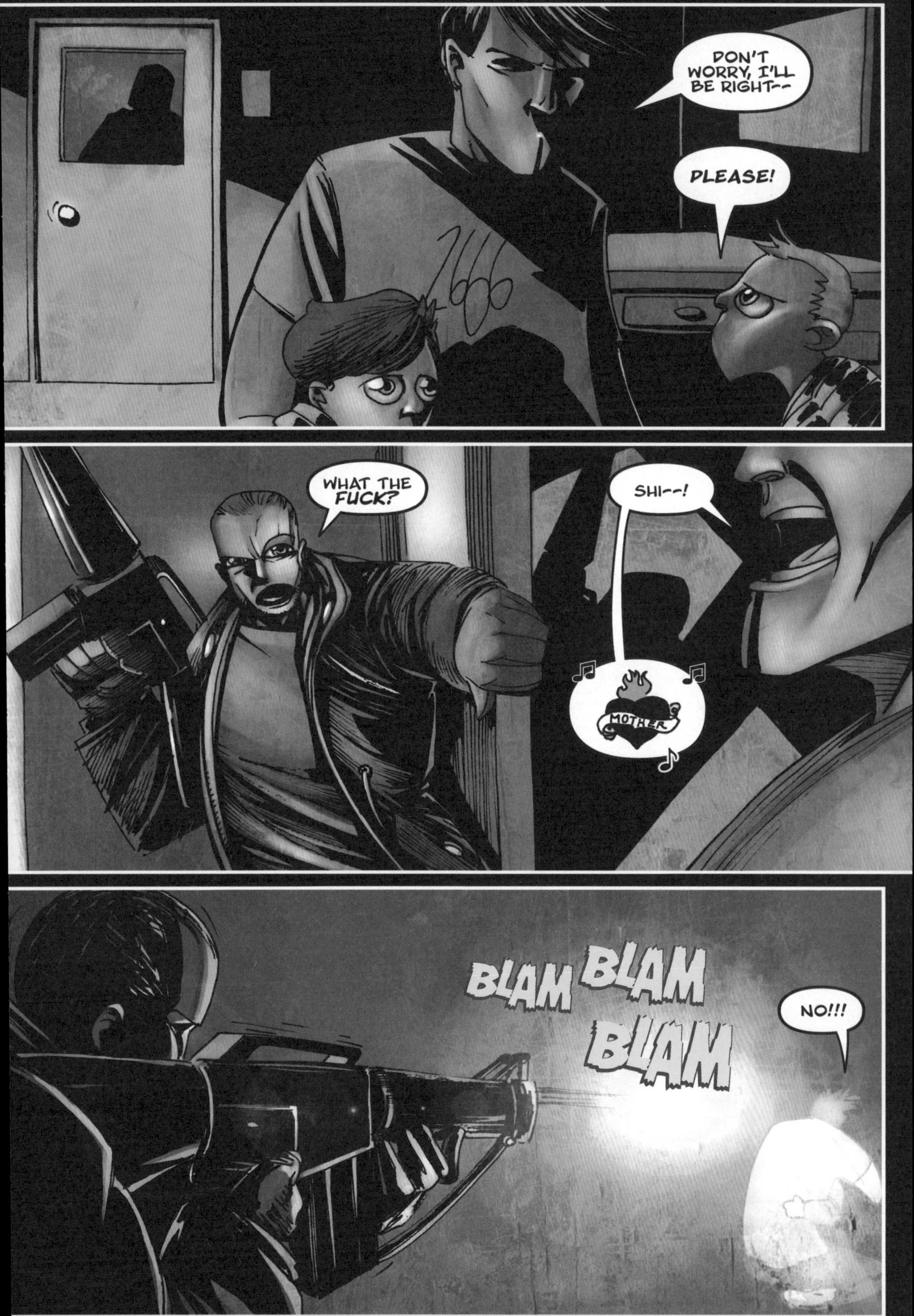

DON'T WORRY, I'LL BE RIGHT--
PLEASE!
WHAT THE FUCK?
SHI--!
MOTHER
BLAM BLAM BLAM
NO!!!

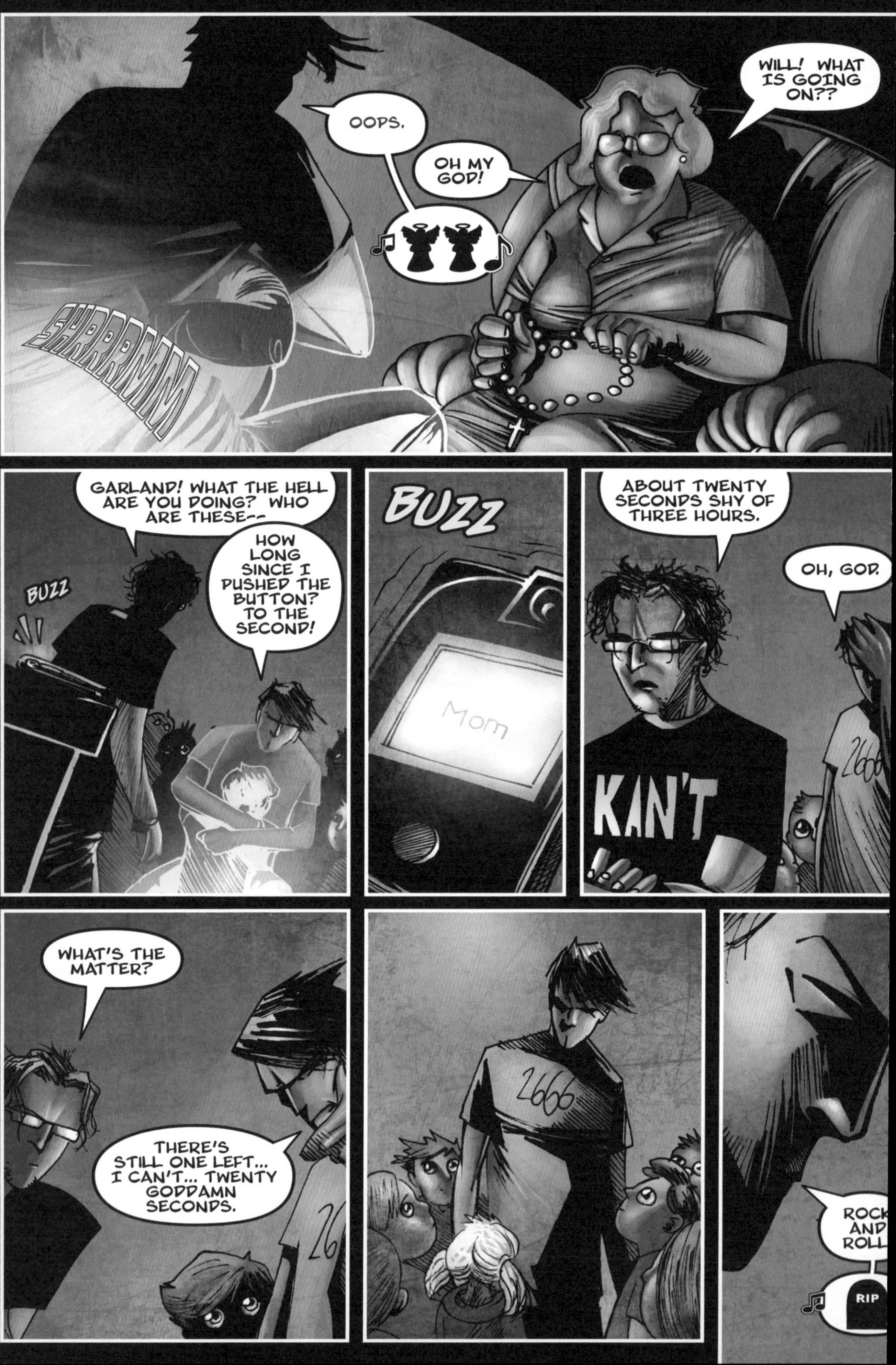
OOPS.
OH MY GOD!
WILL! WHAT IS GOING ON??
SHRRRMM
GARLAND! WHAT THE HELL ARE YOU DOING? WHO ARE THESE--
BUZZ
HOW LONG SINCE I PUSHED THE BUTTON? TO THE SECOND!
BUZZ
Mom
ABOUT TWENTY SECONDS SHY OF THREE HOURS.
OH, GOD.
KAN'T
WHAT'S THE MATTER?
THERE'S STILL ONE LEFT... I CAN'T... TWENTY GODDAMN SECONDS.
2666
ROCK AND ROLL
RIP

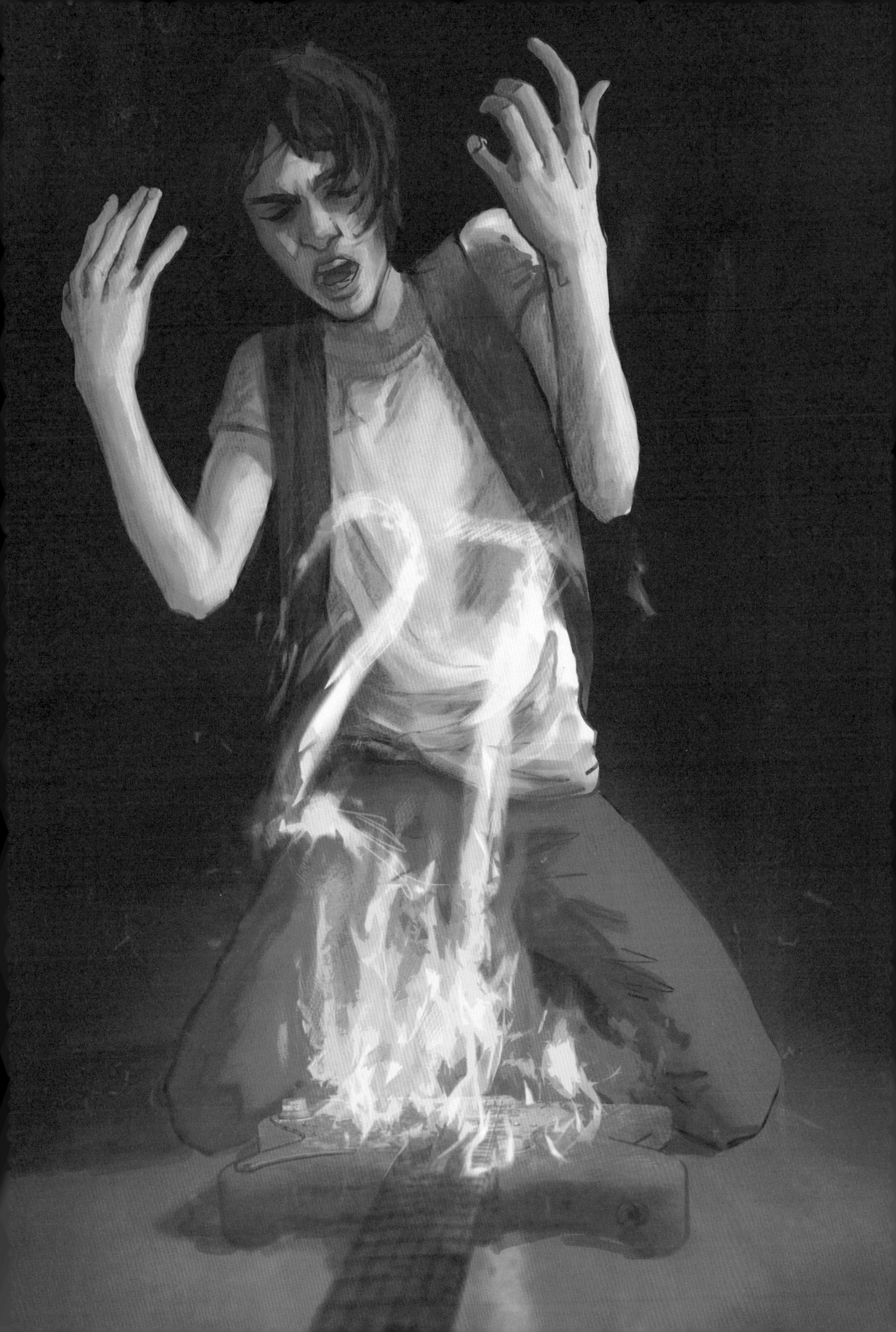

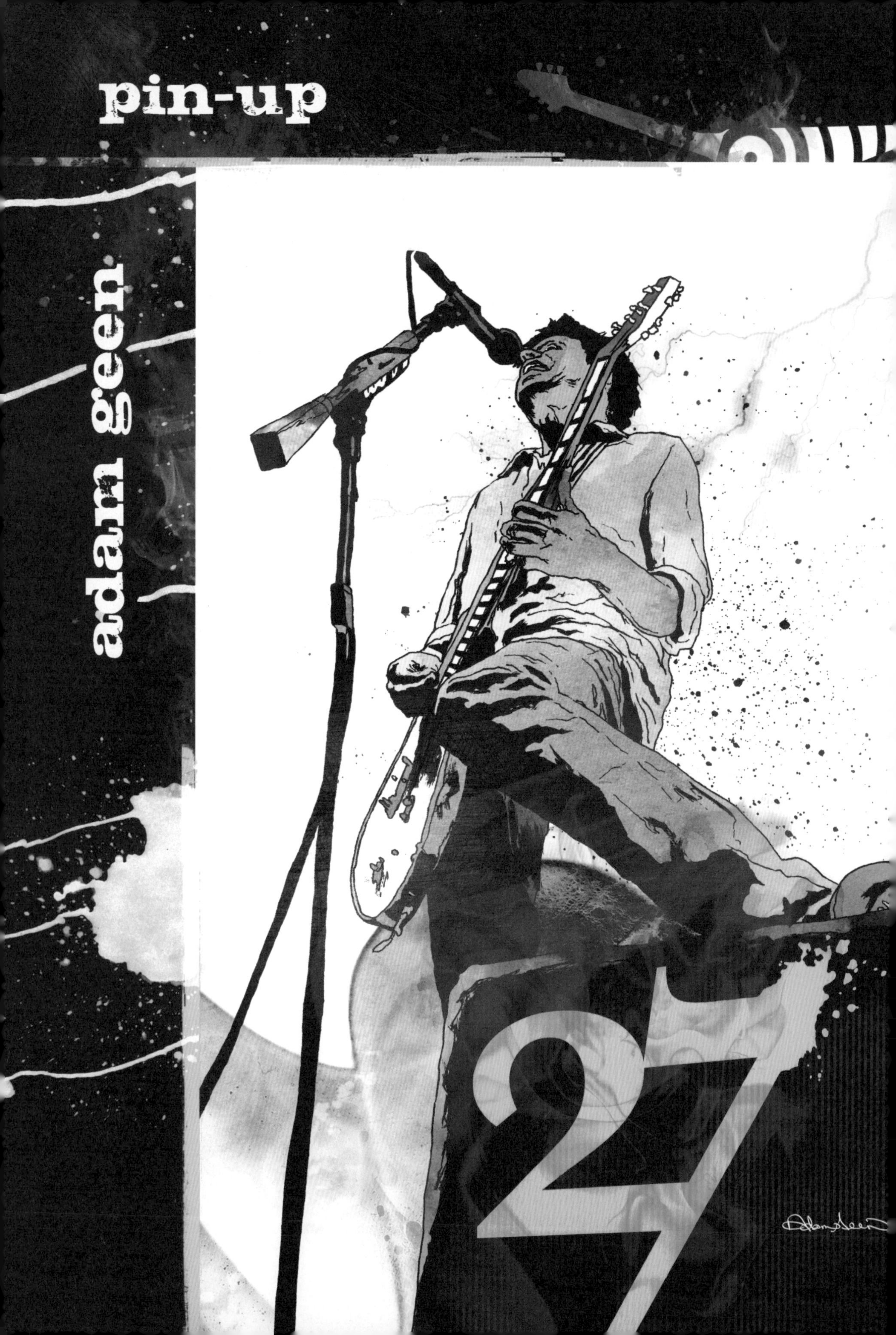
pin-up
adam geen
27

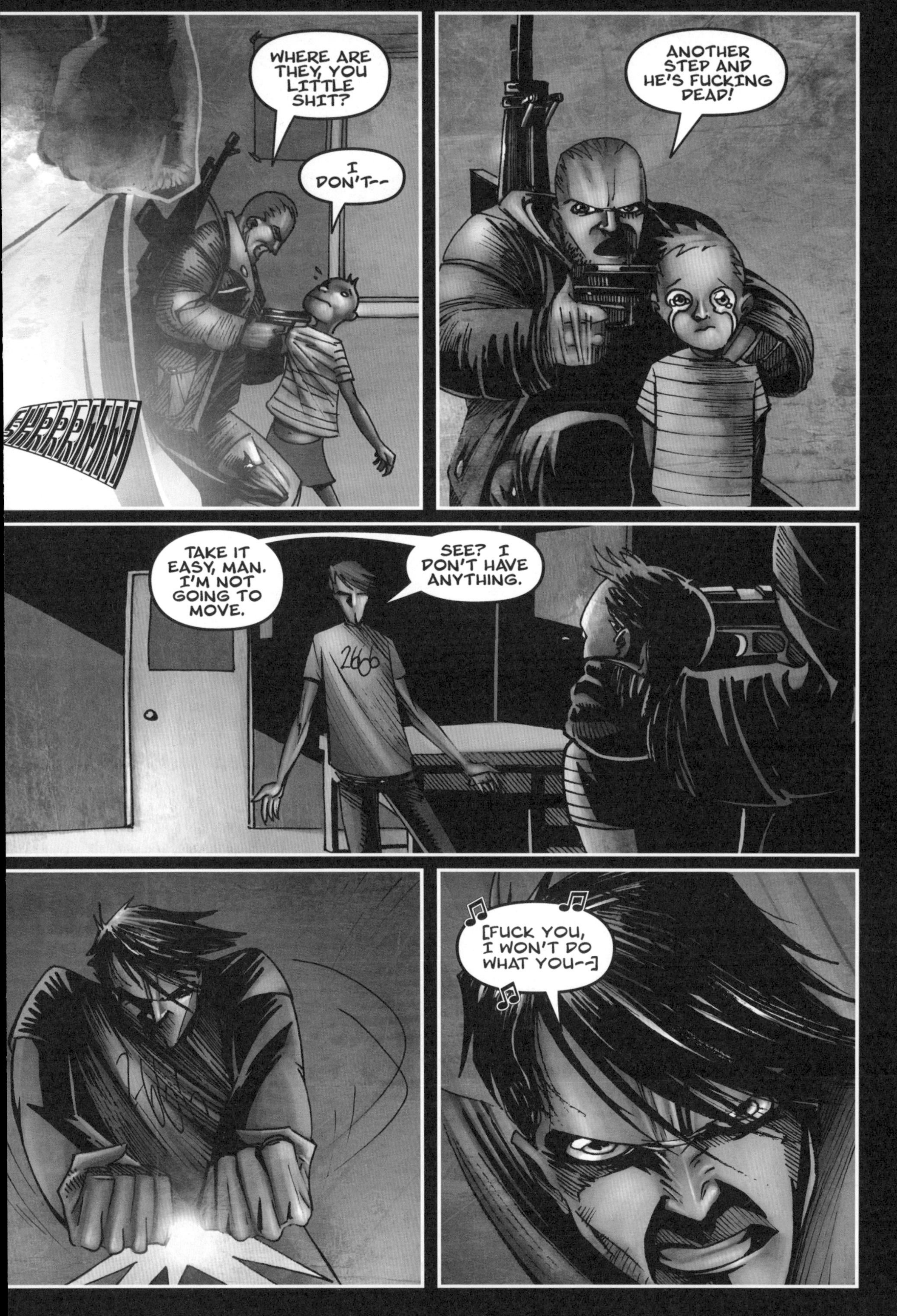
WHERE ARE THEY, YOU LITTLE SHIT?
I DON'T--
ANOTHER STEP AND HE'S FUCKING DEAD!
TAKE IT EASY, MAN. I'M NOT GOING TO MOVE.
SEE? I DON'T HAVE ANYTHING.
2600
[FUCK YOU, I WON'T DO WHAT YOU--]

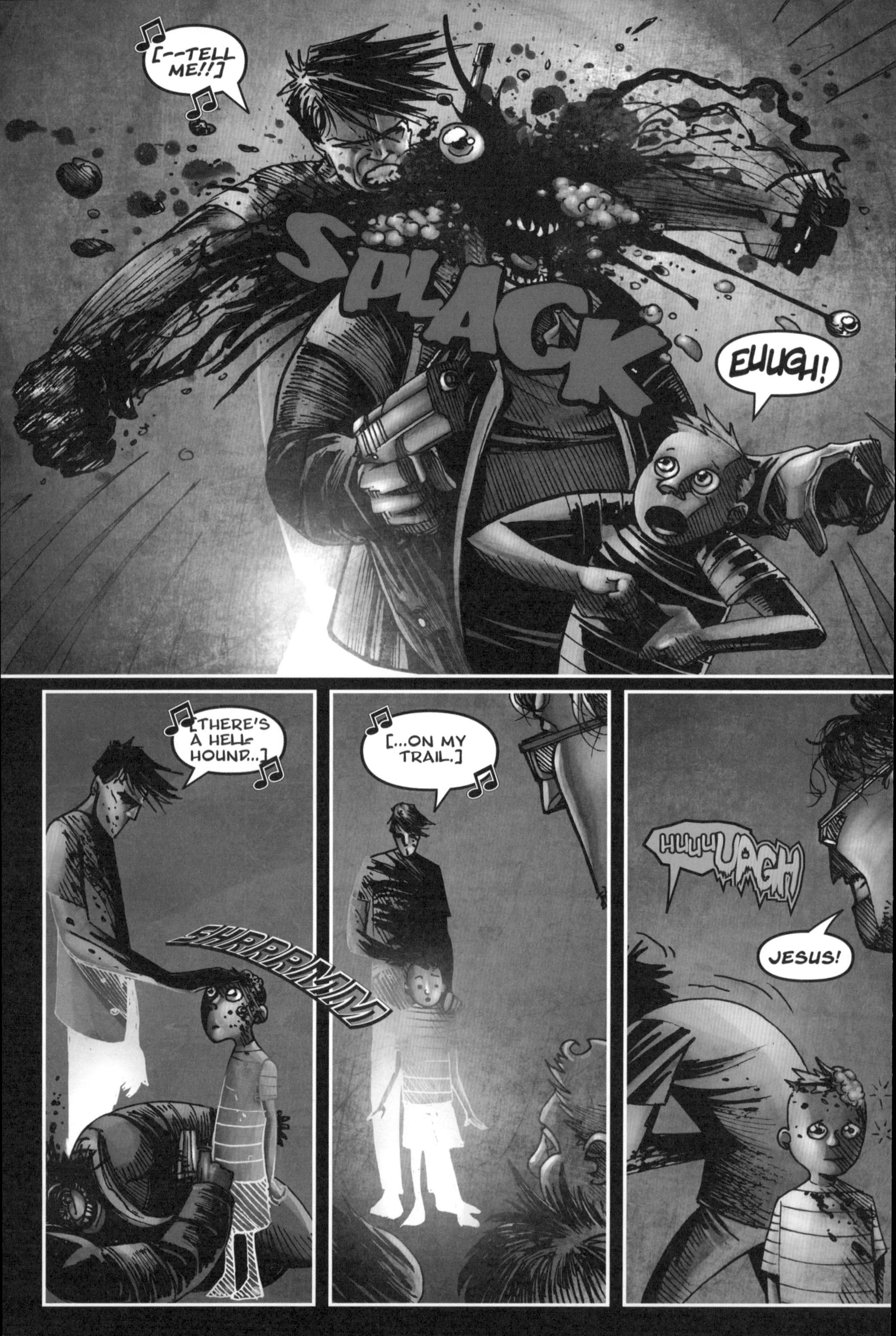
[--TELL ME!!]
SPLACK
EUUGH!
[THERE'S A HELL-HOUND...]
SHRRRMMM
[...ON MY TRAIL.]
HUUUURAGH
JESUS!

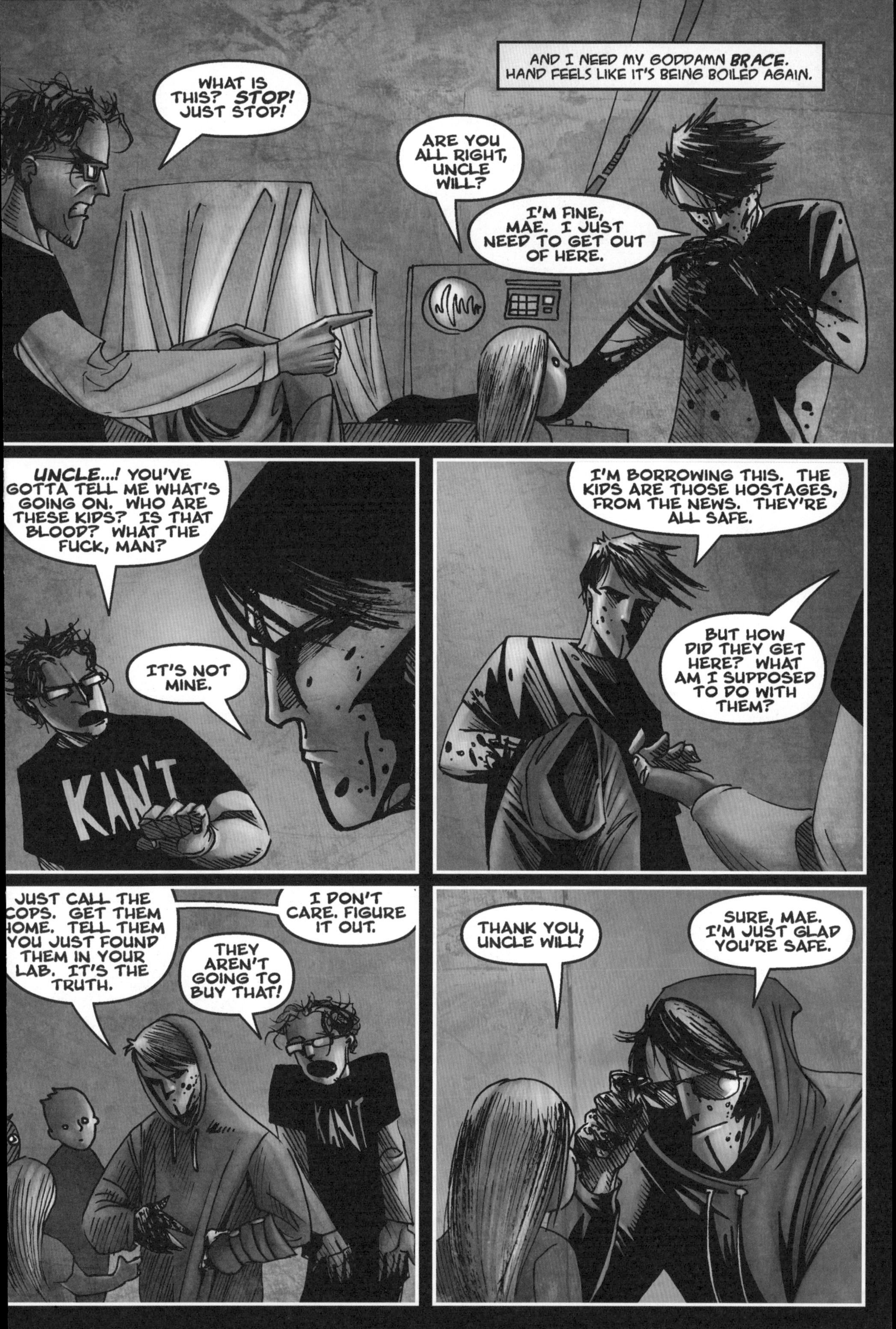
AND I NEED MY GODDAMN BRACE. HAND FEELS LIKE IT'S BEING BOILED AGAIN.
WHAT IS THIS? STOP! JUST STOP!
ARE YOU ALL RIGHT, UNCLE WILL?
I'M FINE, MAE. I JUST NEED TO GET OUT OF HERE.
UNCLE...! YOU'VE GOTTA TELL ME WHAT'S GOING ON. WHO ARE THESE KIDS? IS THAT BLOOD? WHAT THE FUCK, MAN?
IT'S NOT MINE.
KAN'T
I'M BORROWING THIS. THE KIDS ARE THOSE HOSTAGES, FROM THE NEWS. THEY'RE ALL SAFE.
BUT HOW DID THEY GET HERE? WHAT AM I SUPPOSED TO DO WITH THEM?
JUST CALL THE COPS. GET THEM HOME. TELL THEM YOU JUST FOUND THEM IN YOUR LAB. IT'S THE TRUTH.
THEY AREN'T GOING TO BUY THAT!
I DON'T CARE. FIGURE IT OUT.
KANT
THANK YOU, UNCLE WILL!
SURE, MAE. I'M JUST GLAD YOU'RE SAFE.

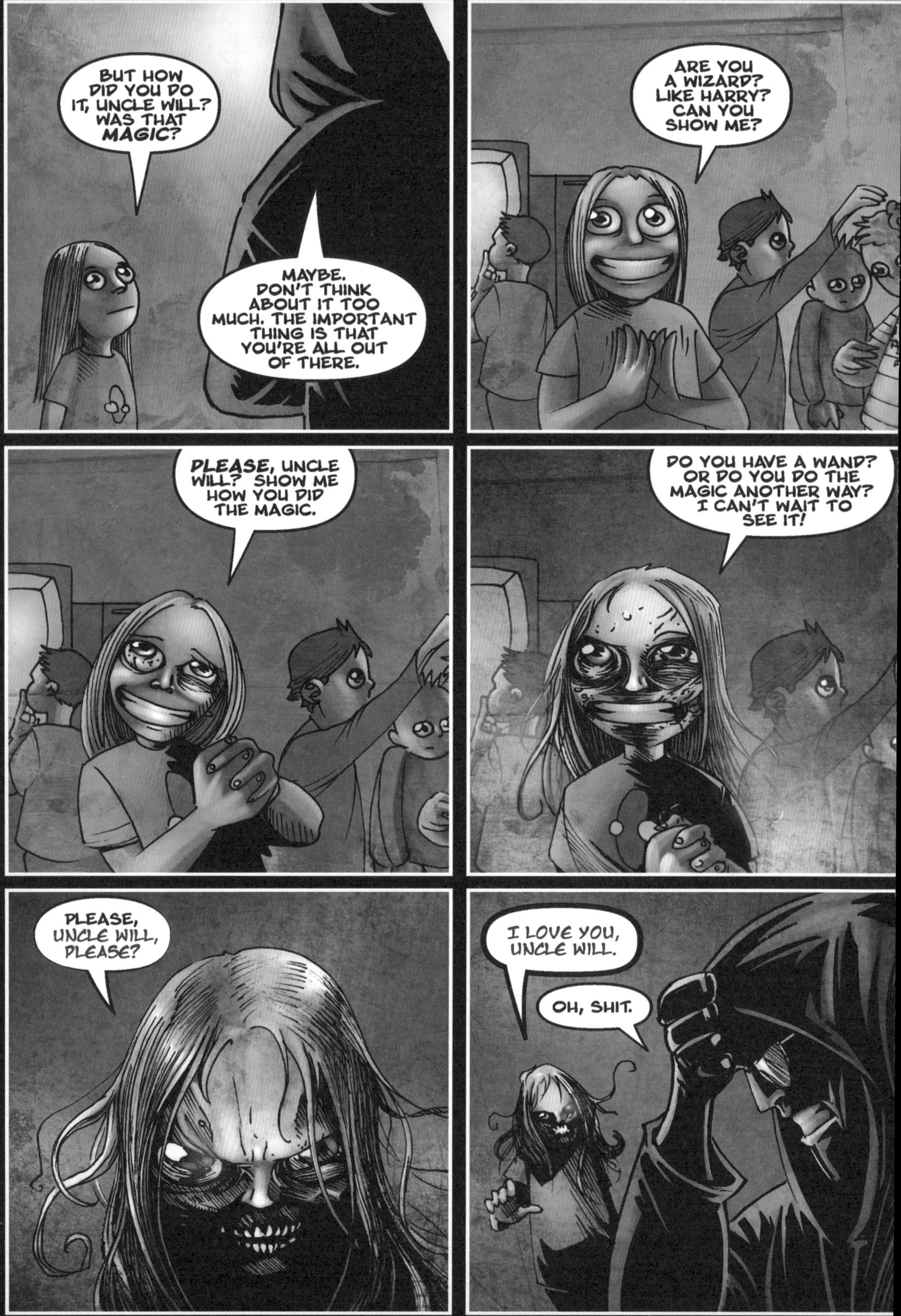
BUT HOW DID YOU DO IT, UNCLE WILL? WAS THAT MAGIC?
MAYBE. DON'T THINK ABOUT IT TOO MUCH. THE IMPORTANT THING IS THAT YOU'RE ALL OUT OF THERE.
ARE YOU A WIZARD? LIKE HARRY? CAN YOU SHOW ME?
PLEASE, UNCLE WILL? SHOW ME HOW YOU DID THE MAGIC.
DO YOU HAVE A WAND? OR DO YOU DO THE MAGIC ANOTHER WAY? I CAN'T WAIT TO SEE IT!
PLEASE, UNCLE WILL, PLEASE?
I LOVE YOU, UNCLE WILL.
OH, SHIT.

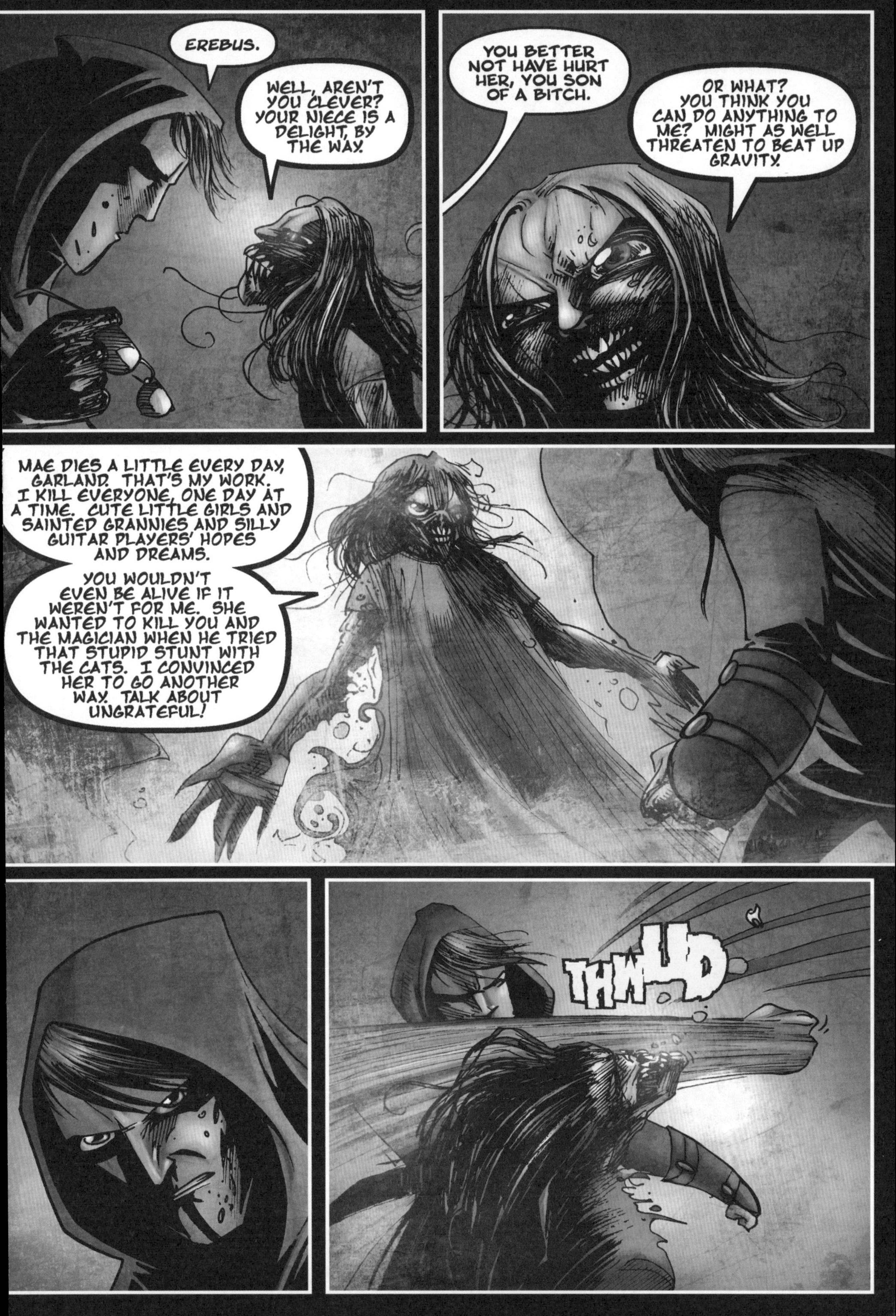
EREBUS.
WELL, AREN'T YOU CLEVER? YOUR NIECE IS A DELIGHT, BY THE WAY.
YOU BETTER NOT HAVE HURT HER, YOU SON OF A BITCH.
OR WHAT? YOU THINK YOU CAN DO ANYTHING TO ME? MIGHT AS WELL THREATEN TO BEAT UP GRAVITY.
MAE DIES A LITTLE EVERY DAY, GARLAND. THAT'S MY WORK. I KILL EVERYONE, ONE DAY AT A TIME. CUTE LITTLE GIRLS AND SAINTED GRANNIES AND SILLY GUITAR PLAYERS' HOPES AND DREAMS.
YOU WOULDN'T EVEN BE ALIVE IF IT WEREN'T FOR ME. SHE WANTED TO KILL YOU AND THE MAGICIAN WHEN HE TRIED THAT STUPID STUNT WITH THE CATS. I CONVINCED HER TO GO ANOTHER WAY. TALK ABOUT UNGRATEFUL!
THWUD

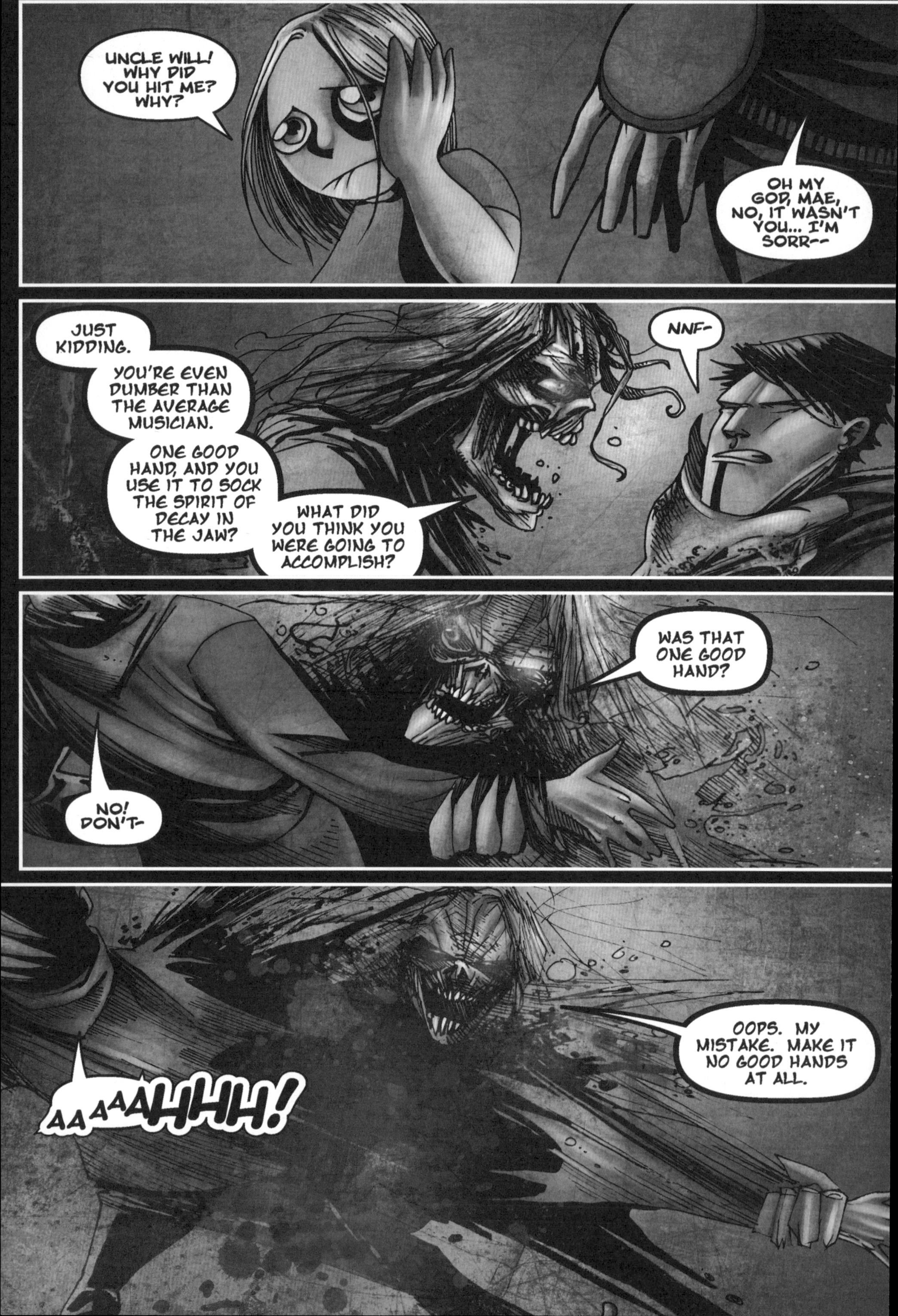
UNCLE WILL! WHY DID YOU HIT ME? WHY?
OH MY GOD, MAE, NO, IT WASN'T YOU... I'M SORR--
JUST KIDDING.
YOU'RE EVEN DUMBER THAN THE AVERAGE MUSICIAN.
ONE GOOD HAND, AND YOU USE IT TO SOCK THE SPIRIT OF DECAY IN THE JAW?
WHAT DID YOU THINK YOU WERE GOING TO ACCOMPLISH?
NNF-
WAS THAT ONE GOOD HAND?
NO! DON'T-
OOPS. MY MISTAKE. MAKE IT NO GOOD HANDS AT ALL.
AAAAAHHHH!

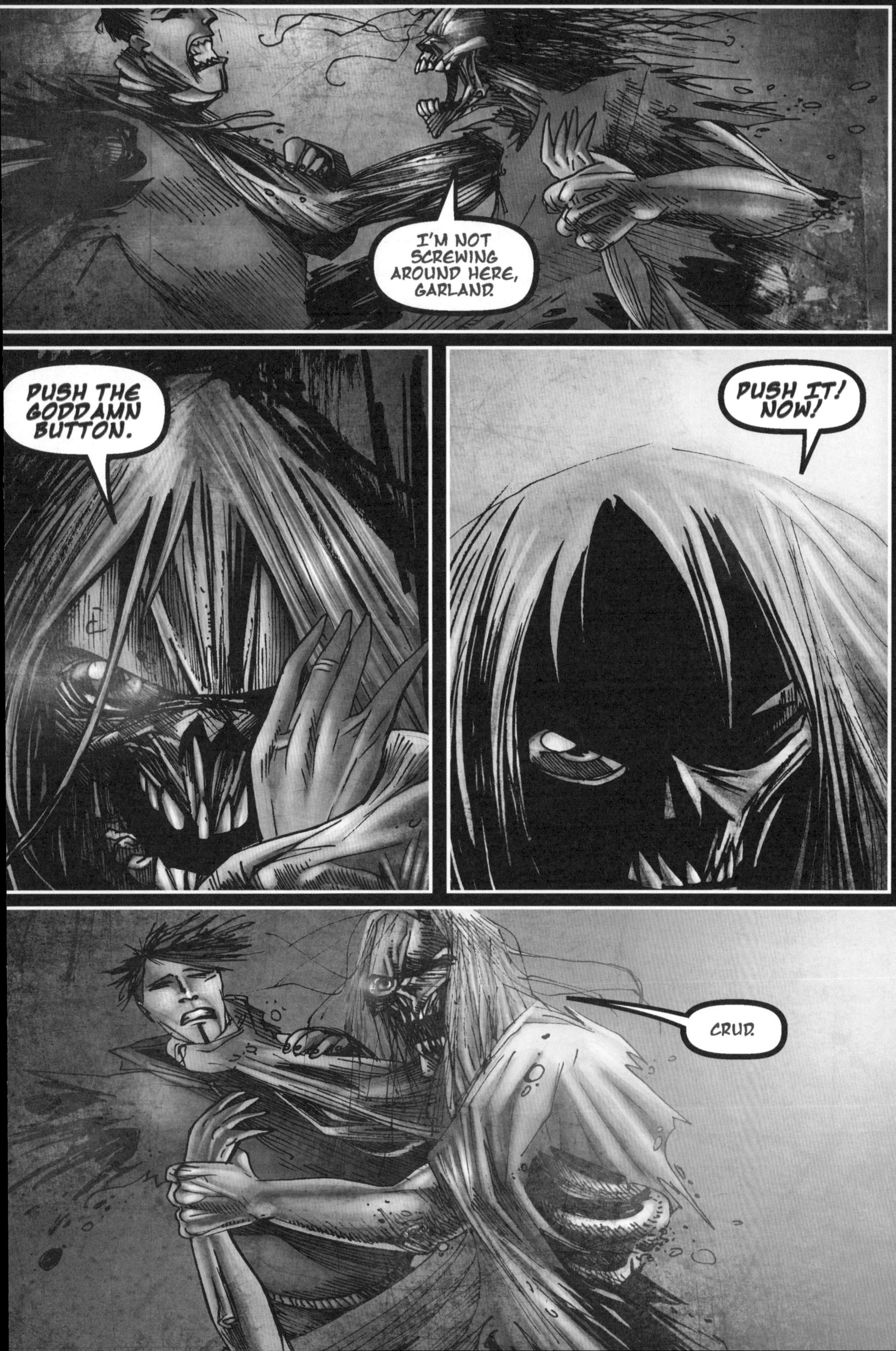
I'M NOT SCREWING AROUND HERE, GARLAND.
PUSH THE GODDAMN BUTTON.
PUSH IT! NOW!
CRUD.

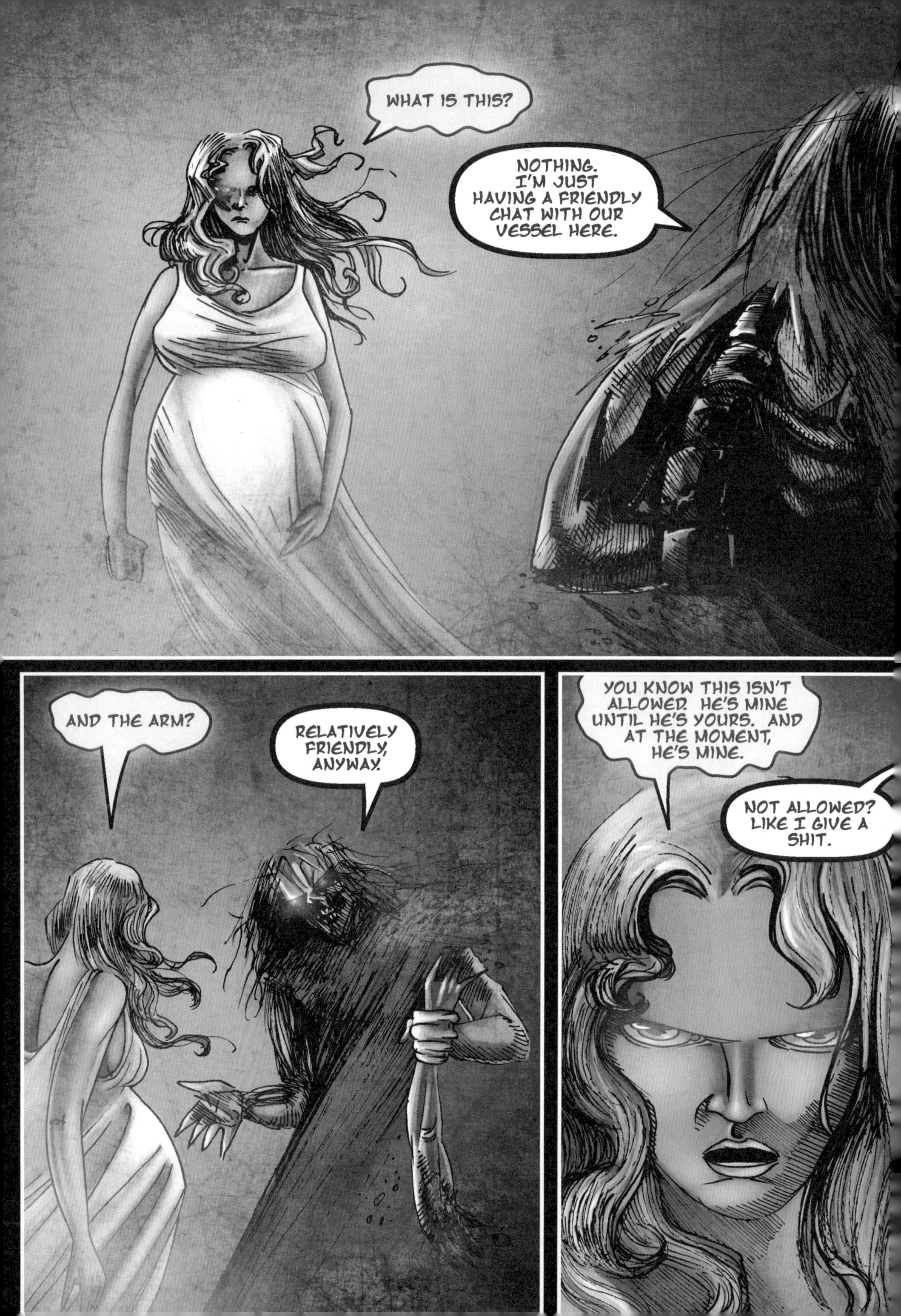
WHAT IS THIS?
NOTHING. I'M JUST HAVING A FRIENDLY CHAT WITH OUR VESSEL HERE.
AND THE ARM?
RELATIVELY FRIENDLY, ANYWAY.
YOU KNOW THIS ISN'T ALLOWED. HE'S MINE UNTIL HE'S YOURS. AND AT THE MOMENT, HE'S MINE.
NOT ALLOWED? LIKE I GIVE A SHIT.

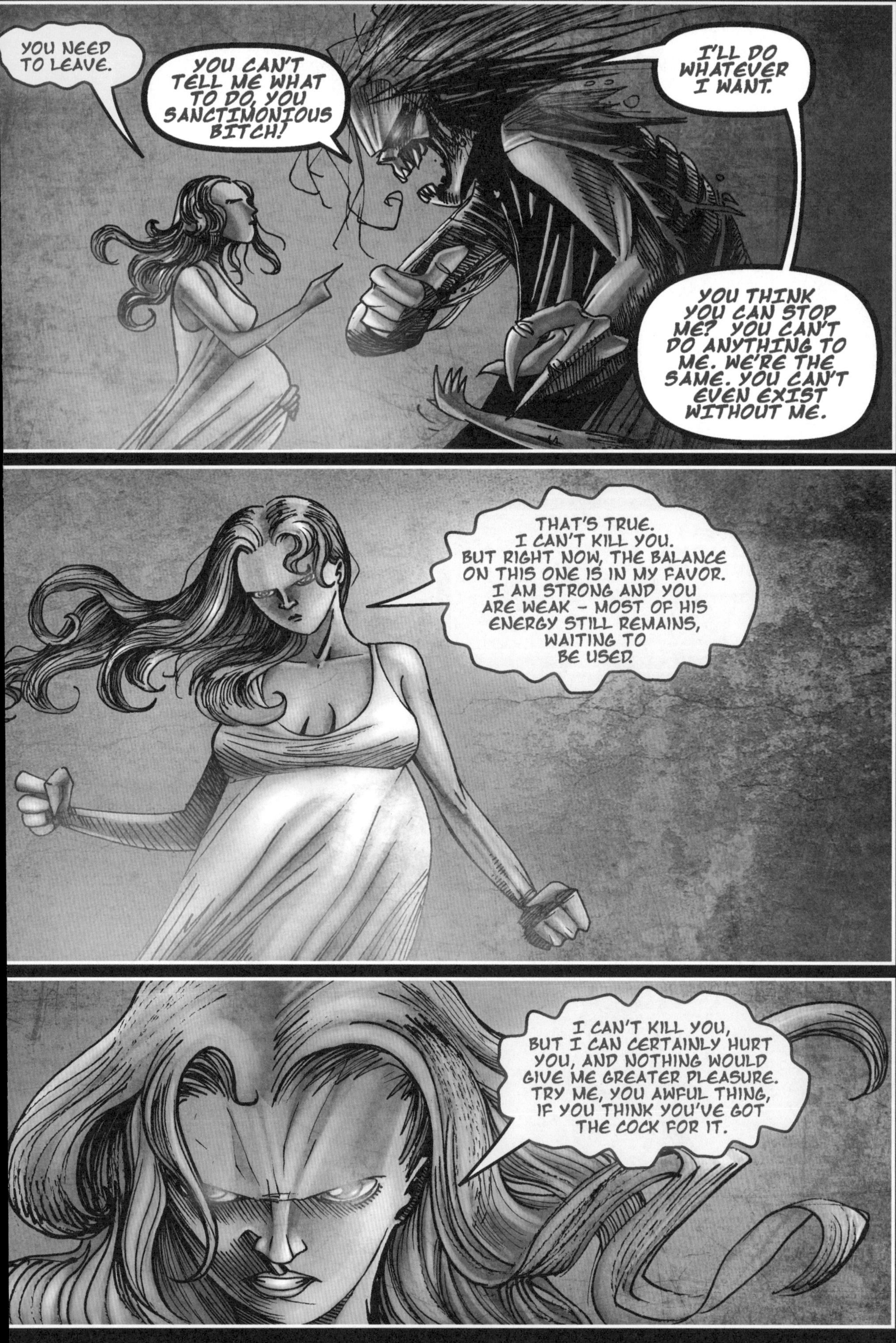
YOU NEED TO LEAVE.
YOU CAN'T TELL ME WHAT TO DO, YOU SANCTIMONIOUS BITCH!
I'LL DO WHATEVER I WANT.
YOU THINK YOU CAN STOP ME? YOU CAN'T DO ANYTHING TO ME. WE'RE THE SAME. YOU CAN'T EVEN EXIST WITHOUT ME.
THAT'S TRUE. I CAN'T KILL YOU. BUT RIGHT NOW, THE BALANCE ON THIS ONE IS IN MY FAVOR. I AM STRONG AND YOU ARE WEAK - MOST OF HIS ENERGY STILL REMAINS, WAITING TO BE USED.
I CAN'T KILL YOU, BUT I CAN CERTAINLY HURT YOU, AND NOTHING WOULD GIVE ME GREATER PLEASURE. TRY ME, YOU AWFUL THING, IF YOU THINK YOU'VE GOT THE COCK FOR IT.

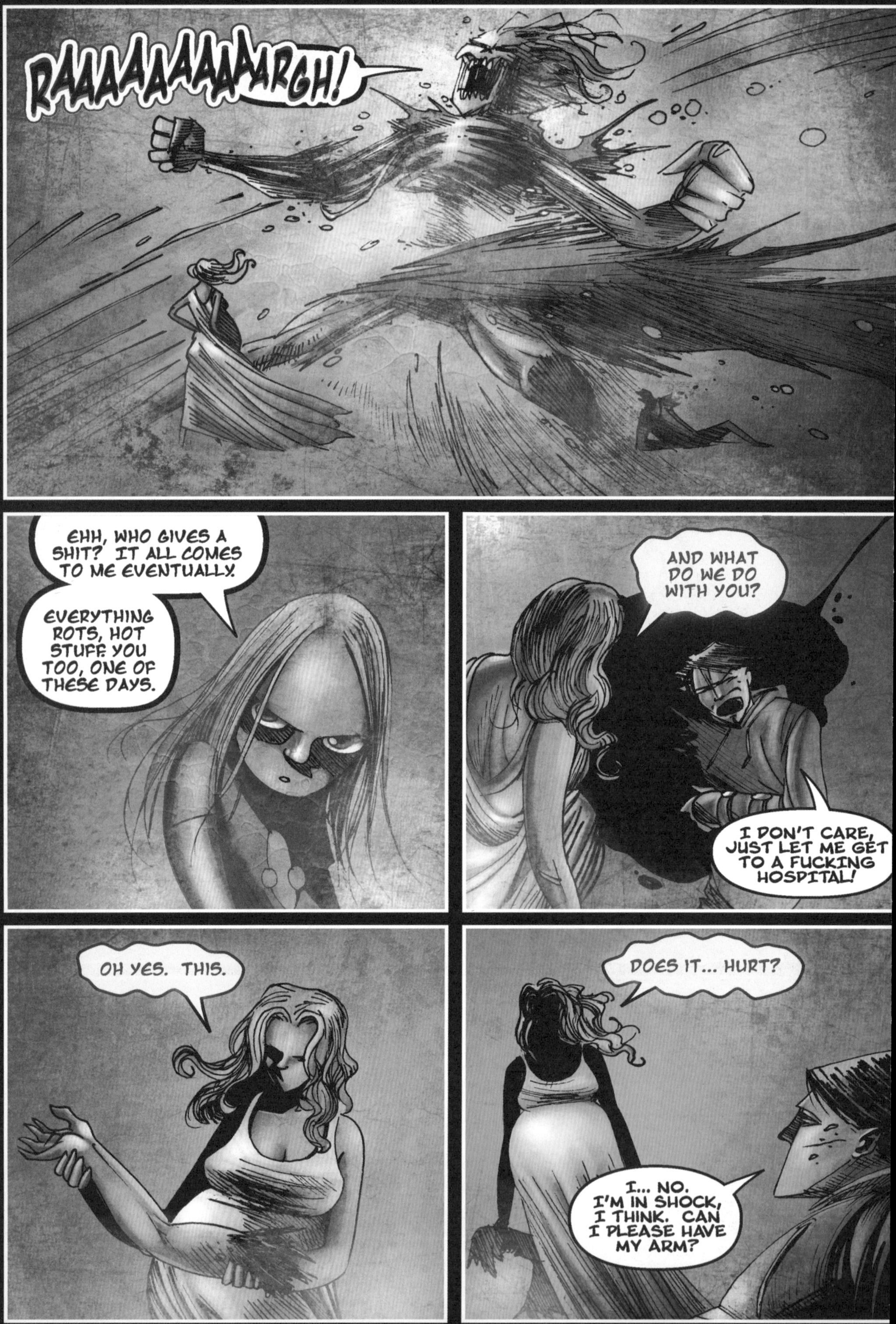
RAAAAAAAAARGH!
EHH, WHO GIVES A SHIT? IT ALL COMES TO ME EVENTUALLY.
EVERYTHING ROTS, HOT STUFF. YOU TOO, ONE OF THESE DAYS.
AND WHAT DO WE DO WITH YOU?
I DON'T CARE, JUST LET ME GET TO A FUCKING HOSPITAL!
OH YES. THIS.
DOES IT... HURT?
I... NO. I'M IN SHOCK, I THINK. CAN I PLEASE HAVE MY ARM?

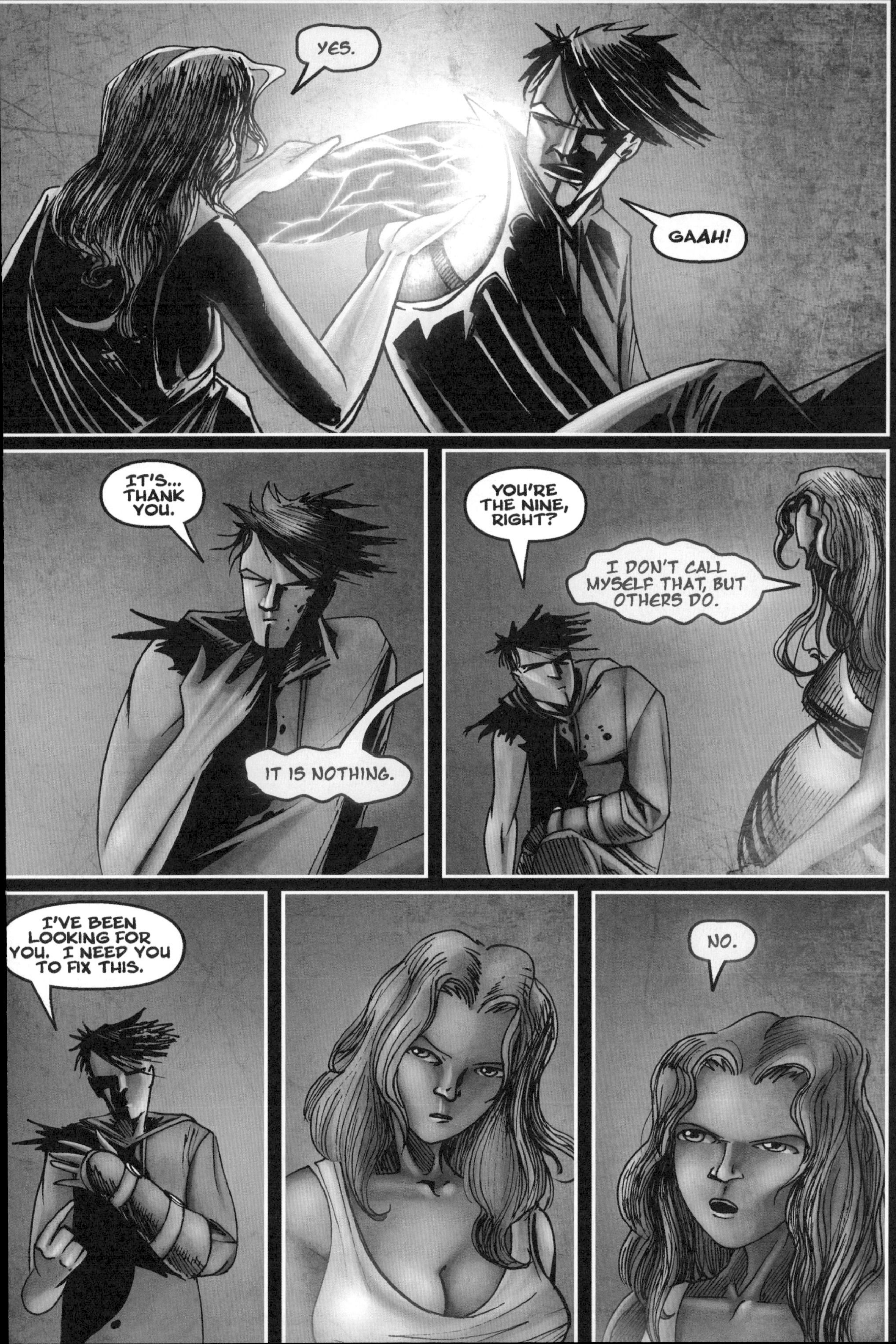
YES.
GAAH!
IT'S... THANK YOU.
IT IS NOTHING.
YOU'RE THE NINE, RIGHT?
I DON'T CALL MYSELF THAT, BUT OTHERS DO.
I'VE BEEN LOOKING FOR YOU. I NEED YOU TO FIX THIS.
NO.

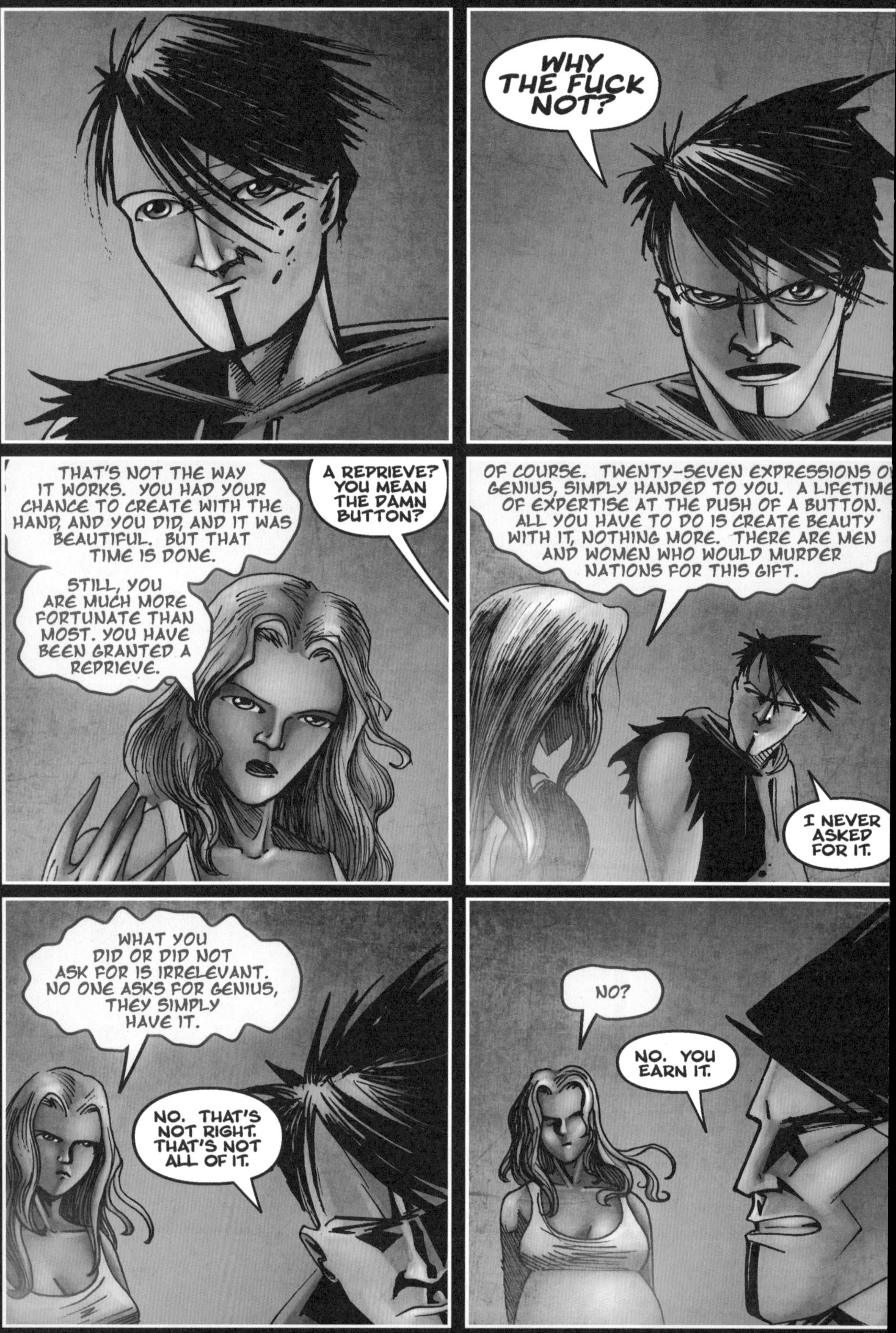
WHY THE FUCK NOT?
THAT'S NOT THE WAY IT WORKS. YOU HAD YOUR CHANCE TO CREATE WITH THE HAND, AND YOU DID, AND IT WAS BEAUTIFUL. BUT THAT TIME IS DONE.
STILL, YOU ARE MUCH MORE FORTUNATE THAN MOST. YOU HAVE BEEN GRANTED A REPRIEVE.
A REPRIEVE? YOU MEAN THE DAMN BUTTON?
OF COURSE. TWENTY-SEVEN EXPRESSIONS OF GENIUS, SIMPLY HANDED TO YOU. A LIFETIME OF EXPERTISE AT THE PUSH OF A BUTTON. ALL YOU HAVE TO DO IS CREATE BEAUTY WITH IT, NOTHING MORE. THERE ARE MEN AND WOMEN WHO WOULD MURDER NATIONS FOR THIS GIFT.
I NEVER ASKED FOR IT.
WHAT YOU DID OR DID NOT ASK FOR IS IRRELEVANT. NO ONE ASKS FOR GENIUS, THEY SIMPLY HAVE IT.
NO. THAT'S NOT RIGHT. THAT'S NOT ALL OF IT.
NO?
NO. YOU EARN IT.

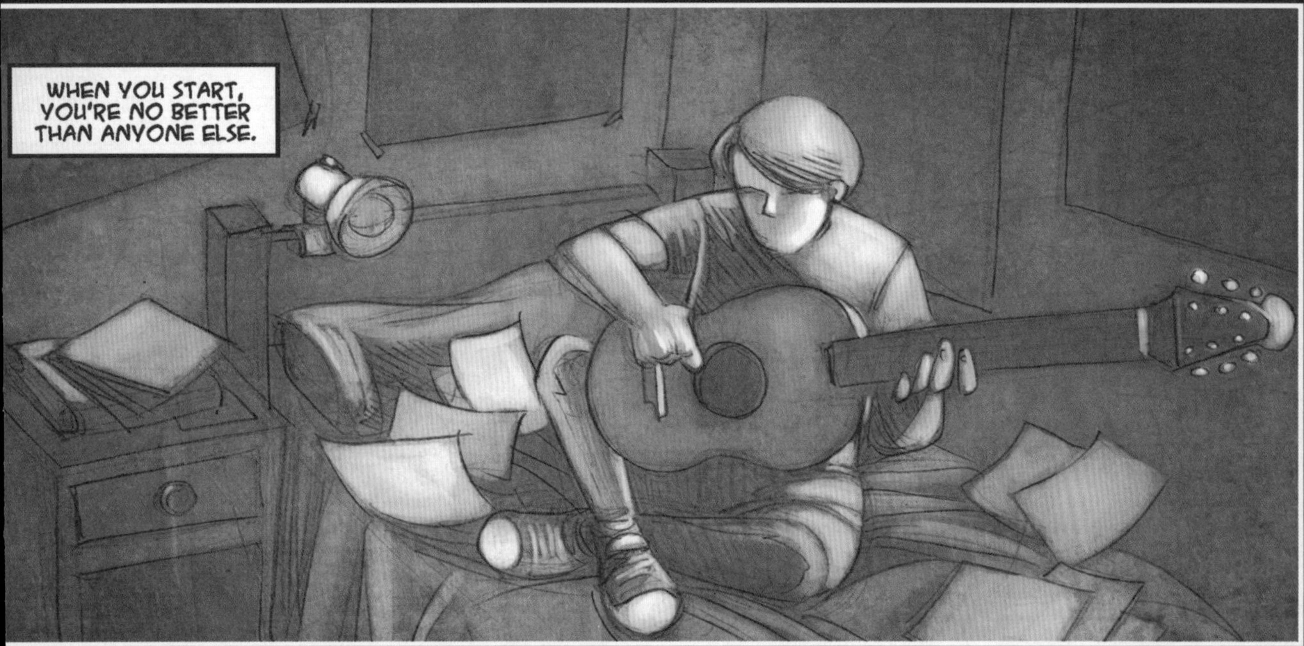
WHEN YOU START, YOU'RE NO BETTER THAN ANYONE ELSE.

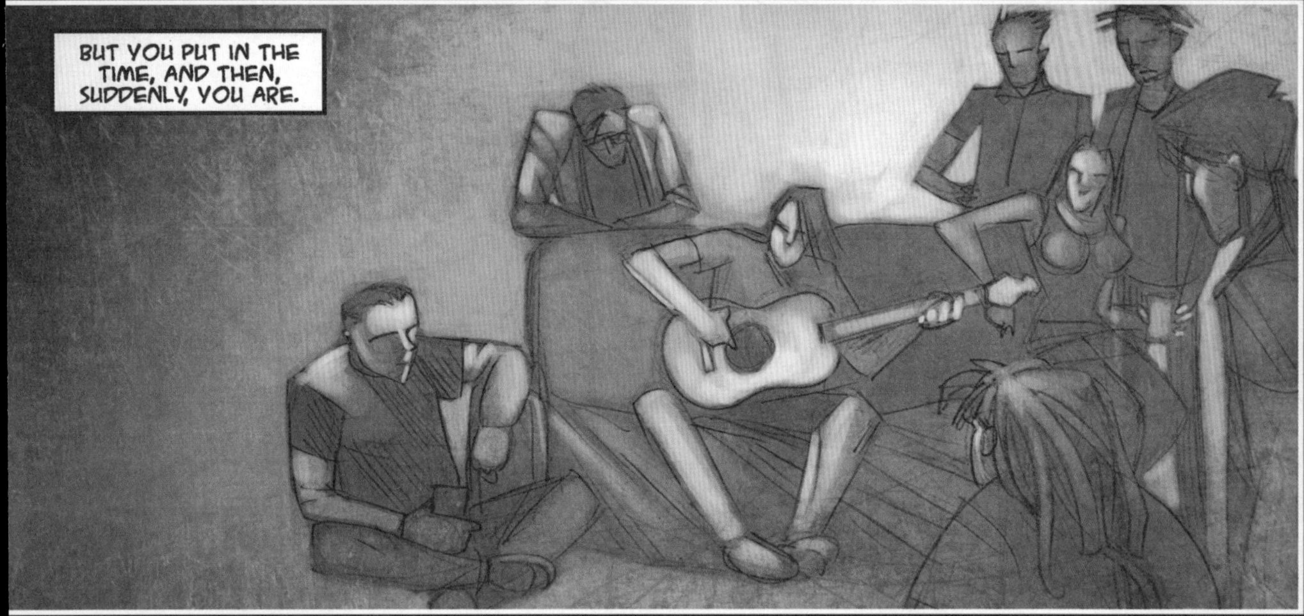
BUT YOU PUT IN THE TIME, AND THEN, SUDDENLY, YOU ARE.

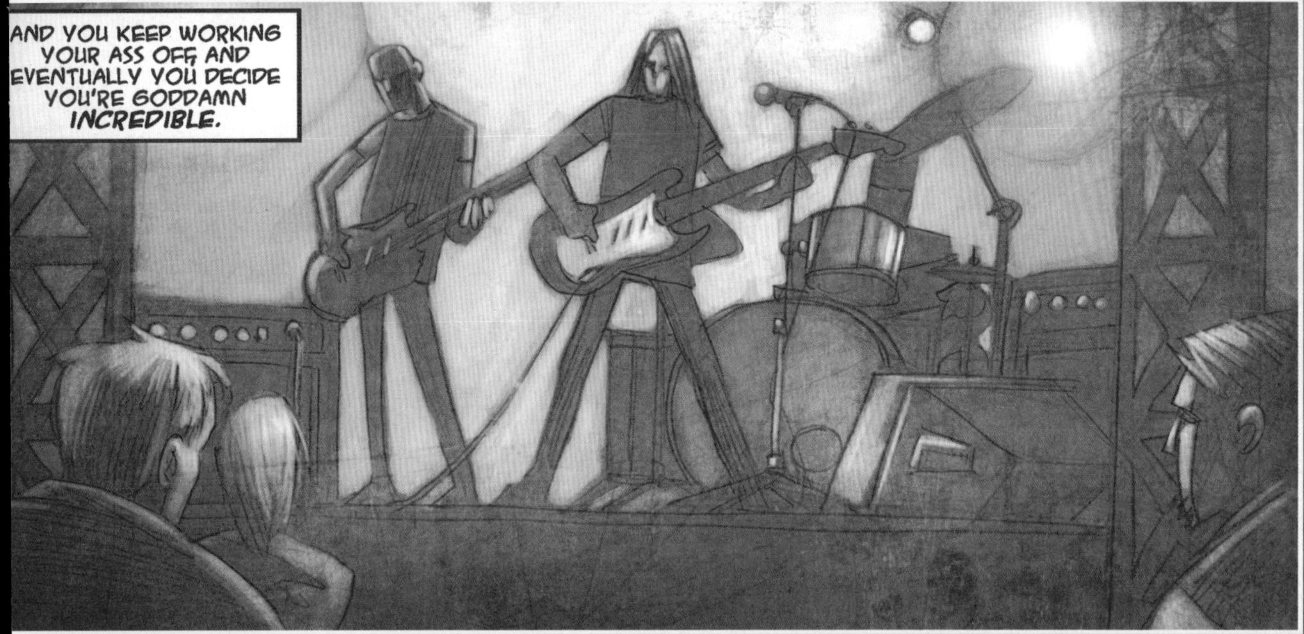
AND YOU KEEP WORKING YOUR ASS OFF AND EVENTUALLY YOU DECIDE YOU'RE GODDAMN *INCREDIBLE*.

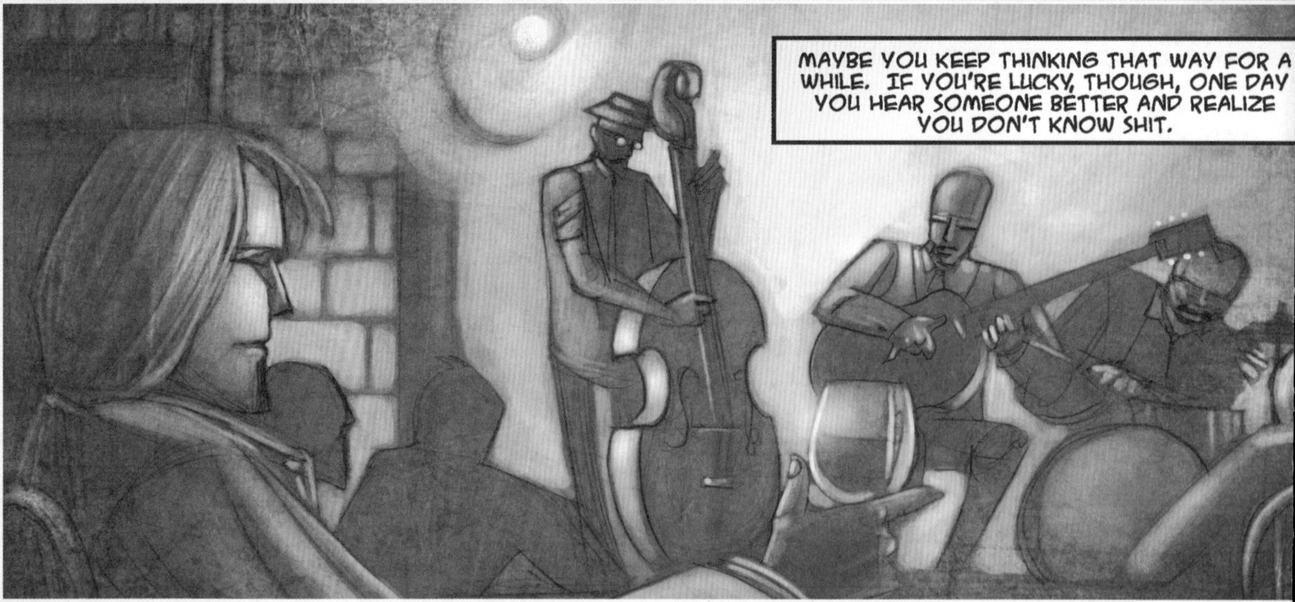
MAYBE YOU KEEP THINKING THAT WAY FOR A WHILE. IF YOU'RE LUCKY, THOUGH, ONE DAY YOU HEAR SOMEONE BETTER AND REALIZE YOU DON'T KNOW SHIT.

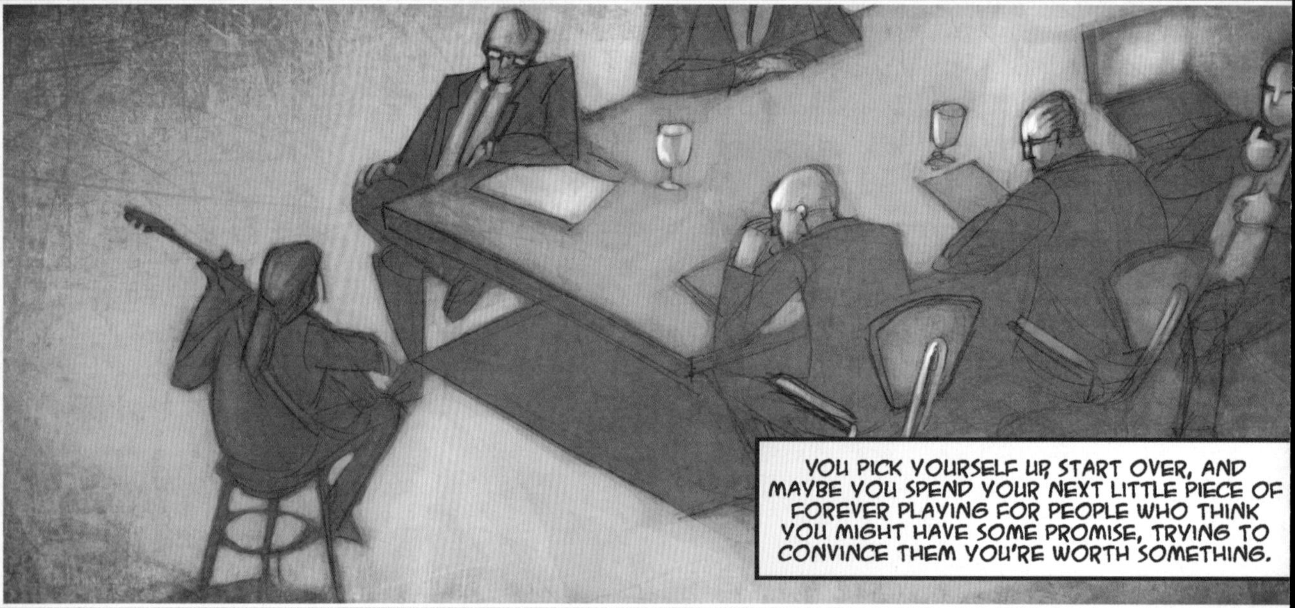
YOU PICK YOURSELF UP, START OVER, AND MAYBE YOU SPEND YOUR NEXT LITTLE PIECE OF FOREVER PLAYING FOR PEOPLE WHO THINK YOU MIGHT HAVE SOME PROMISE, TRYING TO CONVINCE THEM YOU'RE WORTH SOMETHING.

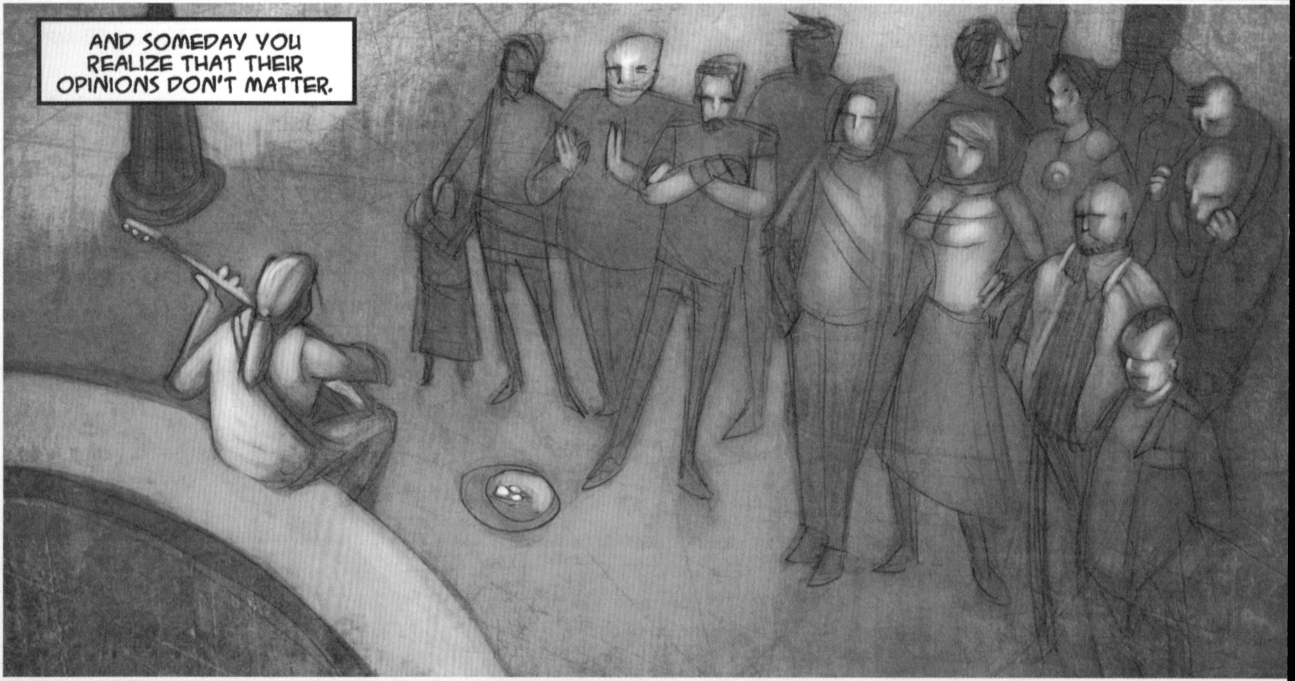
AND SOMEDAY YOU REALIZE THAT THEIR OPINIONS DON'T MATTER.

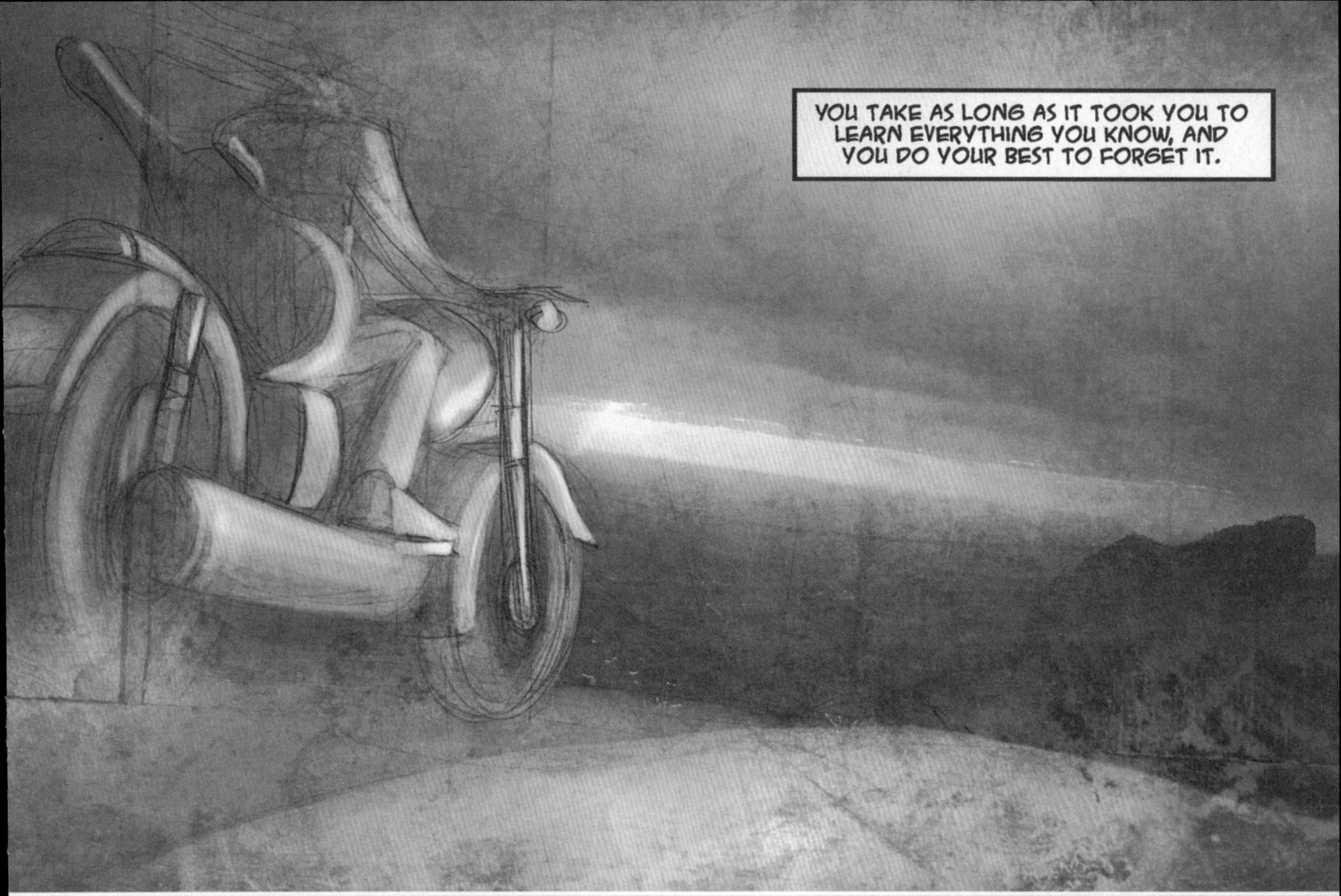
YOU TAKE AS LONG AS IT TOOK YOU TO LEARN EVERYTHING YOU KNOW, AND YOU DO YOUR BEST TO FORGET IT.

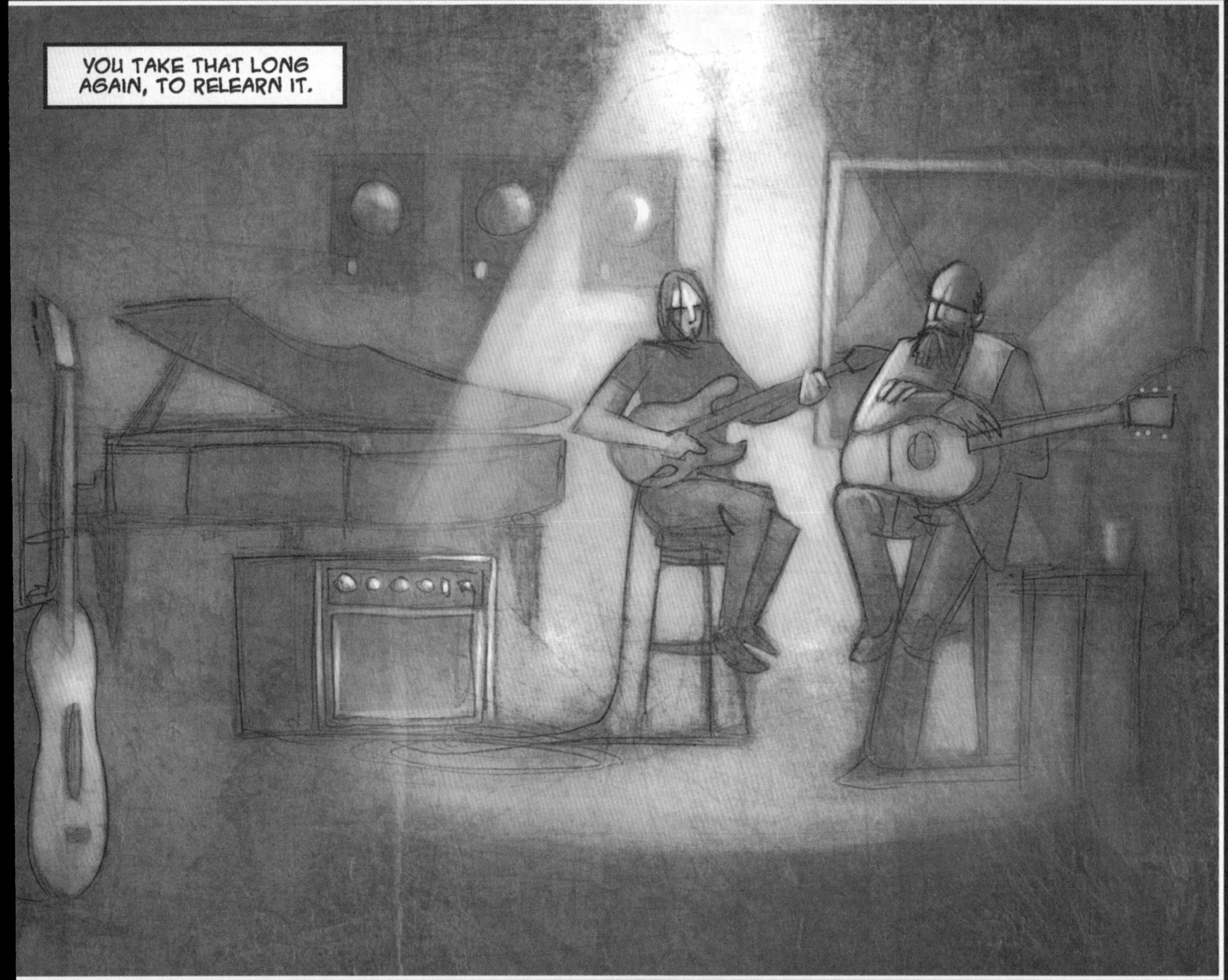
YOU TAKE THAT LONG AGAIN, TO RELEARN IT.

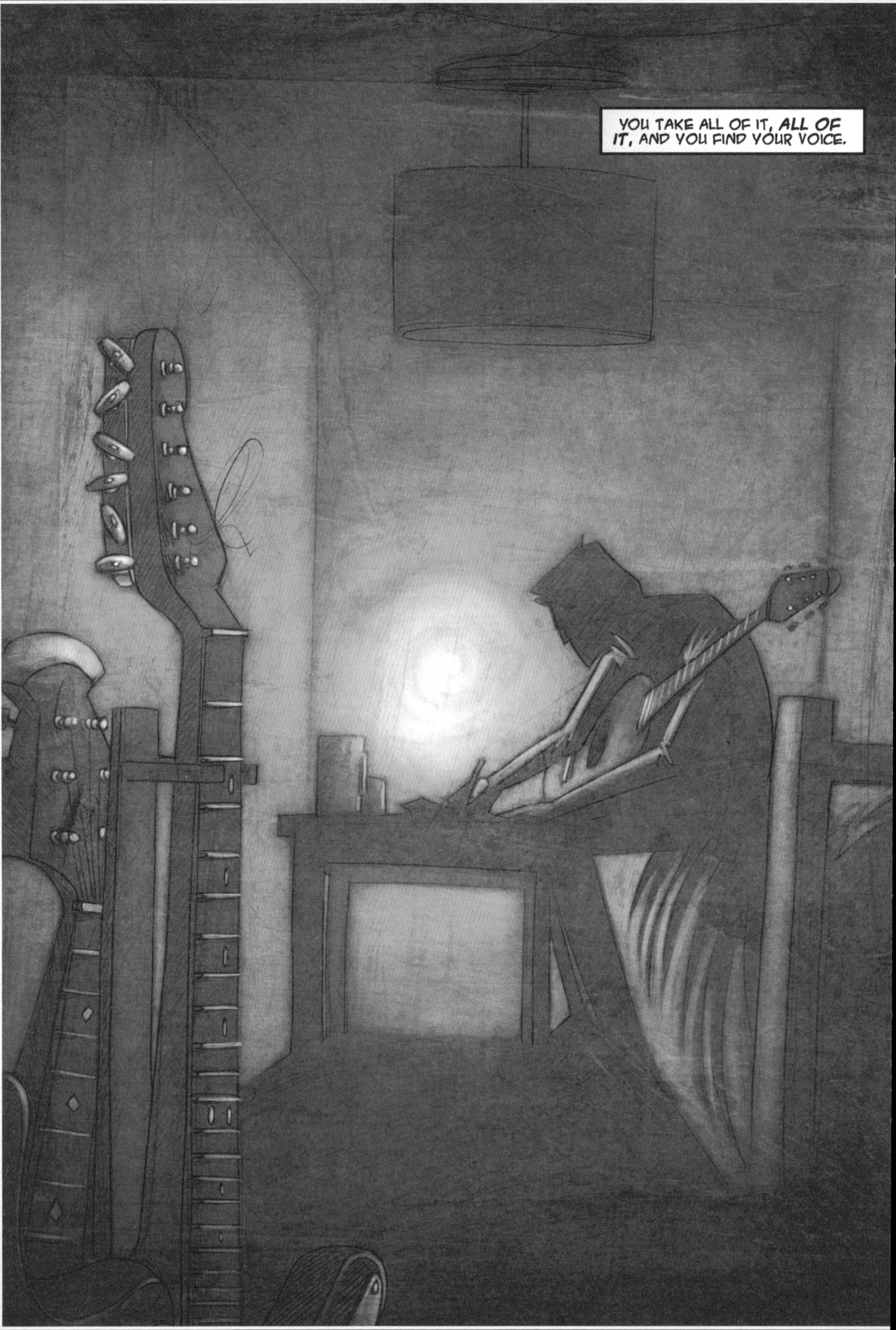
YOU TAKE ALL OF IT, *ALL OF IT,* AND YOU FIND YOUR VOICE.

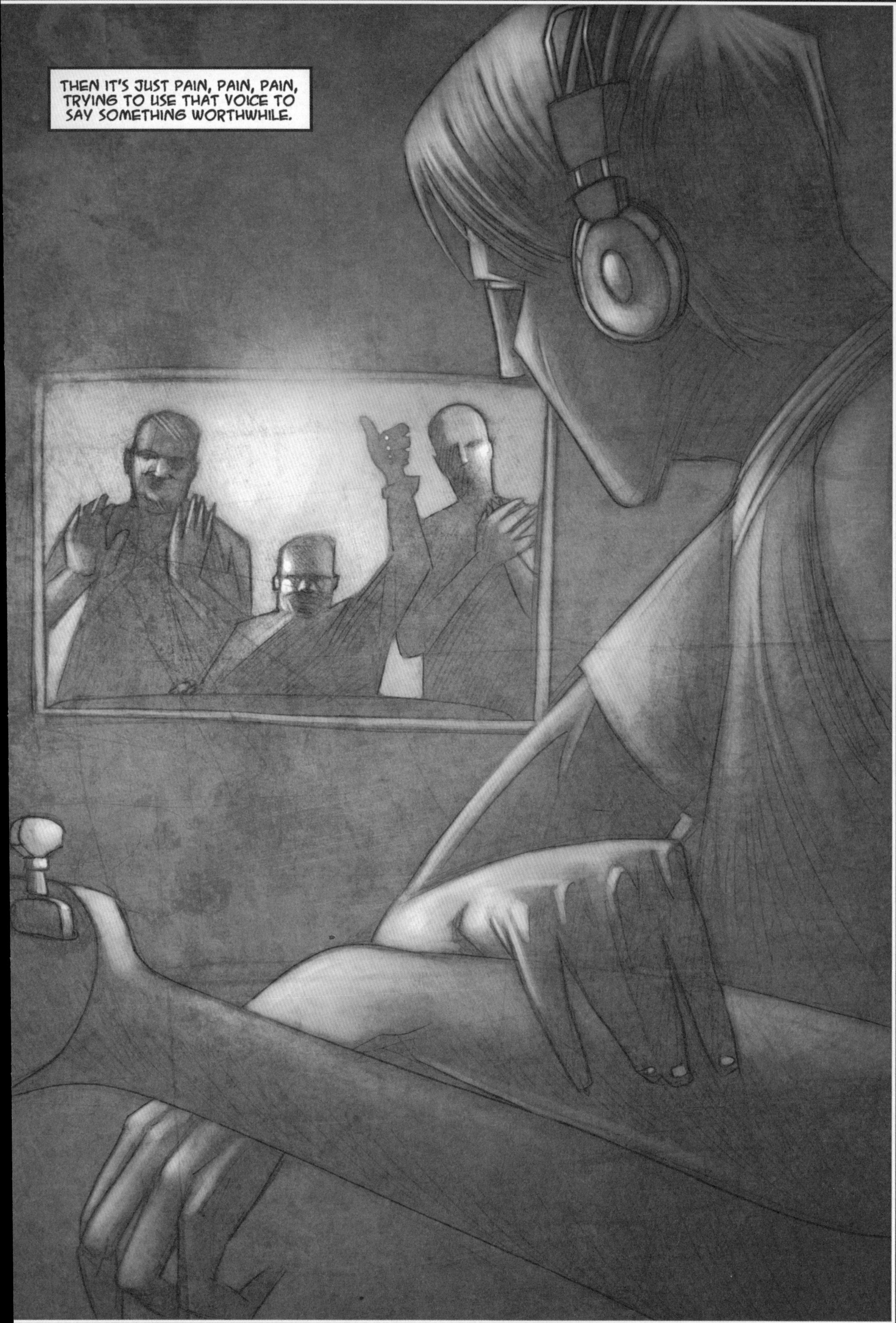
THEN IT'S JUST PAIN, PAIN, PAIN, TRYING TO USE THAT VOICE TO SAY SOMETHING WORTHWHILE.

AND YOU DO IT ALONE.
EVEN AFTER ALL THAT, YOU STILL HAVE TO BE LUCKY.

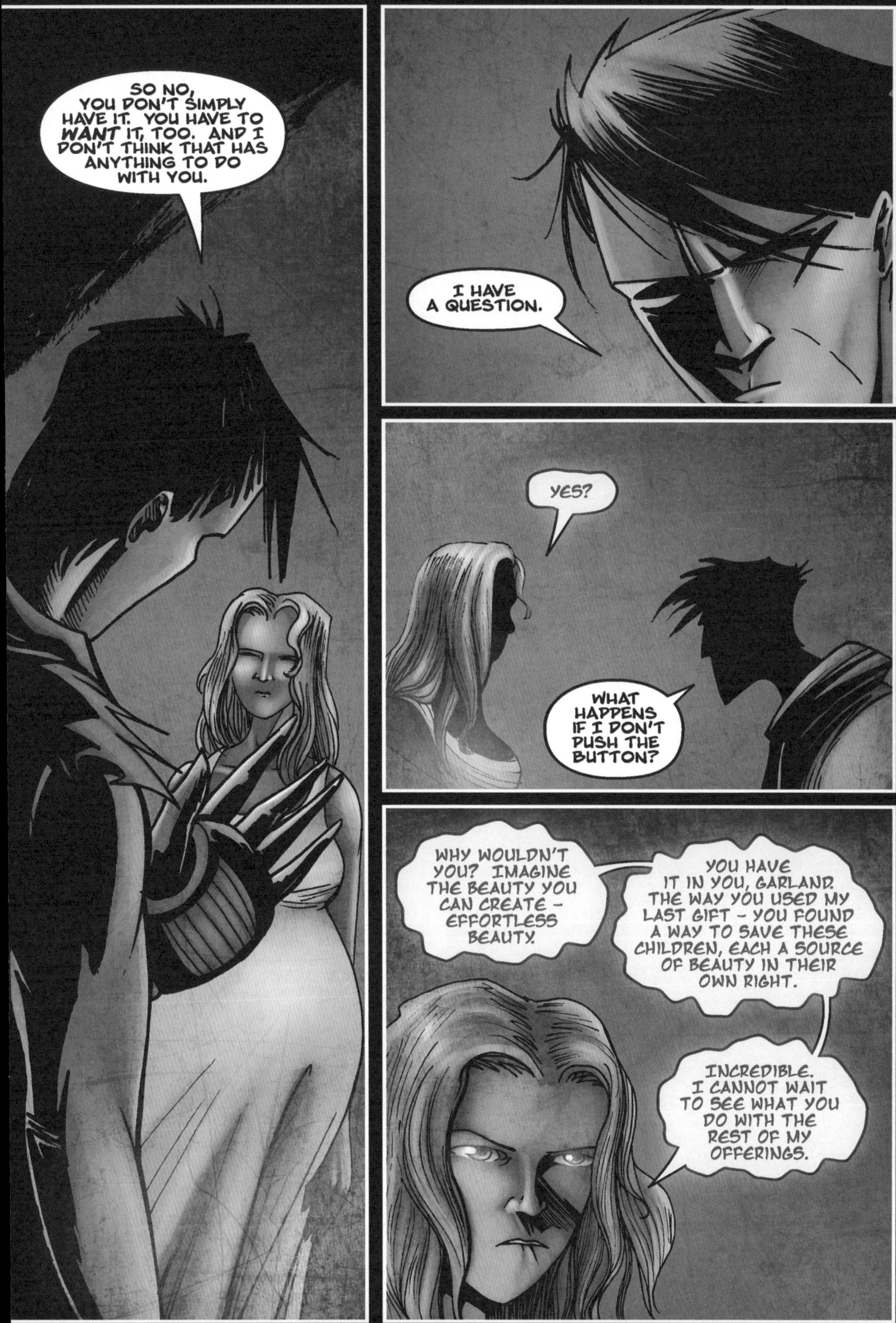
SO NO, YOU DON'T SIMPLY HAVE IT. YOU HAVE TO WANT IT, TOO. AND I DON'T THINK THAT HAS ANYTHING TO DO WITH YOU.
I HAVE A QUESTION.
YES?
WHAT HAPPENS IF I DON'T PUSH THE BUTTON?
WHY WOULDN'T YOU? IMAGINE THE BEAUTY YOU CAN CREATE - EFFORTLESS BEAUTY.
YOU HAVE IT IN YOU, GARLAND. THE WAY YOU USED MY LAST GIFT - YOU FOUND A WAY TO SAVE THESE CHILDREN, EACH A SOURCE OF BEAUTY IN THEIR OWN RIGHT.
INCREDIBLE. I CANNOT WAIT TO SEE WHAT YOU DO WITH THE REST OF MY OFFERINGS.

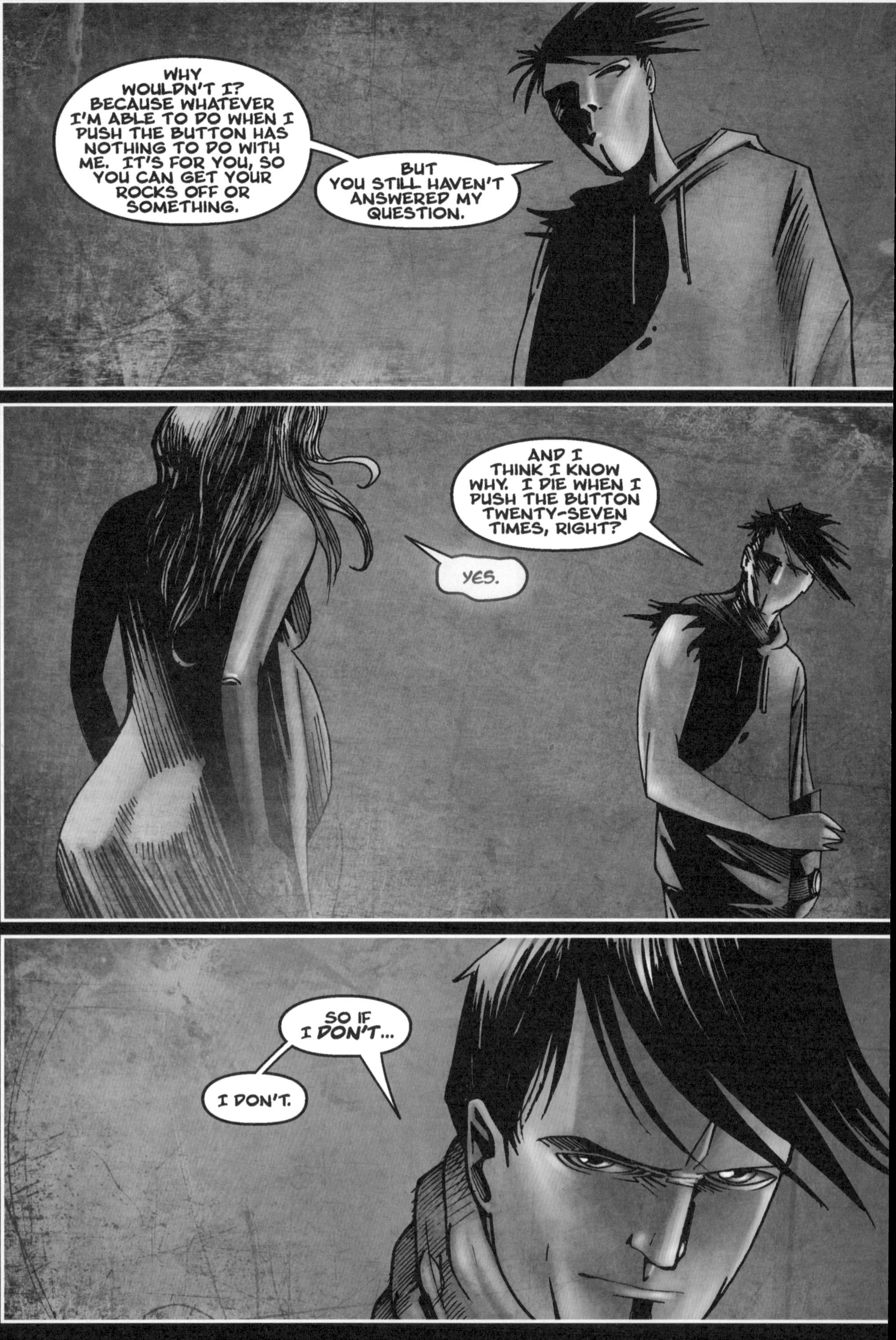
WHY WOULDN'T I? BECAUSE WHATEVER I'M ABLE TO DO WHEN I PUSH THE BUTTON HAS NOTHING TO DO WITH ME. IT'S FOR YOU, SO YOU CAN GET YOUR ROCKS OFF OR SOMETHING.
BUT YOU STILL HAVEN'T ANSWERED MY QUESTION.
AND I THINK I KNOW WHY. I DIE WHEN I PUSH THE BUTTON TWENTY-SEVEN TIMES, RIGHT?
YES.
SO IF I DON'T...
I DON'T.

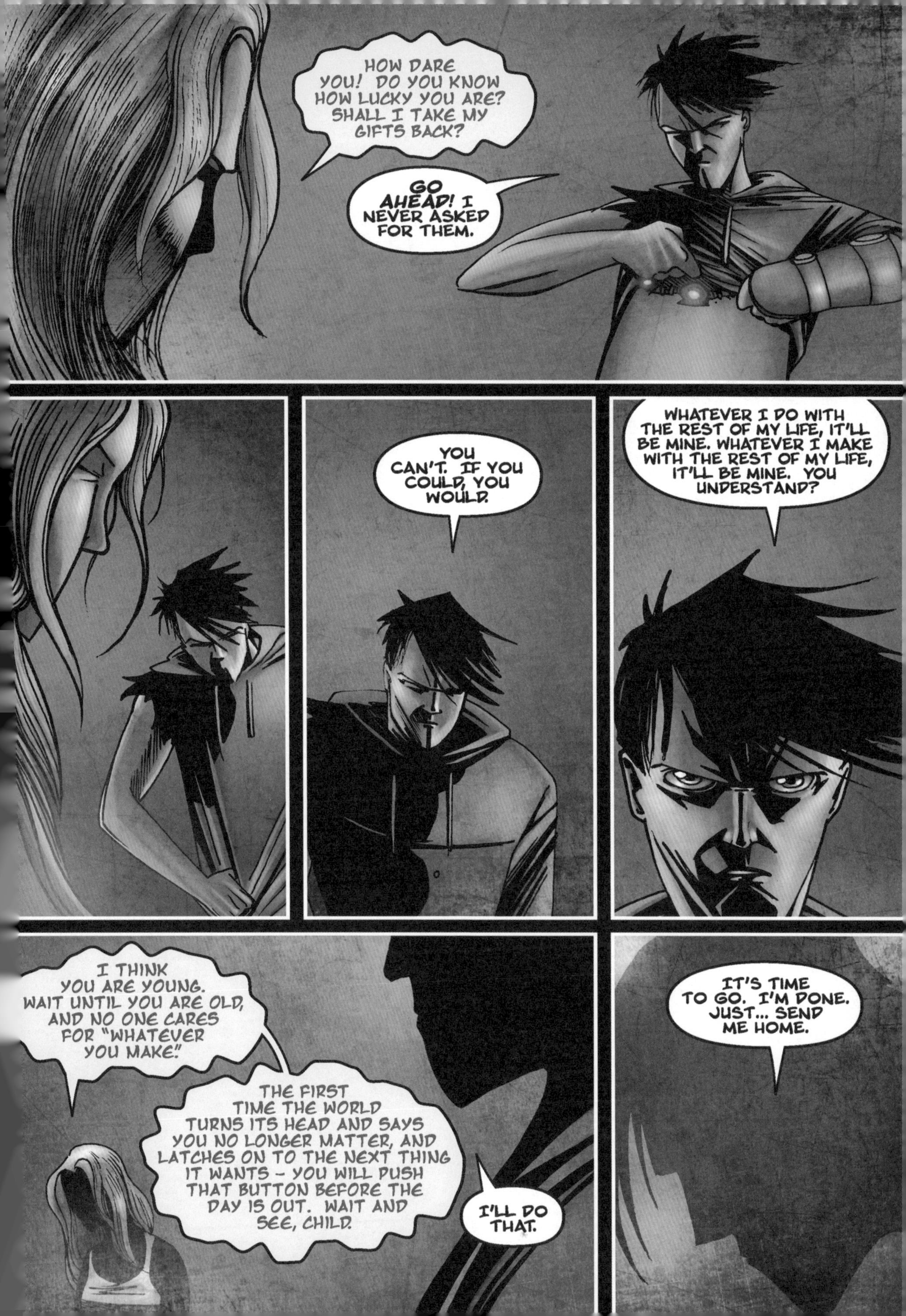
HOW DARE YOU! DO YOU KNOW HOW LUCKY YOU ARE? SHALL I TAKE MY GIFTS BACK?
GO AHEAD! I NEVER ASKED FOR THEM.
YOU CAN'T. IF YOU COULD, YOU WOULD.
WHATEVER I DO WITH THE REST OF MY LIFE, IT'LL BE MINE. WHATEVER I MAKE WITH THE REST OF MY LIFE, IT'LL BE MINE. YOU UNDERSTAND?
I THINK YOU ARE YOUNG. WAIT UNTIL YOU ARE OLD, AND NO ONE CARES FOR "WHATEVER YOU MAKE."
THE FIRST TIME THE WORLD TURNS ITS HEAD AND SAYS YOU NO LONGER MATTER, AND LATCHES ON TO THE NEXT THING IT WANTS – YOU WILL PUSH THAT BUTTON BEFORE THE DAY IS OUT. WAIT AND SEE, CHILD.
I'LL DO THAT.
IT'S TIME TO GO. I'M DONE. JUST... SEND ME HOME.

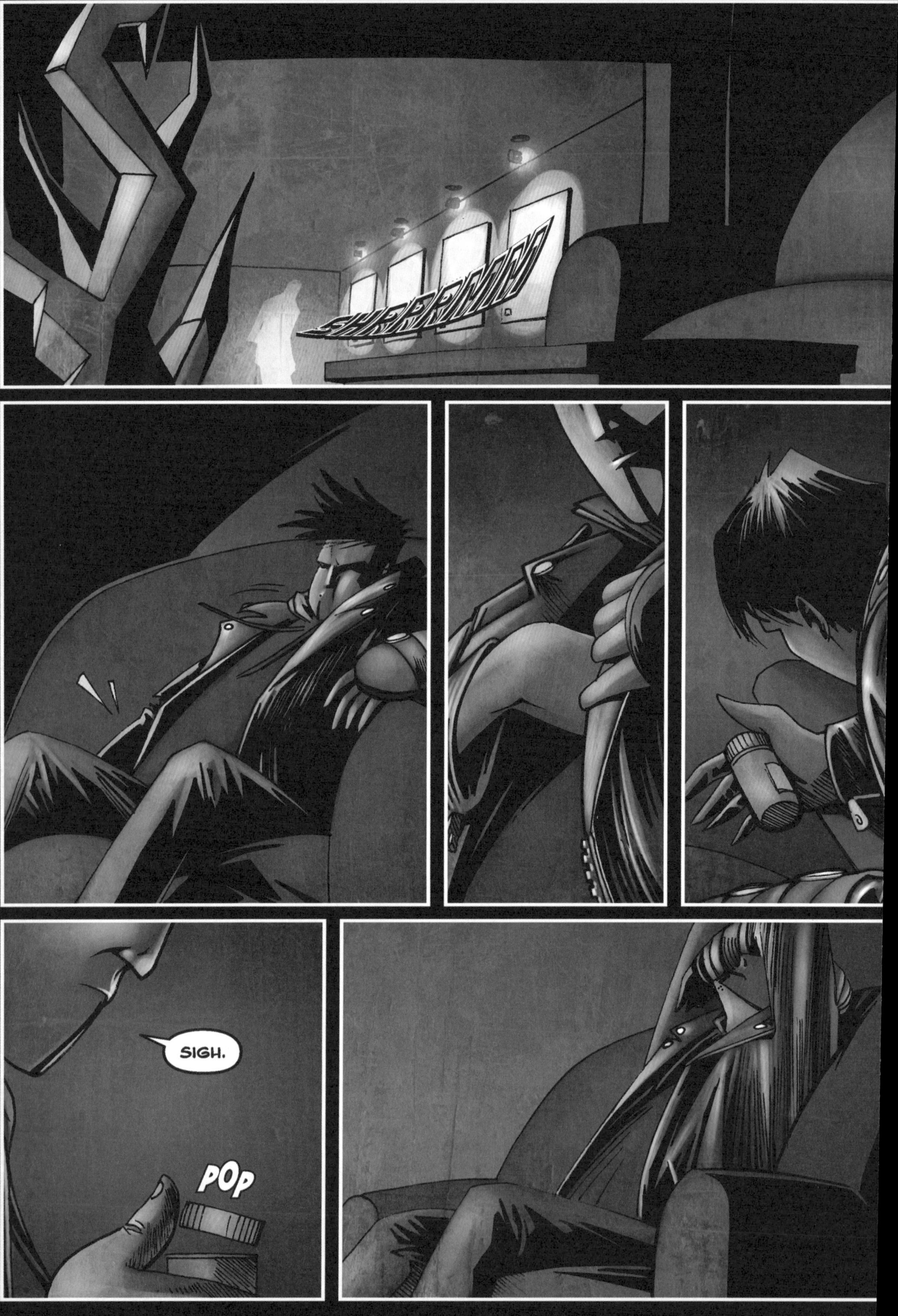
SHRRRMM
SIGH.
POP

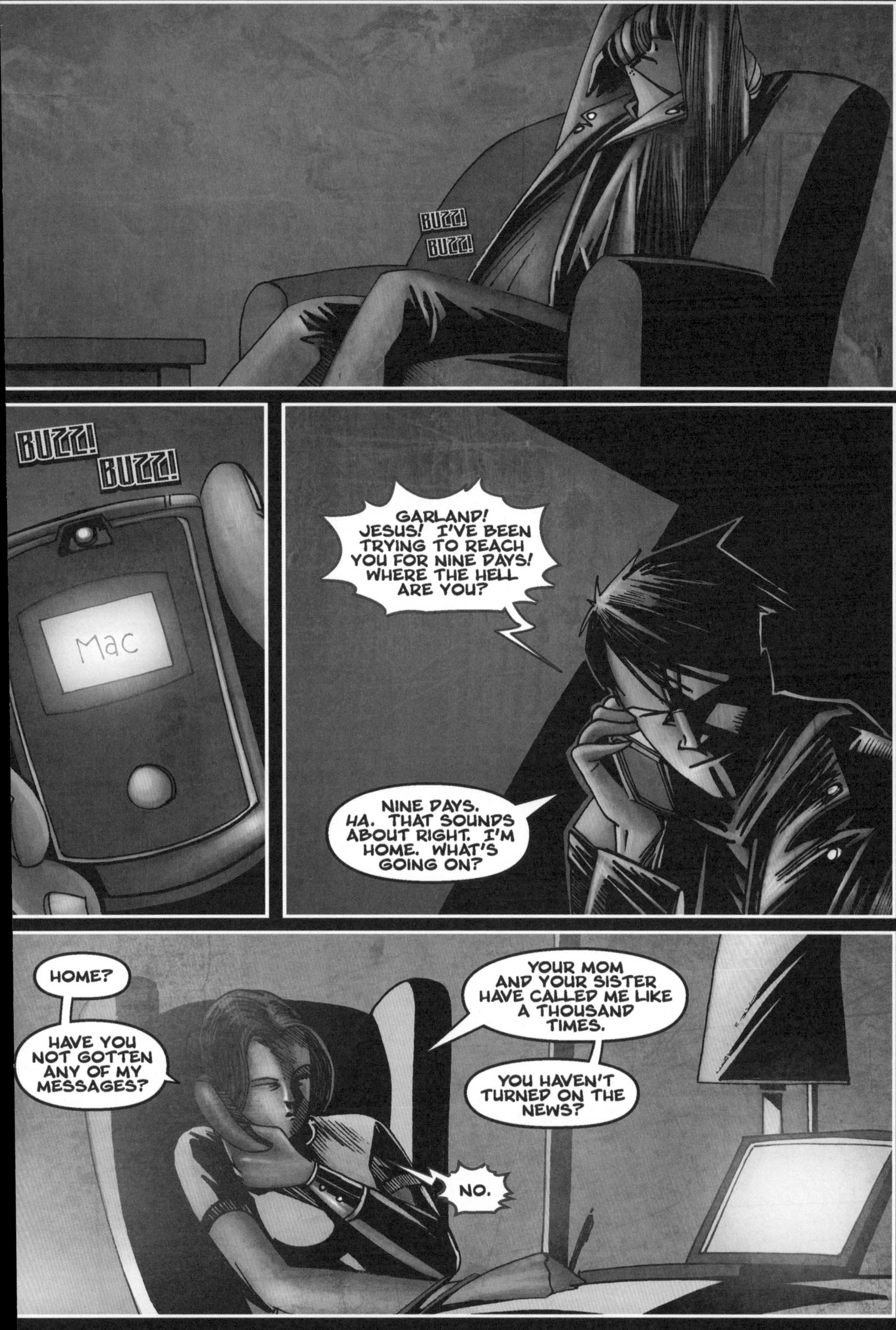
BUZZ!
BUZZ!
BUZZ!
BUZZ!
Mac
GARLAND! JESUS! I'VE BEEN TRYING TO REACH YOU FOR NINE DAYS! WHERE THE HELL ARE YOU?
NINE DAYS. HA. THAT SOUNDS ABOUT RIGHT. I'M HOME. WHAT'S GOING ON?
HOME?
HAVE YOU NOT GOTTEN ANY OF MY MESSAGES?
YOUR MOM AND YOUR SISTER HAVE CALLED ME LIKE A THOUSAND TIMES.
YOU HAVEN'T TURNED ON THE NEWS?
NO.

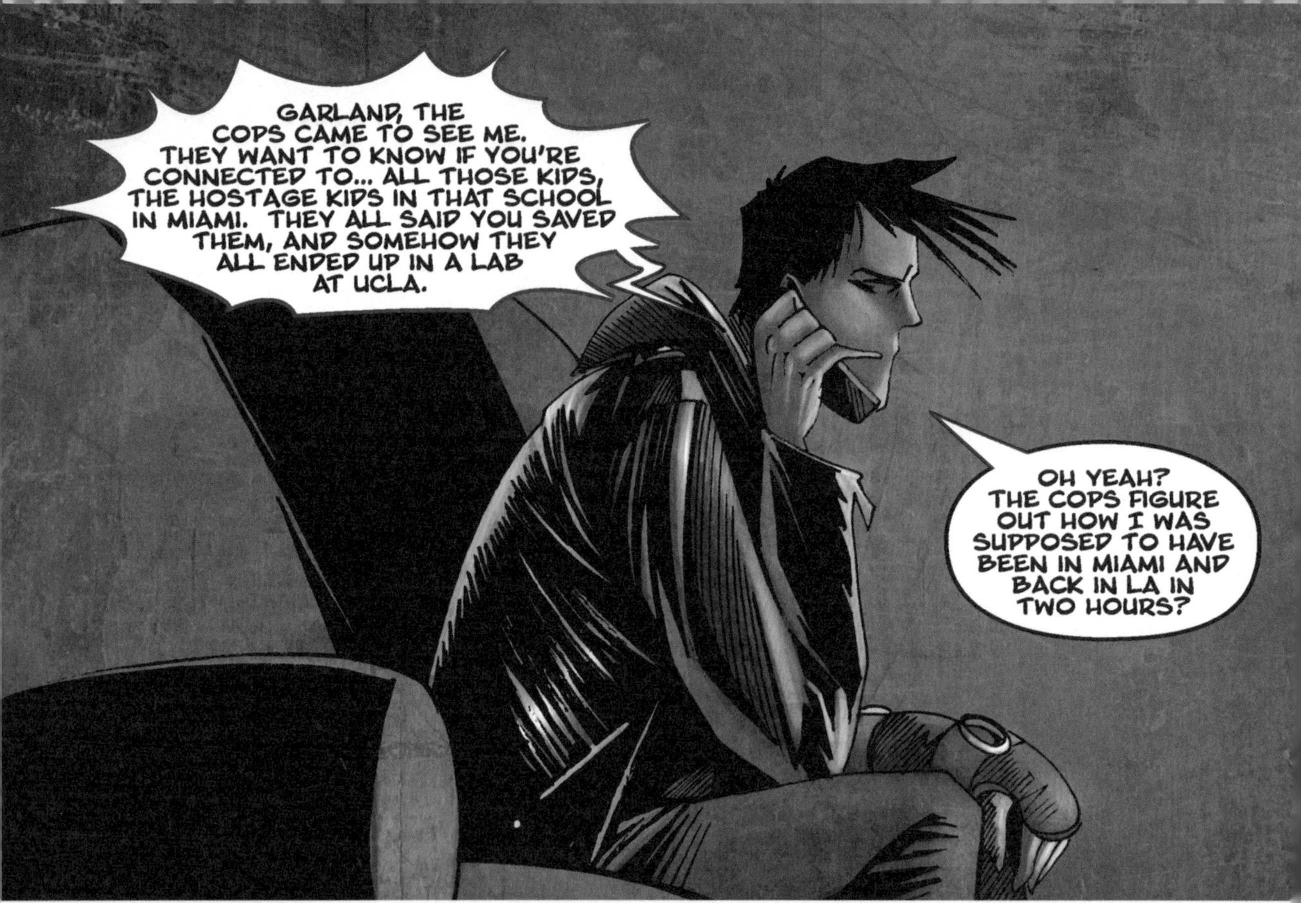
GARLAND, THE COPS CAME TO SEE ME. THEY WANT TO KNOW IF YOU'RE CONNECTED TO... ALL THOSE KIDS, THE HOSTAGE KIDS IN THAT SCHOOL IN MIAMI. THEY ALL SAID YOU SAVED THEM, AND SOMEHOW THEY ALL ENDED UP IN A LAB AT UCLA.
OH YEAH? THE COPS FIGURE OUT HOW I WAS SUPPOSED TO HAVE BEEN IN MIAMI AND BACK IN LA IN TWO HOURS?

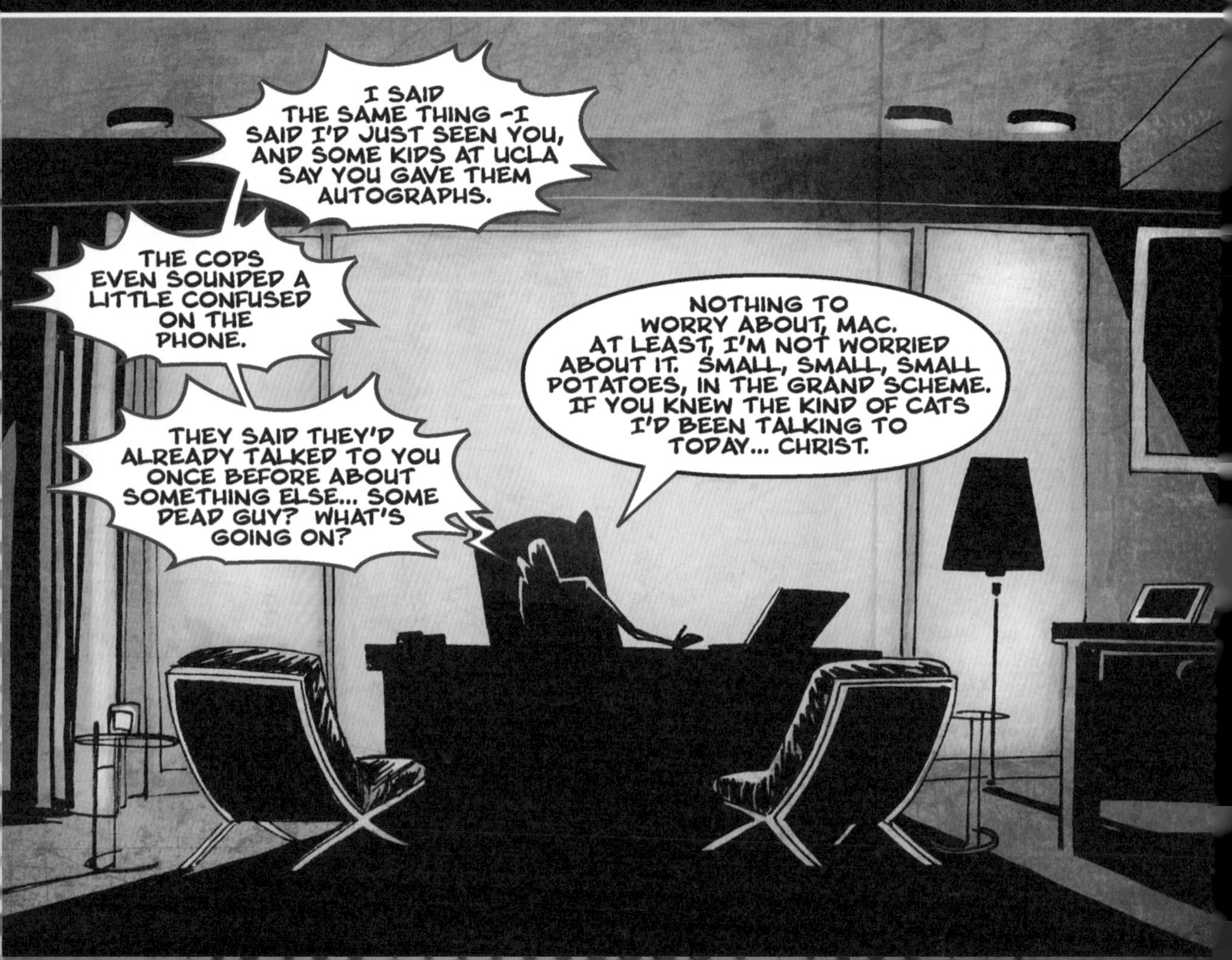
I SAID THE SAME THING -I SAID I'D JUST SEEN YOU, AND SOME KIDS AT UCLA SAY YOU GAVE THEM AUTOGRAPHS.
THE COPS EVEN SOUNDED A LITTLE CONFUSED ON THE PHONE.
THEY SAID THEY'D ALREADY TALKED TO YOU ONCE BEFORE ABOUT SOMETHING ELSE... SOME DEAD GUY? WHAT'S GOING ON?
NOTHING TO WORRY ABOUT, MAC. AT LEAST, I'M NOT WORRIED ABOUT IT. SMALL, SMALL, SMALL POTATOES, IN THE GRAND SCHEME. IF YOU KNEW THE KIND OF CATS I'D BEEN TALKING TO TODAY... CHRIST.

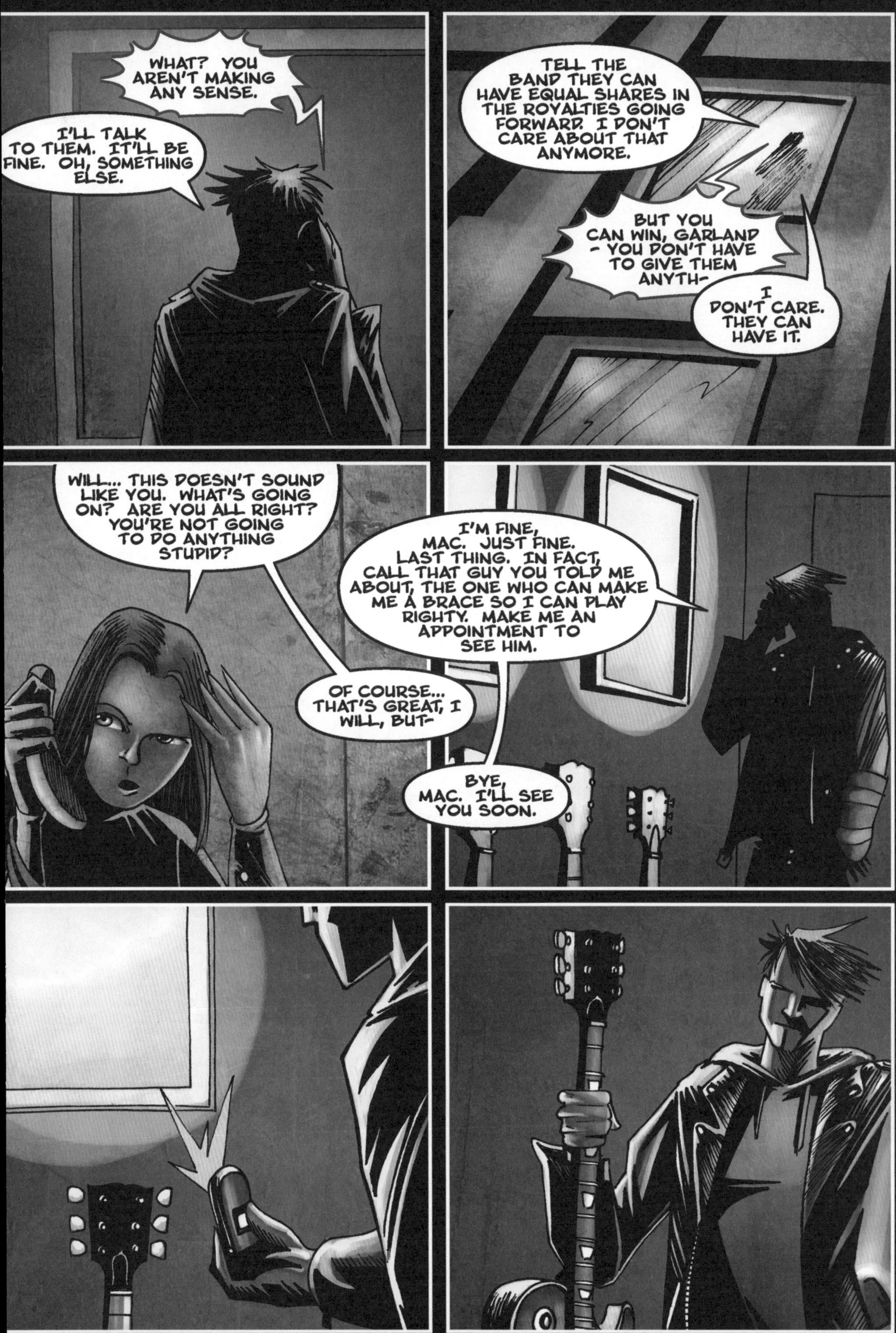
WHAT? YOU AREN'T MAKING ANY SENSE.
I'LL TALK TO THEM. IT'LL BE FINE. OH, SOMETHING ELSE.
TELL THE BAND THEY CAN HAVE EQUAL SHARES IN THE ROYALTIES GOING FORWARD. I DON'T CARE ABOUT THAT ANYMORE.
BUT YOU CAN WIN, GARLAND - YOU DON'T HAVE TO GIVE THEM ANYTH-
I DON'T CARE. THEY CAN HAVE IT.
WILL... THIS DOESN'T SOUND LIKE YOU. WHAT'S GOING ON? ARE YOU ALL RIGHT? YOU'RE NOT GOING TO DO ANYTHING STUPID?
I'M FINE, MAC. JUST FINE. LAST THING. IN FACT, CALL THAT GUY YOU TOLD ME ABOUT, THE ONE WHO CAN MAKE ME A BRACE SO I CAN PLAY RIGHTY. MAKE ME AN APPOINTMENT TO SEE HIM.
OF COURSE... THAT'S GREAT, I WILL, BUT-
BYE, MAC. I'LL SEE YOU SOON.

FLIP

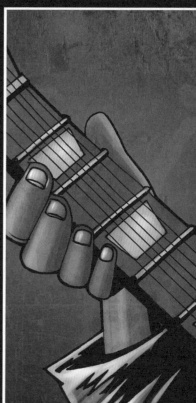

VVBRRRANG

SOUNDS AWFUL.

BUT I'LL GET BETTER.

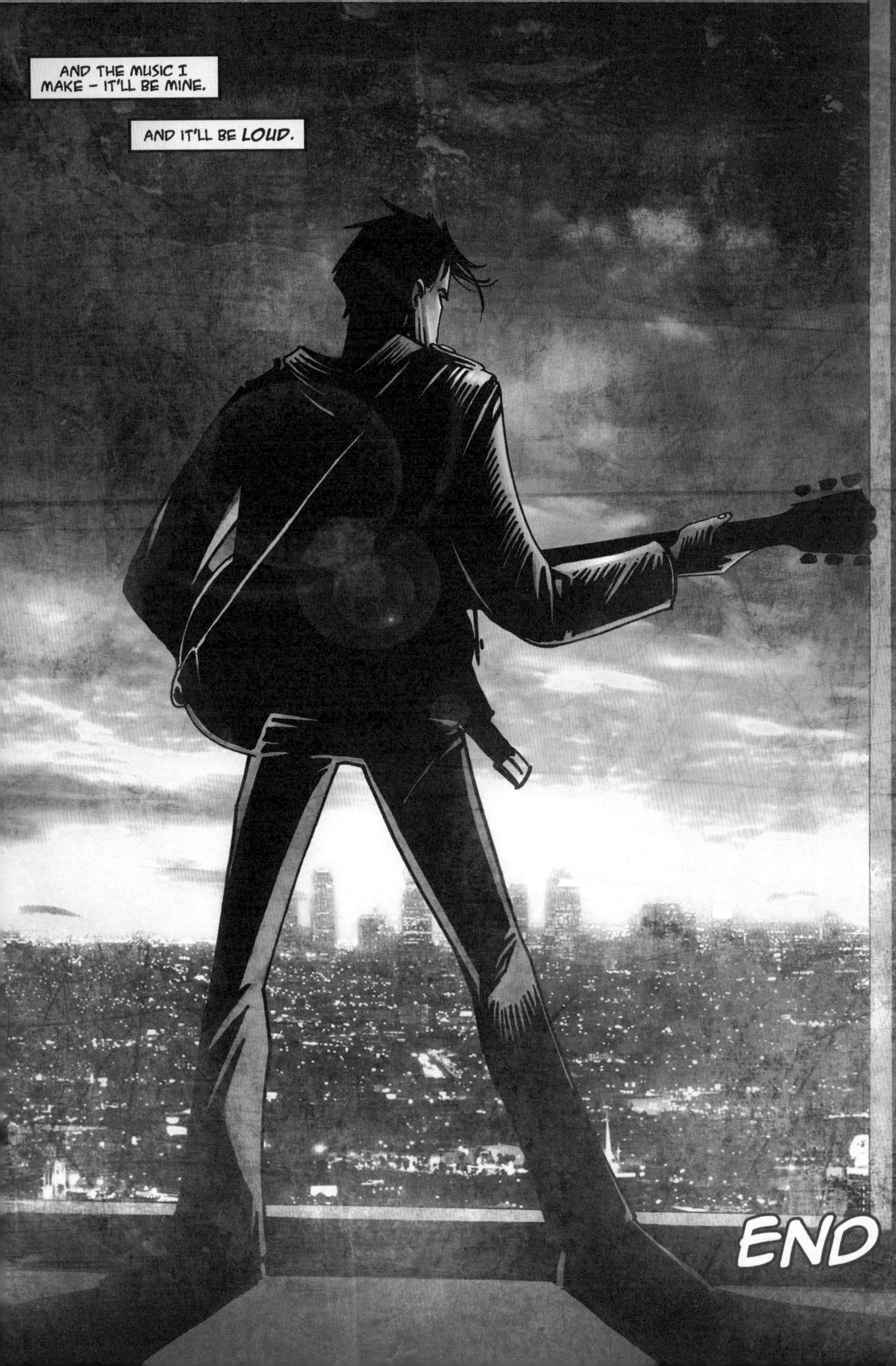
AND THE MUSIC I MAKE – IT'LL BE MINE.
AND IT'LL BE LOUD.
END

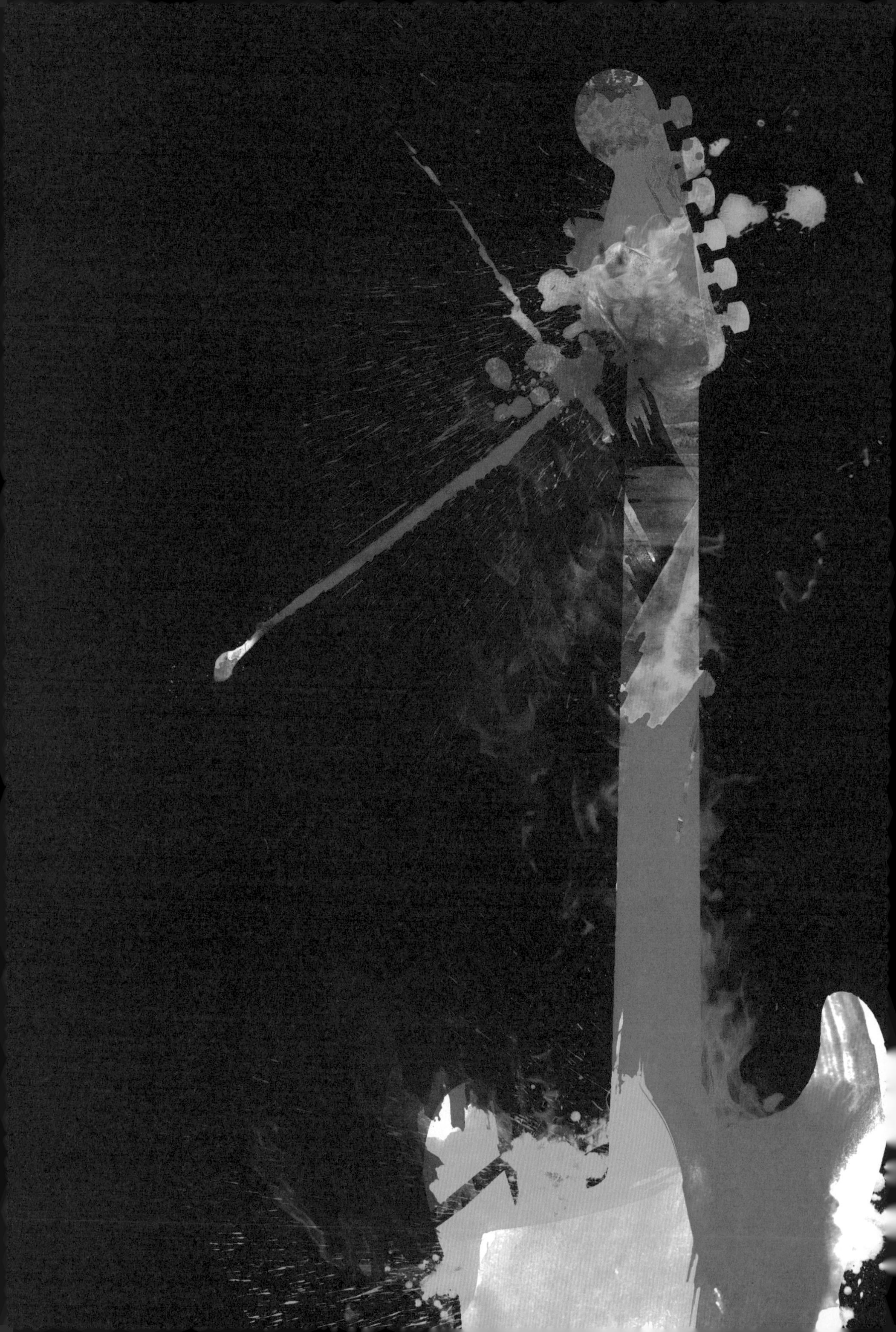

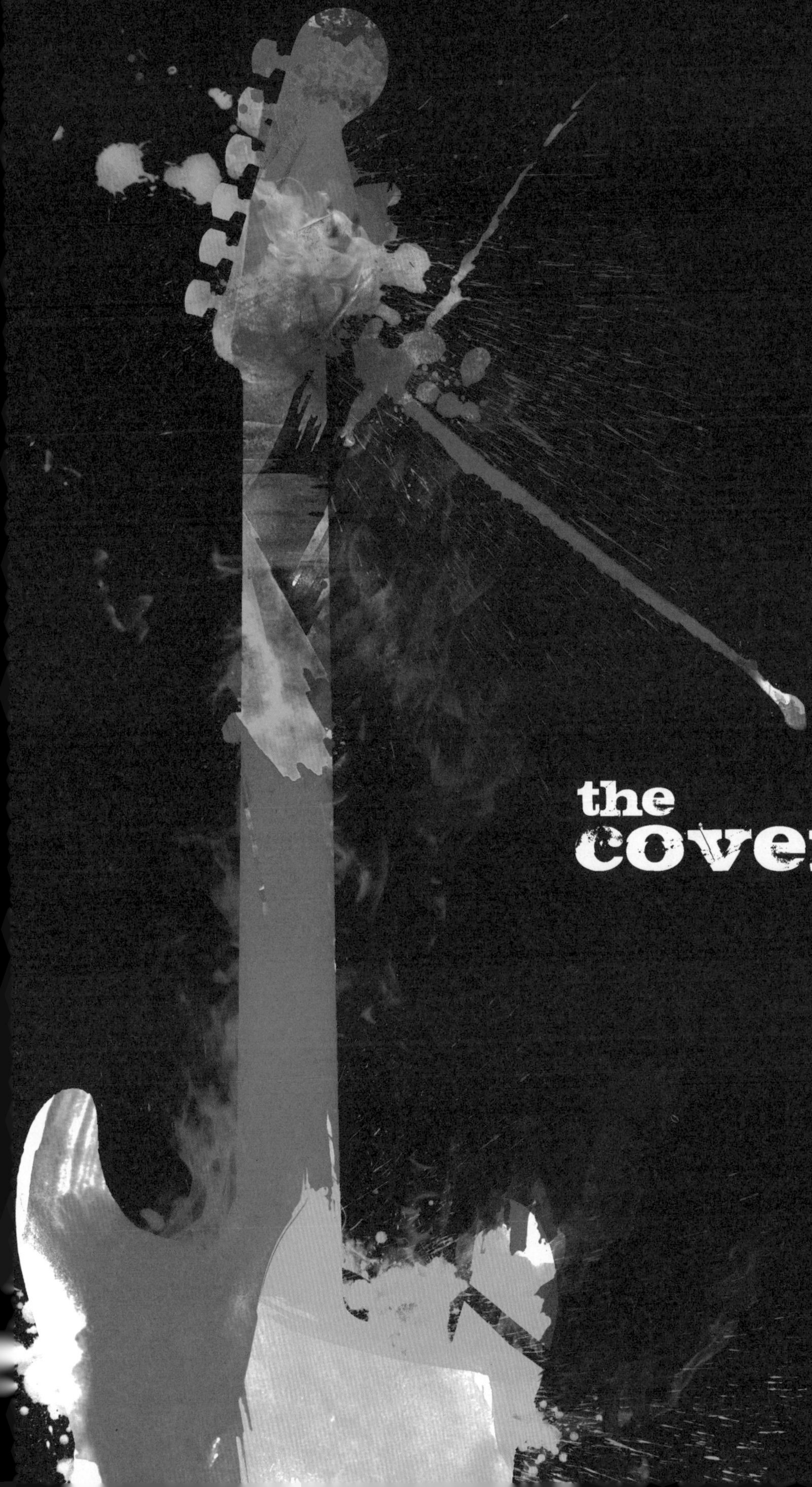

the covers

issue 1//cover

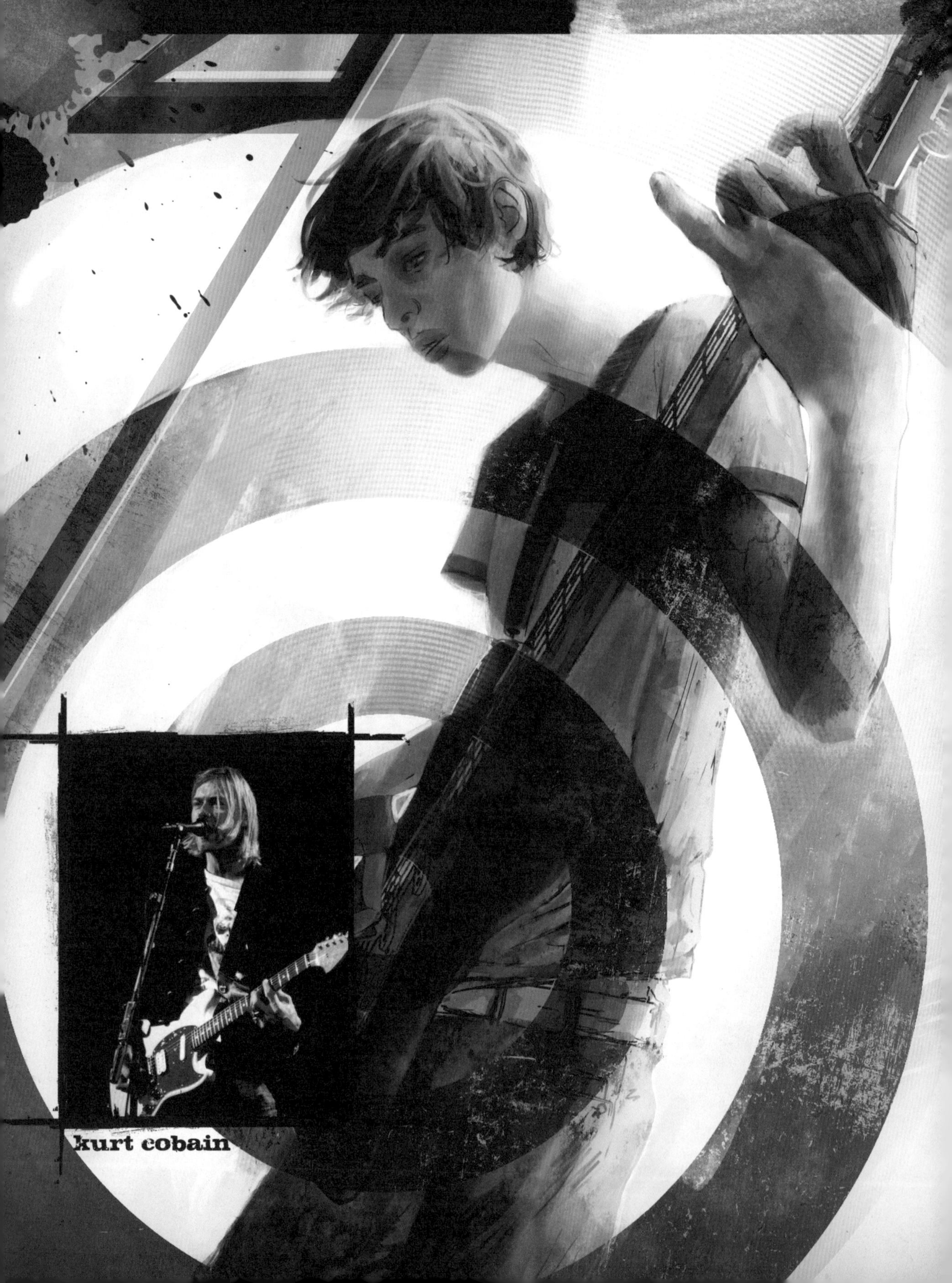

kurt cobain

issue 2//cover

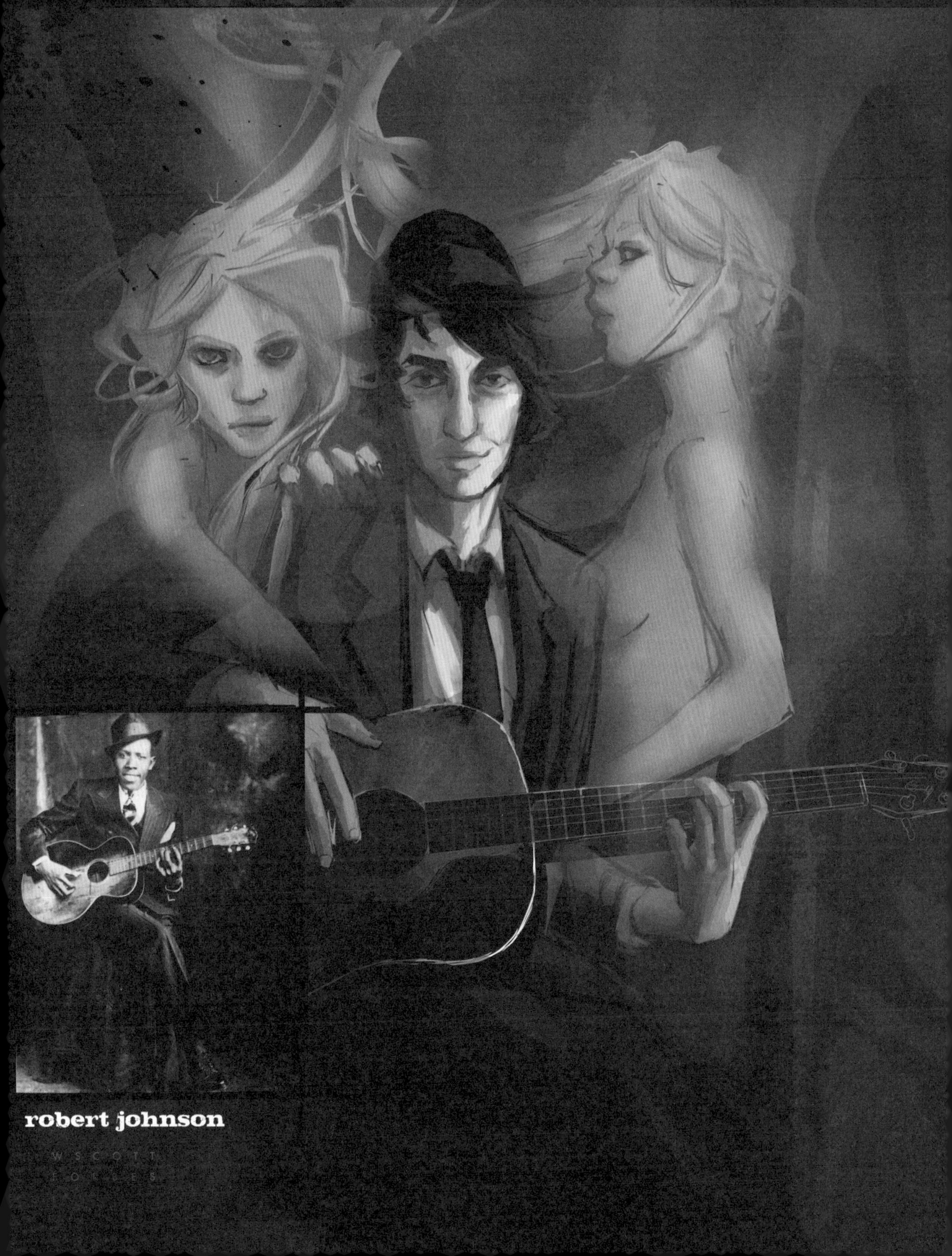

robert johnson

W SCOTT
FORBES

issue 3//cover

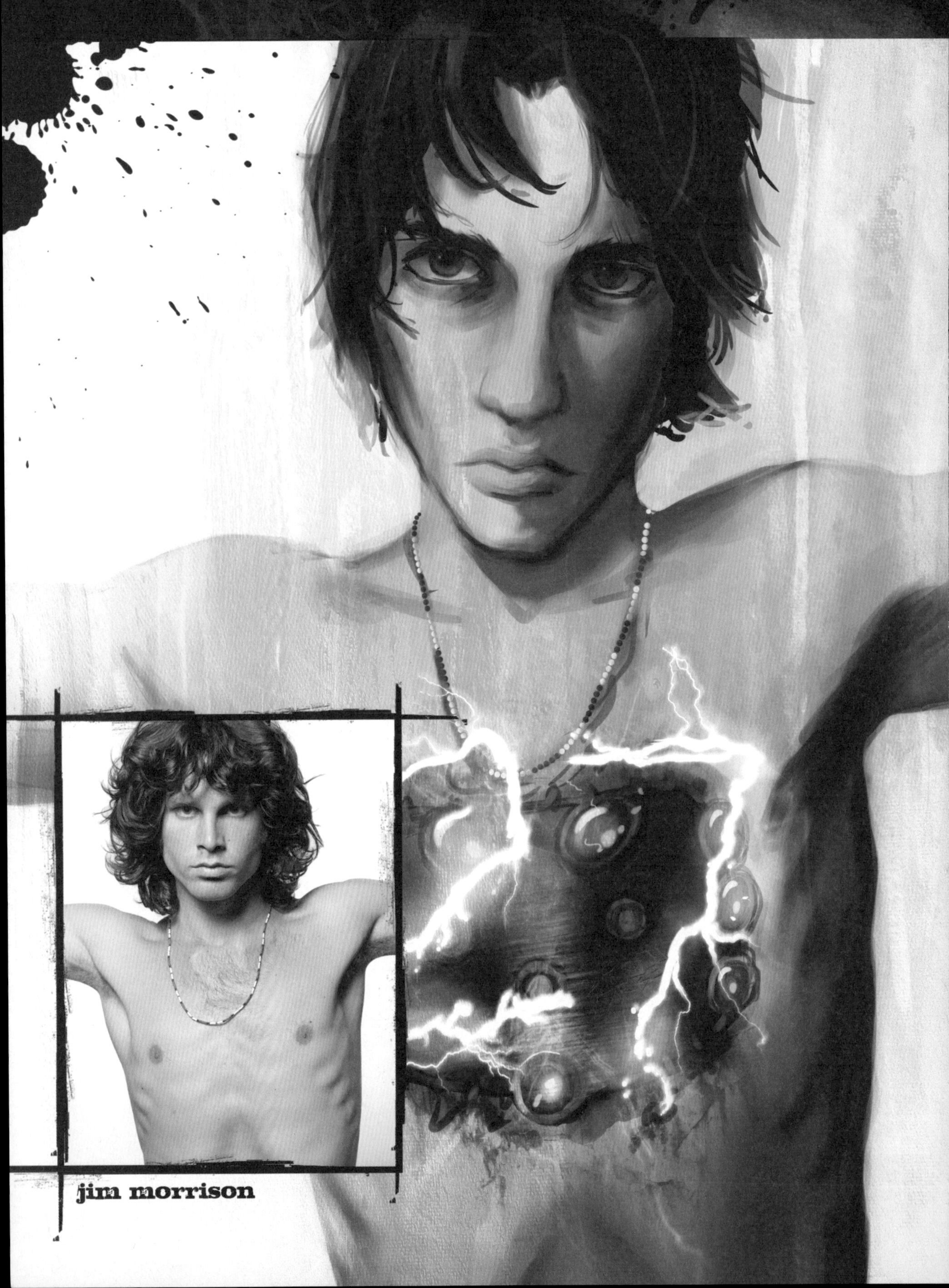

jim morrison

issue 4//cover

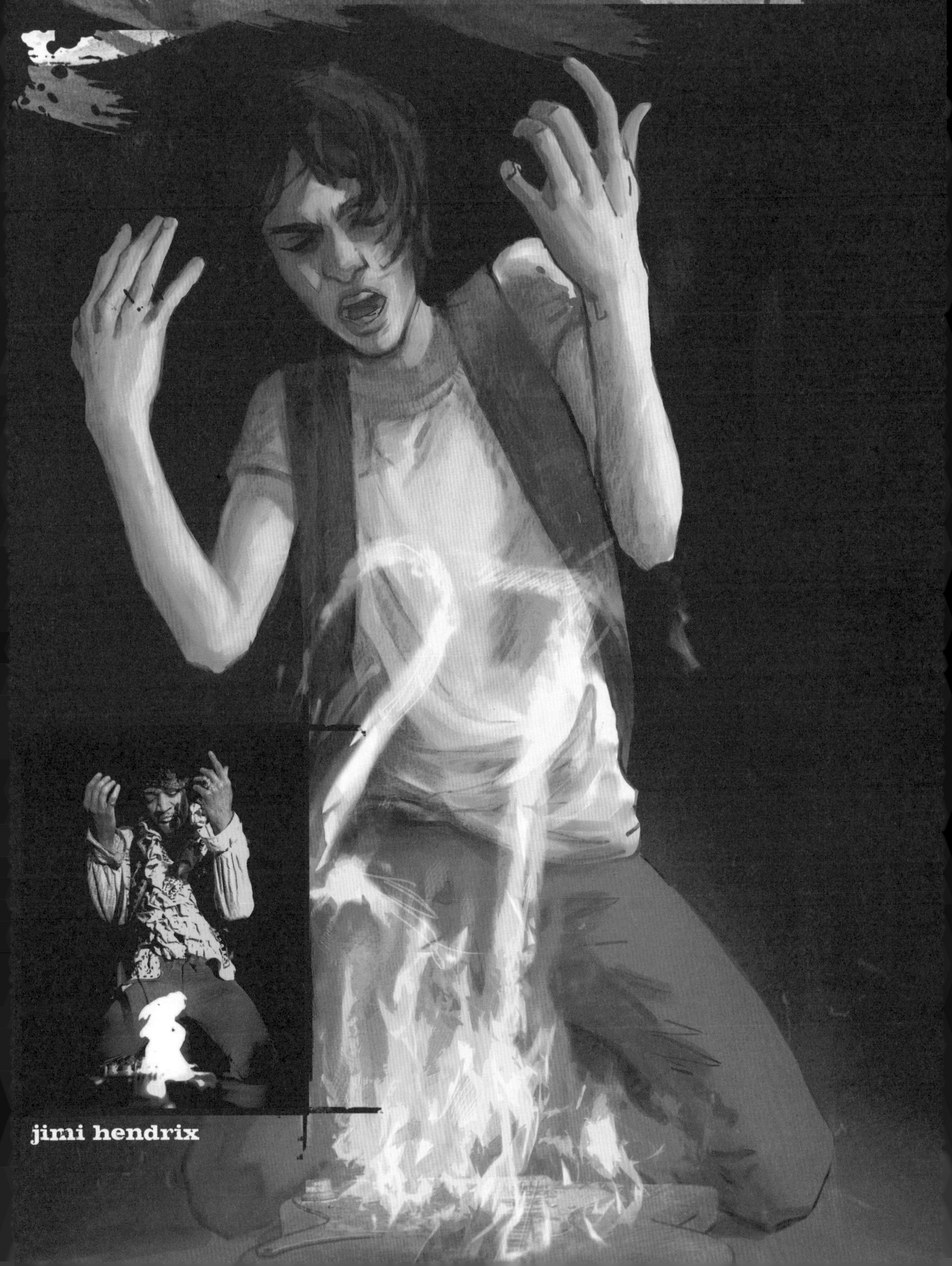

jimi hendrix

issue 1//interior front cover

A Shadowline™ PRODUCTION

LIVE! TONIGHT! SOLD OUT!

TWENTY SEVEN

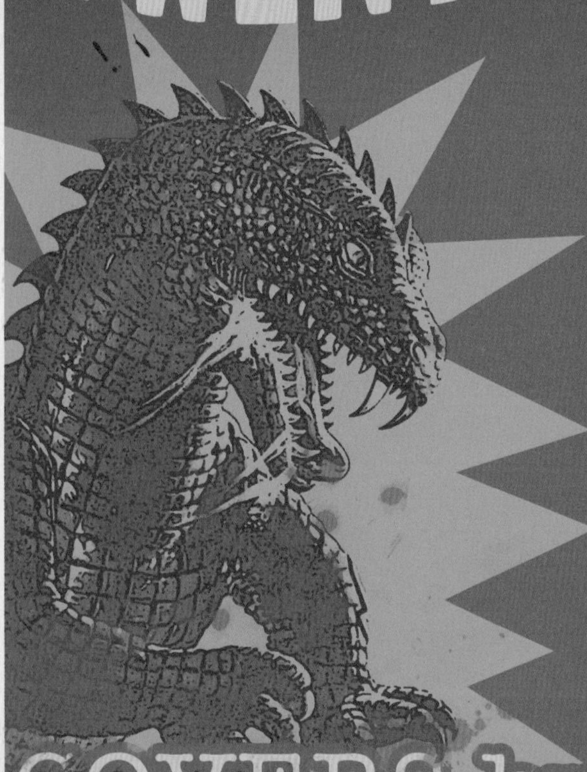

written by
CHARLES SOULE

art by
RENZO PODESTA

letters by
SHAWN DePASQUALE

editor
KRISTEN SIMON

JIM VALENTINO
publisher

COVERS by
W. SCOTT FORBES

TIM DANIEL
design

FRIFEB_9 SHOWBOX
$4 COVER - ALL AGES

TWENTY SEVEN #1. OCTOBER, 2010. Published by Image Comics, Inc. Office of publication: 2134 Allston Way, Second Floor, Berkeley, California 94704.

inspired by nirvna's pine st. concert poster

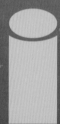

issue 2//interior front cover

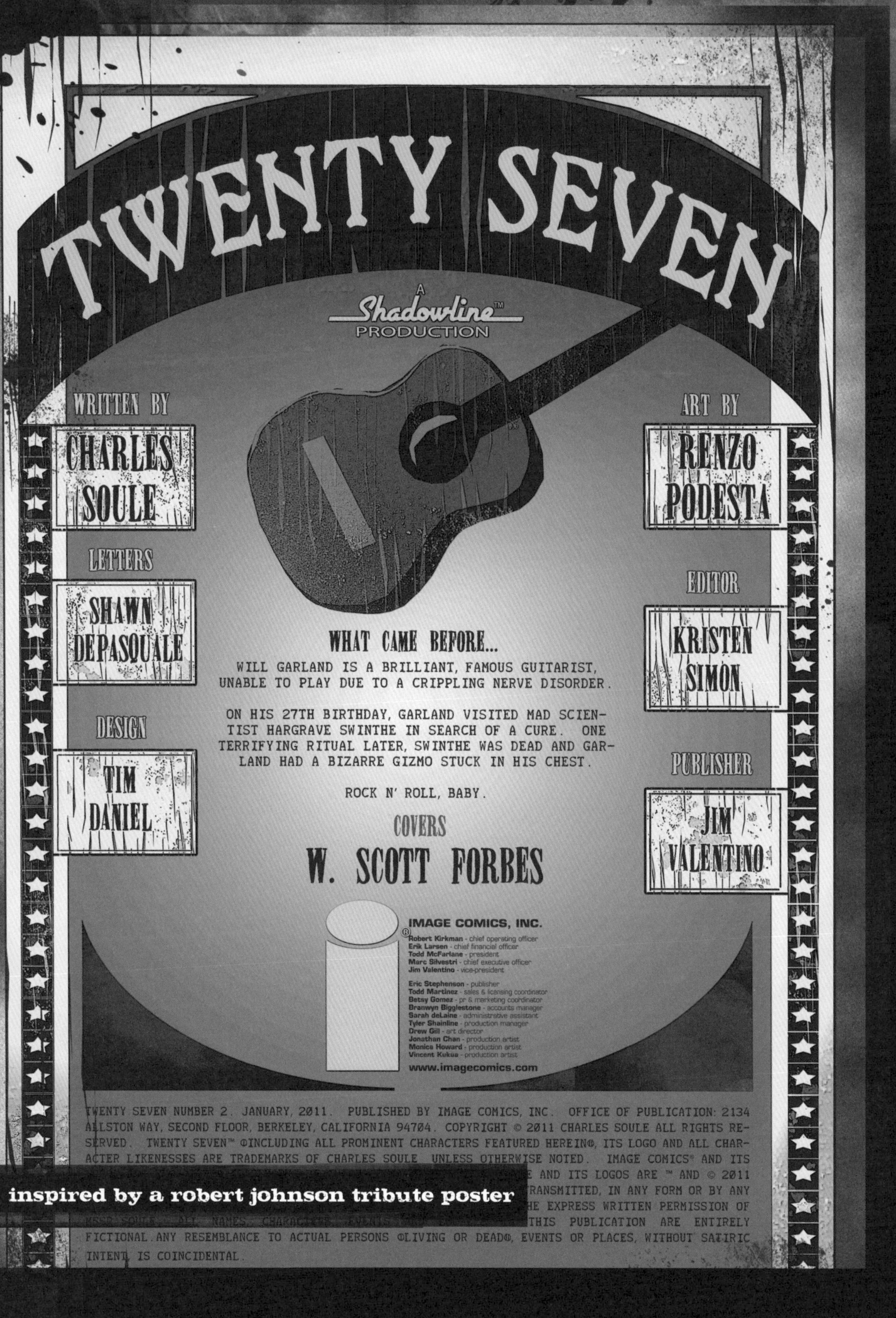

TWENTY SEVEN
A Shadowline™ PRODUCTION
WRITTEN BY
CHARLES SOULE
ART BY
RENZO PODESTA
LETTERS
SHAWN DEPASQUALE
EDITOR
KRISTEN SIMON
DESIGN
TIM DANIEL
PUBLISHER
JIM VALENTINO
WHAT CAME BEFORE...
WILL GARLAND IS A BRILLIANT, FAMOUS GUITARIST, UNABLE TO PLAY DUE TO A CRIPPLING NERVE DISORDER.
ON HIS 27TH BIRTHDAY, GARLAND VISITED MAD SCIENTIST HARGRAVE SWINTHE IN SEARCH OF A CURE. ONE TERRIFYING RITUAL LATER, SWINTHE WAS DEAD AND GARLAND HAD A BIZARRE GIZMO STUCK IN HIS CHEST.
ROCK N' ROLL, BABY.
COVERS
W. SCOTT FORBES
IMAGE COMICS, INC.
Robert Kirkman - chief operating officer
Erik Larsen - chief financial officer
Todd McFarlane - president
Marc Silvestri - chief executive officer
Jim Valentino - vice-president
Eric Stephenson - publisher
Todd Martinez - sales & licensing coordinator
Betsy Gomez - pr & marketing coordinator
Branwyn Bigglestone - accounts manager
Sarah deLaine - administrative assistant
Tyler Shainline - production manager
Drew Gill - art director
Jonathan Chan - production artist
Monica Howard - production artist
Vincent Kukua - production artist
www.imagecomics.com
TWENTY SEVEN NUMBER 2. JANUARY, 2011. PUBLISHED BY IMAGE COMICS, INC. OFFICE OF PUBLICATION: 2134 ALLSTON WAY, SECOND FLOOR, BERKELEY, CALIFORNIA 94704. COPYRIGHT © 2011 CHARLES SOULE ALL RIGHTS RESERVED. TWENTY SEVEN™ (INCLUDING ALL PROMINENT CHARACTERS FEATURED HEREIN), ITS LOGO AND ALL CHARACTER LIKENESSES ARE TRADEMARKS OF CHARLES SOULE UNLESS OTHERWISE NOTED. IMAGE COMICS® AND ITS
E AND ITS LOGOS ARE ™ AND © 2011
TRANSMITTED, IN ANY FORM OR BY ANY
HE EXPRESS WRITTEN PERMISSION OF
THIS PUBLICATION ARE ENTIRELY
FICTIONAL. ANY RESEMBLANCE TO ACTUAL PERSONS (LIVING OR DEAD), EVENTS OR PLACES, WITHOUT SATIRIC INTENT, IS COINCIDENTAL.

inspired by a robert johnson tribute poster

issue 3//interior front cover

twenty seven

written by
CHARLES SOULE

art by
RENZO PODESTA

letters by
SHAWN DePASQUALE

editor
JADE DODGE

publisher
JIM VALENTINO

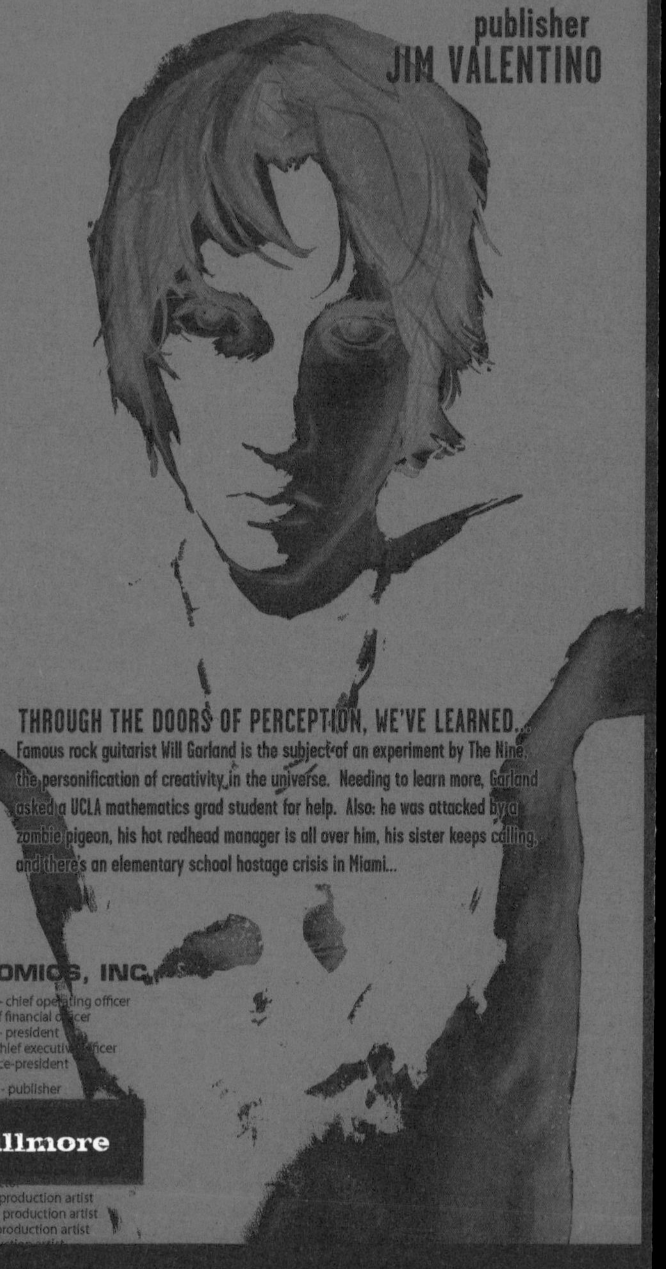

THROUGH THE DOORS OF PERCEPTION, WE'VE LEARNED...
Famous rock guitarist Will Garland is the subject of an experiment by The Nine, the personification of creativity in the universe. Needing to learn more, Garland asked a UCLA mathematics grad student for help. Also: he was attacked by a zombie pigeon, his hot redhead manager is all over him, his sister keeps calling, and there's an elementary school hostage crisis in Miami...

image

IMAGE COMICS, INC.
Robert Kirkman - chief operating officer
Erik Larsen - chief financial officer
Todd McFarlane - president
Marc Silvestri - chief executive officer
Jim Valentino - vice-president

Eric Stephenson - publisher
Todd Martinez ...

Jonathan Chan - production artist
Monica Howard - production artist
Vincent Kukua - production artist
Kevin Yuen - production artist

designed by T... ANIE

inspired by the doors live at the fillmore

issue 4//interior front cover

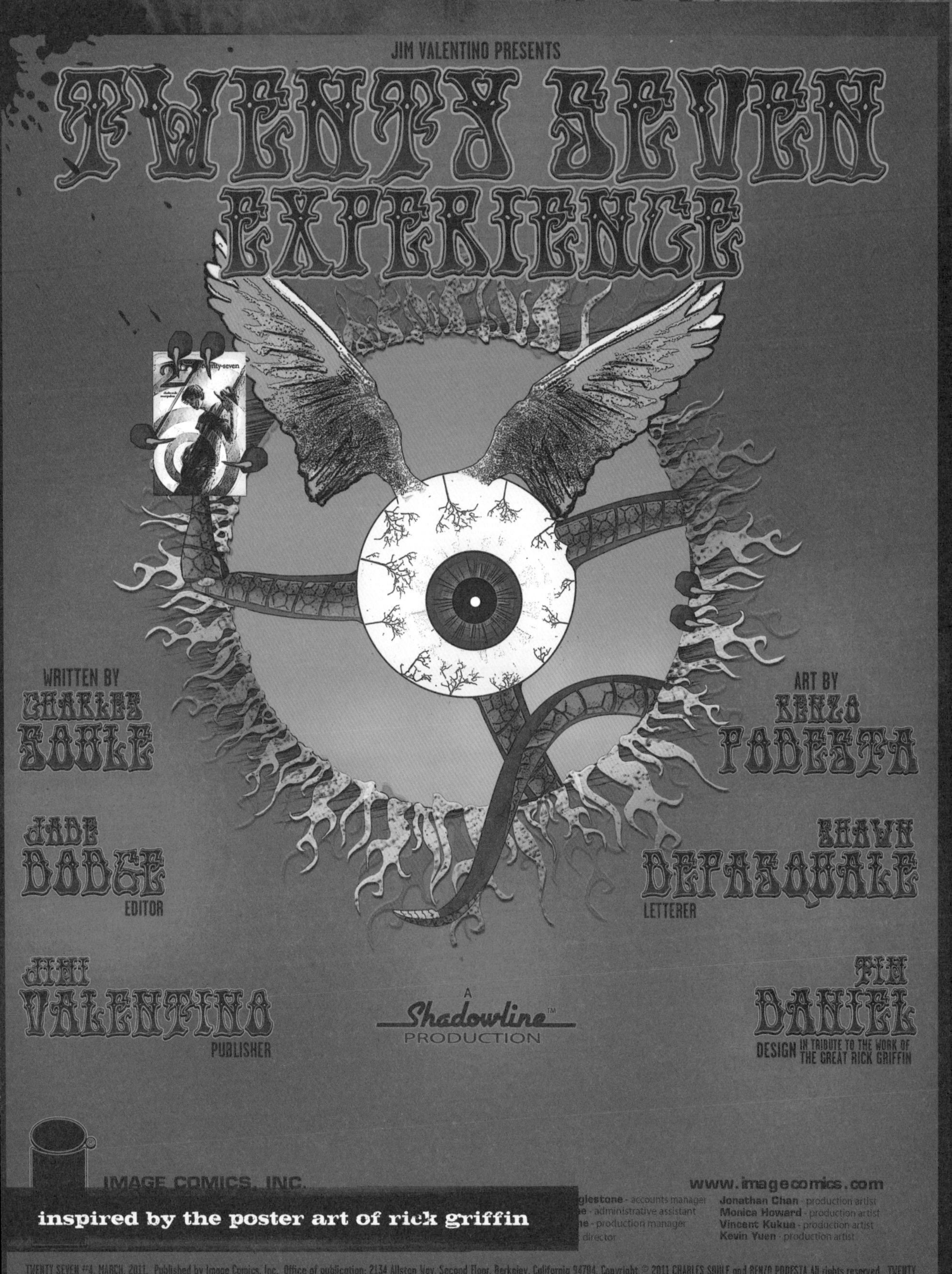

JIM VALENTINO PRESENTS
TWENTY SEVEN EXPERIENCE
WRITTEN BY CHARLES SOULE
ART BY RENZO PODESTA
JADE DODGE EDITOR
SHAWN DEPASQUALE LETTERER
JIM VALENTINO PUBLISHER
A Shadowline™ PRODUCTION
TIM DANIEL DESIGN IN TRIBUTE TO THE WORK OF THE GREAT RICK GRIFFIN
IMAGE COMICS, INC.
www.imagecomics.com
...glestone - accounts manager
...e - administrative assistant
...ne - production manager
... director
Jonathan Chan - production artist
Monica Howard - production artist
Vincent Kukua - production artist
Kevin Yuen - production artist
TWENTY SEVEN #4. MARCH, 2011. Published by Image Comics, Inc. Office of publication: 2134 Allston Way, Second Floor, Berkeley, California 94704. Copyright © 2011 CHARLES SOULE and RENZO PODESTA All rights reserved. TWENTY SEVEN™ (including all prominent characters featured herein), its logo and all character likenesses are trademarks of CHARLES SOULE, unless otherwise noted. Image Comics® and its logos are registered trademarks of Image Comics.

inspired by the poster art of rick griffin

27 has a lot going on. Numerology, music history, weird magic, exploding heads, dead cats – it get
pretty thick at times. Still, when the book was finished, and I could look at the story as a whole wit
the gorgeous finished art, only one word came to mind, and that one word was MORE. So, I decide
to stick a puzzle in there. You know, for the kids. And for the grownups too, since I put out the wor
that the first person to solve the puzzle would get a plane ticket to a con of their choice, on me. As c
right now (or, the publication date of this trade, to be more accurate), the puzzle game is officiall
closed – because I'm revealing the solution, right here, right now.

the
puzzle

On certain pages of the book, little guitar chord symbols could b
found in the gutters between the panels. I placed these in all fou
issues, and when I could I put them on pages numbered with mu
tiples of nine (9, 18, etc.). There were twenty-seven chords in al
When you put them together, they worked as a substitutio
cipher, with each chord representing a letter. However, I didn
want to make it a straight substitution code, since those are rela
tively easy to crack. Instead, it's (slightly) more thoughtful. /
single letter might be represented by any number of differer
chords. The route to figuring out which letter a given chor
equates to is based in good old music theory.

To figure out a chord, you first take the root.   That's the big letter o
the left, and it's your starting point.

If a chord only has a root, with nothing else, then that's the letter it rep
resents in the code.

If it has an indication that it's a minor, major, sharp or flat chord, ther
you have to move up or down the alphabet from the root some numbe
of spaces to determine the letter. Minor and flat chords were down
and major or sharp chords were up.

How many spaces?

Well, that's determined by the number on the right, which refers to th
chord's harmonization beyond the basic triad. So, a seventh chor
means you move seven spots in the alphabet, whether up or dow
Some examples follow on the next page.

f the chord was E by itself, then the referenced letter was E.
f the chord was Eminor7, then the referenced letter was E minus seven spots on the alphabet, or X.
f the chord was a G#13, then you would move up thirteen spots from G, and the letter you need is T.
From there, it's pretty easy.

The full, decoded message is:

THEGIFTOFNINEAWAITSGMAILCOM

The first person to email me at thegiftofnineawaits@gmail.com would be the winner.

As I write this, Issue 4 hasn't been released, so I don't know if anyone will crack it, but I hope so. I think the puzzle was difficult, but not impossible, and I had a blast designing it and putting it into the book. Hope you enjoyed it, if you tried to work it out.

-CDS

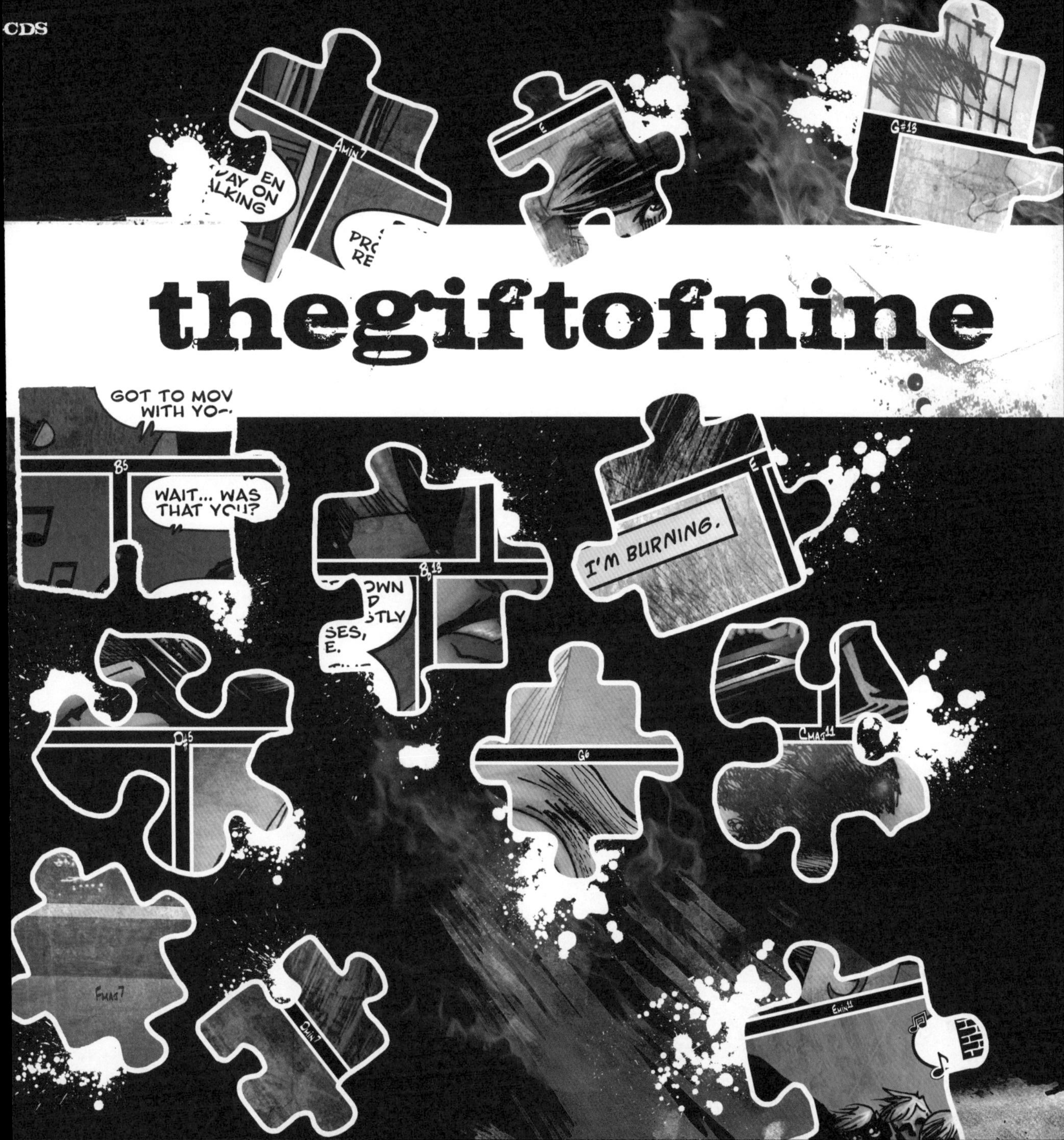

Amin7
E
G#13
thegiftofnine
GOT TO MOV WITH YO-
B5
WAIT... WAS THAT YOU?
Bb13
E
I'M BURNING.
D#5
G6
Cmaj11
Fmaj7
Dmin7
Emin11

liner notes

An early version of the Twenty-Seven story had nothing to do with music.

The first character Renzo drew for the book was Swinthe.

When putting together the cover for Issue 1, we were surprised by the fact that there aren't many iconic pictures of Kurt Cobain.

Garland usually plays Fender Stratocasters and Taylor acoustics. His style is reminiscent of Jonny Greenwood, Eric Johnson and Eddie Van Halen.

Renzo plays bass.

Charles has been playing violin since he was 3 and guitar since about 14.

The homage to Robert Johnson on the cover of Issue 2 is based on one of only two photos of the legendary blues guitarist known to exist.

The sum of the digits in any number that's a multiple of nine add up to nine. Go ahead, kids, try it!

The grey man dispelled by Jim in Issue 3 is Hargrave Swinthe. The idea is that he's been there in the background since Issue 1, just hanging around, watching.

Garland's pose in the last panel of Issue 4 is meant to mirror his pose in the first panel of Issue 1.

The first character Renzo drew for the book was Swinthe.

Everyone who worked on the book has beaten the 27 Club curse – except for cover artist Scott Forbes.

influences

Each of the lyric bubbles used in issues 3 and 4 when Garland is teleporting from place to place represents an actual song. Clearing the lyrics would have been prohibitively expensive, and in the end, I think the pictograms were more fun. They gave readers an extra layer of fun to puzzle out. No special significance to any of them – they're just tunes I like that worked for the story. The songs used, in order, are:

London Calling – The Clash

Mother – Danzig

Home Sweet Home – Motley Crue

Beautiful Girls – Van Halen

For the Love of Money – The O'Jays

Crossroads Blues – Robert Johnson

Break On Through (to the Other Side) – The Doors

Another Brick in the Wall – Pink Floyd

She Blinded Me with Science – Thomas Dolby

Hot for Teacher – Van Halen
(Yes, I know that's two. I love VH – sue me.)

Mama I'm Coming Home – Ozzy Osbourne

I Love L.A. – Randy Newman
(Garland's under pressure here – this is the first LA-related song he can think of.)

[gravestone song] – every song about death, sung all at once.

Killing in the Name Of – Rage Against the Machine
(Garland's singing the bit that repeats at the end – you know the line I mean.)

Hellhound On My Trail – Robert Johnson

bonus tracks

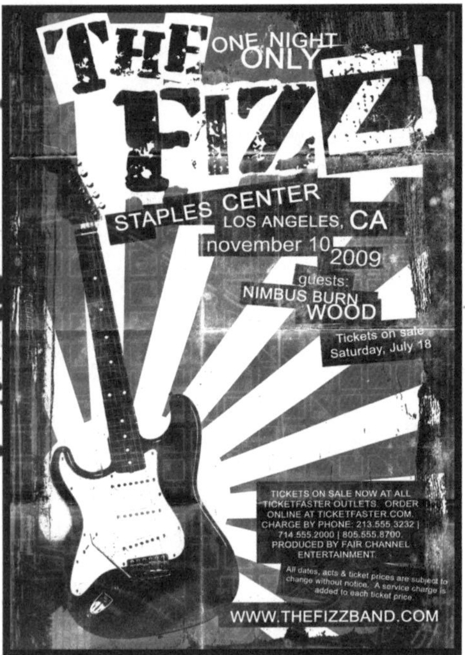
THE FIZZ
ONE NIGHT ONLY
STAPLES CENTER
LOS ANGELES, CA
november 10 2009
guests:
NIMBUS BURN
WOOD
Tickets on sale Saturday, July 18
TICKETS ON SALE NOW AT ALL TICKETFASTER OUTLETS. ORDER ONLINE AT TICKETFASTER.COM. CHARGE BY PHONE: 213.555.3232 | 714.555.2000 | 805.555.8700. PRODUCED BY FAIR CHANNEL ENTERTAINMENT.
All dates, acts & ticket prices are subject to change without notice. A service charge is added to each ticket price.
WWW.THEFIZZBAND.COM

The concert poster that begins Issue 1 includes a number of easter eg Wood and Nimbus Burn were two of Charles' college bands, and July 18 his birthday. The date of the concert is exactly one year before the origina solicited release date of Issue 1. The guitar itself is a right-handed guit flipped and re-strung to play lefty, which foreshadows the book's ending.

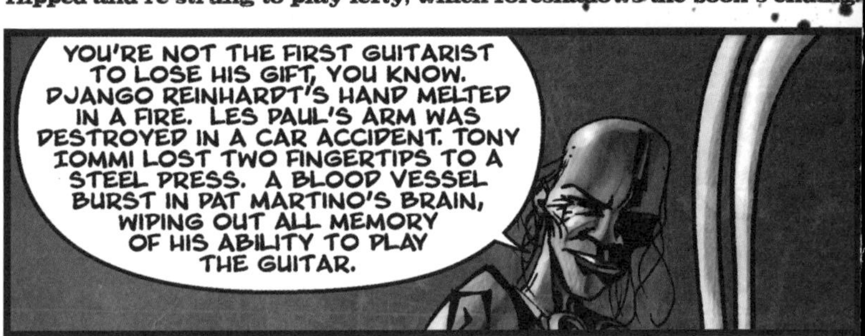
YOU'RE NOT THE FIRST GUITARIST TO LOSE HIS GIFT, YOU KNOW. DJANGO REINHARDT'S HAND MELTED IN A FIRE. LES PAUL'S ARM WAS DESTROYED IN A CAR ACCIDENT. TONY IOMMI LOST TWO FINGERTIPS TO A STEEL PRESS. A BLOOD VESSEL BURST IN PAT MARTINO'S BRAIN, WIPING OUT ALL MEMORY OF HIS ABILITY TO PLAY THE GUITAR.

The story about Tony Iommi making himself false fingertips is even better than the tidbit included in the book. When he lost his fingertips in a steel press, his doctors told him he was done with guitar forever. Tony, however, knew how crucial it would be that he work with Black Sabbath to unleash upon the world the many super-riffs boiling inside him. So, he made himself new fingertips by melting down empty bottles of dish soap and molding them into fake fingers until they worked as replacements. Metal.

There's more to the story about Les Paul, too. He got in a car crash back in the 1950s while his wife Mary Ford, the great singer, was in the car. Back in those days, the windshields and such weren't made from safety glass they were more like plate glass, which tends to shatter into awful, flying daggers. Les threw up his right arm to protect Mary's face, and got a shredded elbow and hand for his trouble. Still, he recovered, and played the Iridium in New York City well into his 90s, every Monday night.

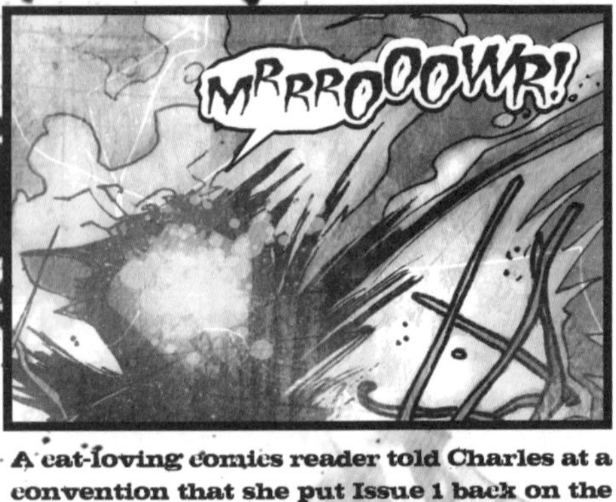
MRRROOOOWR!

A cat-loving comics reader told Charles at a convention that she put Issue 1 back on the shelf after flipping through it and seeing the blatant cat murders on page nine and they are after all murdered on page nine...

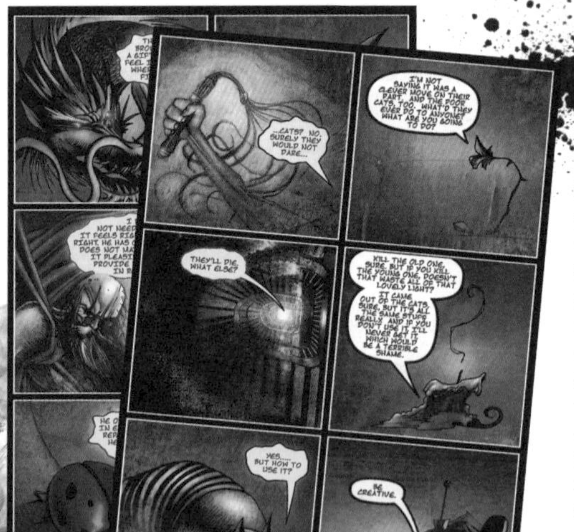
...CATS? NO. SURELY THEY WOULD NOT DARE...
I'M NOT SAYING IT WAS A CLEVER MOVE ON THEIR PART. AND THE POOR CATS, TOO. WHAT'D THEY EVER DO TO ANYONE? WHAT ARE YOU GOING TO DO?
THEY'LL DIE. WHAT ELSE?
KILL THE OLD ONE, SURE. BUT IF YOU KILL THE YOUNG ONE, DOESN'T THAT WASTE ALL OF THAT LOVELY LIGHT?
IT CAME OUT OF THE CATS, SURE, BUT IT'S ALL THE SAME STUFF REALLY. AND IF YOU DON'T USE IT, IT'LL NEVER GET IT WHICH WOULD BE A TERRIBLE SHAME.
YES..... BUT HOW TO USE IT?
BE CREATIVE.

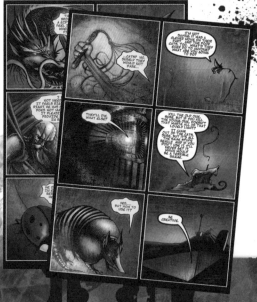

Pages 10 and 11 of Issue include manifestation of The Nine tied to th number nine. They are in order, a Chines dragon (of which ther are nine types), Nors god Odin (who hung o the world-tree for nin days to achieve wisdom a nine-spot ladybug, cat o'nine tails, Dante' nine circles of hell and nine-banded armadillo.

The homage to Robert Johnson on the cover of Issue 2 is based on one of only two photos of the legendary blues guitarist known to exist.

OKAY. I'M TALKING TO THE GHOST OF THE MAD SCIENTIST GUY I SAW TORN APART ABOUT 5 HOURS AGO AFTER HE TRIED TO SELL MY SOUL TO THE DEVIL OR SOMETHING AND KILLED SOME CATS AND PUT SOME F'ED UP BUTTON IN MY CHEST THAT APPARENTLY SOMETIMES MAKES MY HAND WORK SO I CAN PLAY GUITAR AGAIN, UNLESS IT DOESN'T.
WHO AM I SUPPOSED TO BE? ALICE COOPER?

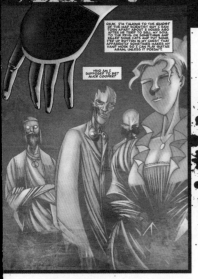

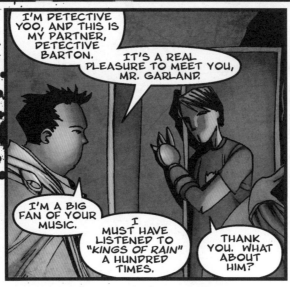

I'M DETECTIVE YOO, AND THIS IS MY PARTNER, DETECTIVE BARTON.
IT'S A REAL PLEASURE TO MEET YOU, MR. GARLAND.
I'M A BIG FAN OF YOUR MUSIC.
I MUST HAVE LISTENED TO "KINGS OF RAIN" A HUNDRED TIMES.
THANK YOU. WHAT ABOUT HIM?

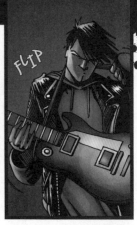

FLIP

he ghosts in Issues 1 & 2 are inspired y the film The Sixth Sense, particu-arly the unsettling concept that there re ghosts around us everywhere, all he time, watching with jealous, bitter, ostile eyes. That's why they have lothes from different eras – they're os Angelenos who died in or near arland's apartment over the years.

The song "Kings of Rain," as referred to in Issue 2, exists. Here's the first line: "I remember when I held your hand, first time since I was a child."* It's a Tom Waits-style booze and regrets ballad, with, as one might expect, room for one hell of a guitar solo.

The idea of playing lefty has a long history in rock guitar. To briefly explain, guitars are built to be played either left-handed or right-handed, and you can t really just change it up on a whim. If you learn righty, then switching to lefty basically means starting from scratch. (Brief aside: Jimi Hendrix played lefty. However, he used a right-handed guitar that he flipped over and re-strung so that it could technically be played lefty. Wacky.)

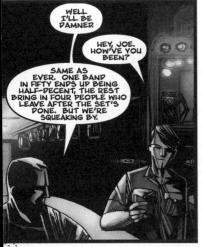

WELL I'LL BE DAMNED.
HEY, JOE. HOW'VE YOU BEEN?
SAME AS EVER. ONE BAND IN FIFTY ENDS UP BEING HALF-DECENT, THE REST BRING IN FOUR PEOPLE WHO LEAVE AFTER THE SET'S DONE. BUT WE'RE SQUEAKING BY.

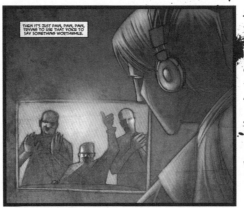

THEN IT'S JUST PAIN, PAIN, PAIN, TRYING TO USE THAT VOICE TO SAY SOMETHING WORTHWHILE.

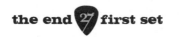

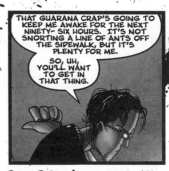

THAT GUARANA CRAP'S GOING TO KEEP ME AWAKE FOR THE NEXT NINETY- SIX HOURS. IT'S NOT SNORTING A LINE OF ANTS OFF THE SIDEWALK, BUT IT'S PLENTY FOR ME.
SO, UH, YOU'LL WANT TO GET IN THAT THING.

Garland's monologue in Issue 4 about the nature of talent vs. hard work depicts a scene where he's shown playing in what looks like some sort of boardroom to a conference table full of suits. This closely mirrors experiences some of my up-and-coming musician friends have had while trying to break into a major label. Worst possible audience – I'd take a gig in Folsom Prison over that one.

arland greets the bartender at The ting in Issue 2 with a "Hey, Joe." lany of you will recognize that as the tle of a famous bluesy Hendrix tune. Vhat you may not know is that Hey oe's chord progression is built round the Circle of Fifths, one of the ost fundamental principles in music heory. Learned or instinctive, Jimi lendrix knew his stuff.

Ozzy Osbourne snorted a line of ants off a sidewalk, in response to some boast about a big night from a member of Motley Crue (maybe Nikki Sixx). His point (and very elegantly made) was that no matter whatever shenanigans he could get up to, Ozzy would not be topped.

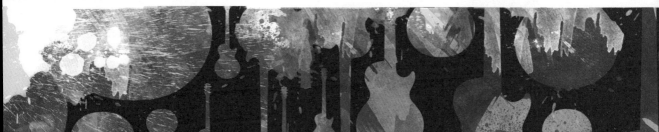

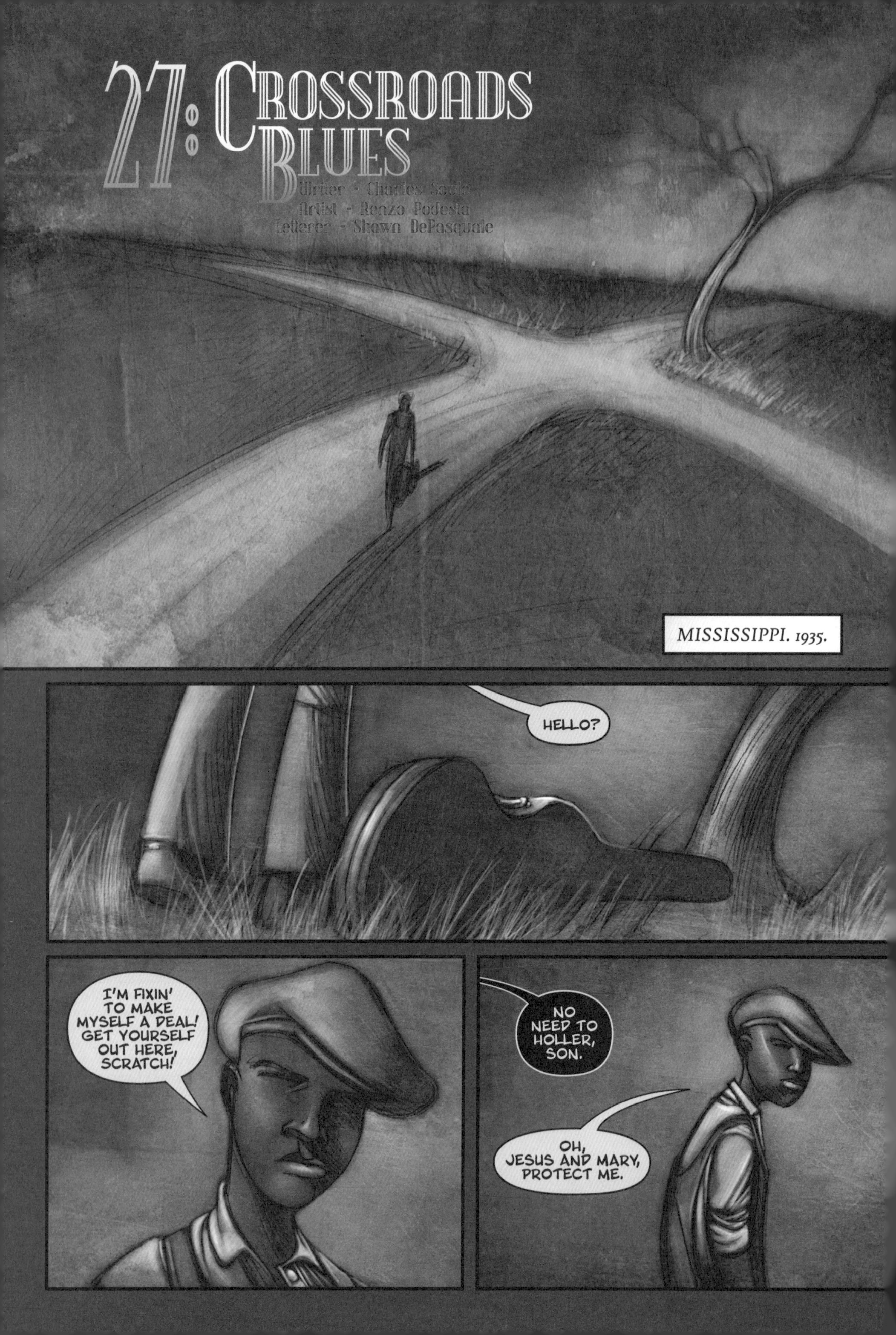
27: Crossroads Blues
Writer - Charles Soule
Artist - Renzo Podesta
Letterer - Shawn DePasquale
MISSISSIPPI. 1935.
HELLO?
I'M FIXIN' TO MAKE MYSELF A DEAL! GET YOURSELF OUT HERE, SCRATCH!
NO NEED TO HOLLER, SON.
OH, JESUS AND MARY, PROTECT ME.

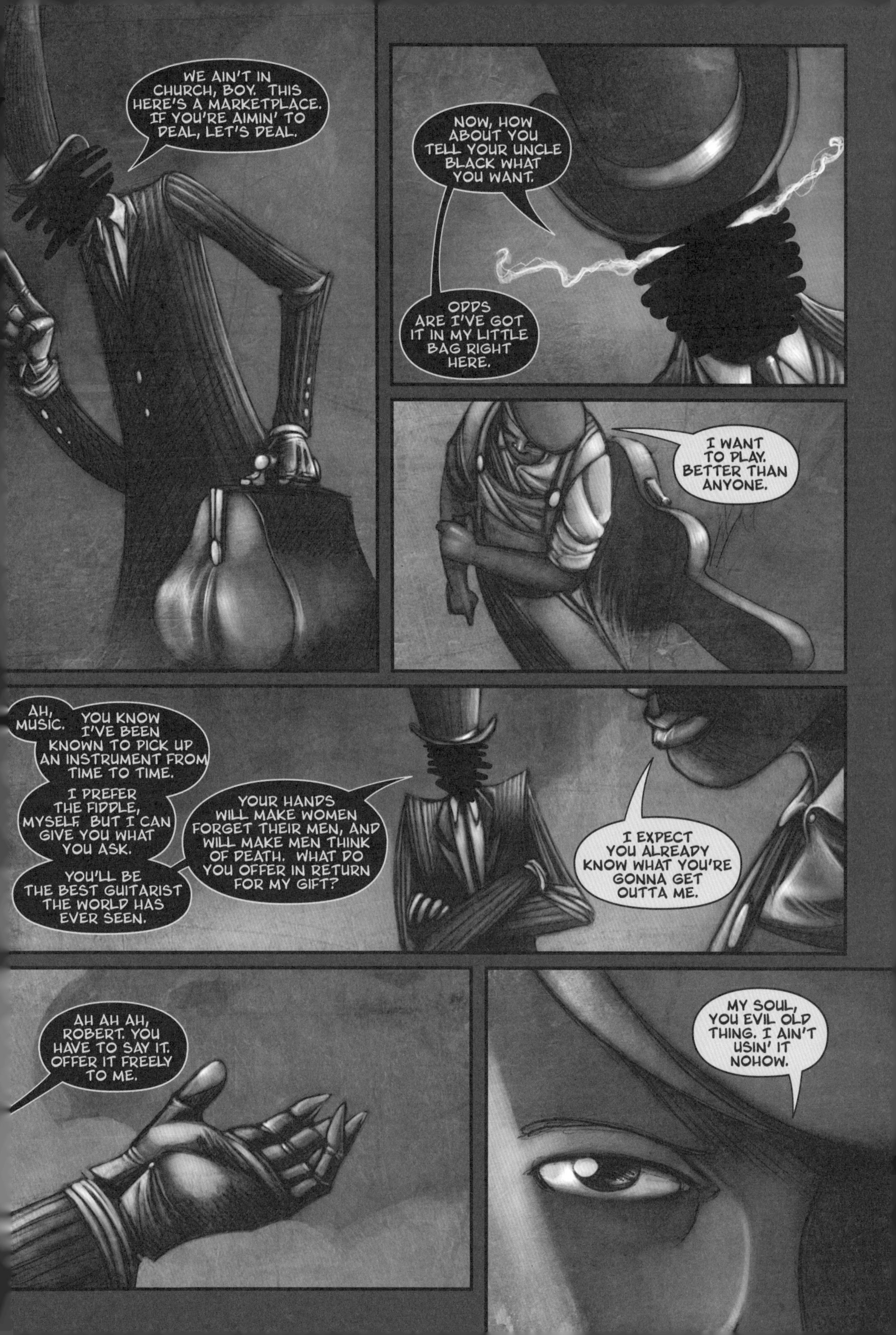
WE AIN'T IN CHURCH, BOY. THIS HERE'S A MARKETPLACE. IF YOU'RE AIMIN' TO DEAL, LET'S DEAL.
NOW, HOW ABOUT YOU TELL YOUR UNCLE BLACK WHAT YOU WANT.
ODDS ARE I'VE GOT IT IN MY LITTLE BAG RIGHT HERE.
I WANT TO PLAY. BETTER THAN ANYONE.
AH, MUSIC. YOU KNOW I'VE BEEN KNOWN TO PICK UP AN INSTRUMENT FROM TIME TO TIME.
I PREFER THE FIDDLE, MYSELF. BUT I CAN GIVE YOU WHAT YOU ASK.
YOU'LL BE THE BEST GUITARIST THE WORLD HAS EVER SEEN.
YOUR HANDS WILL MAKE WOMEN FORGET THEIR MEN, AND WILL MAKE MEN THINK OF DEATH. WHAT DO YOU OFFER IN RETURN FOR MY GIFT?
I EXPECT YOU ALREADY KNOW WHAT YOU'RE GONNA GET OUTTA ME.
AH AH AH, ROBERT. YOU HAVE TO SAY IT. OFFER IT FREELY TO ME.
MY SOUL, YOU EVIL OLD THING. I AIN'T USIN' IT NOHOW.

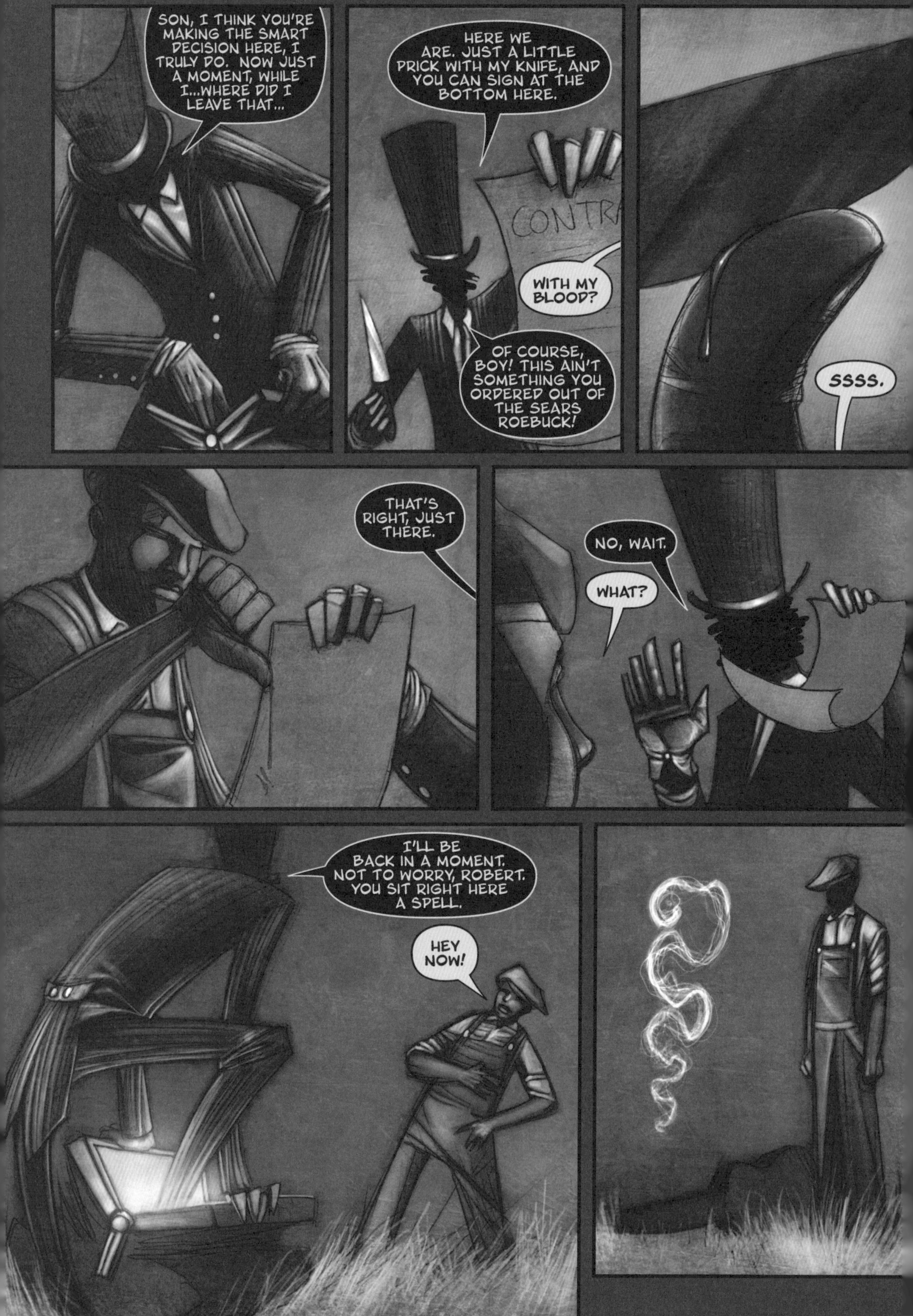
SON, I THINK YOU'RE MAKING THE SMART DECISION HERE, I TRULY DO. NOW JUST A MOMENT, WHILE I...WHERE DID I LEAVE THAT...
HERE WE ARE. JUST A LITTLE PRICK WITH MY KNIFE, AND YOU CAN SIGN AT THE BOTTOM HERE.
CONTRA
WITH MY BLOOD?
OF COURSE, BOY! THIS AIN'T SOMETHING YOU ORDERED OUT OF THE SEARS ROEBUCK!
SSSS.
THAT'S RIGHT, JUST THERE.
NO, WAIT.
WHAT?
I'LL BE BACK IN A MOMENT. NOT TO WORRY, ROBERT. YOU SIT RIGHT HERE A SPELL.
HEY NOW!

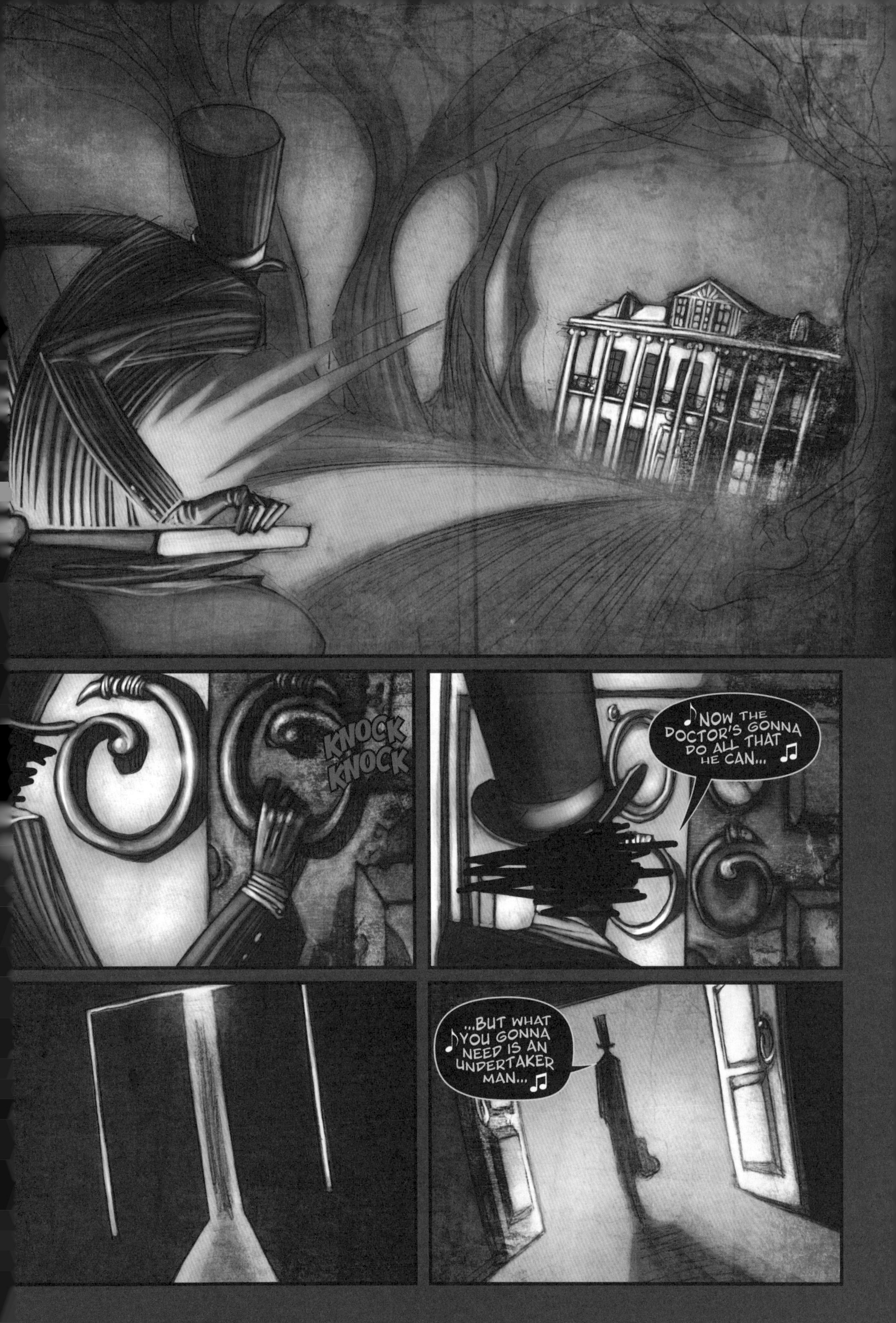
KNOCK KNOCK
♪NOW THE DOCTOR'S GONNA DO ALL THAT HE CAN... ♫
...BUT WHAT ♪YOU GONNA NEED IS AN UNDERTAKER MAN... ♫

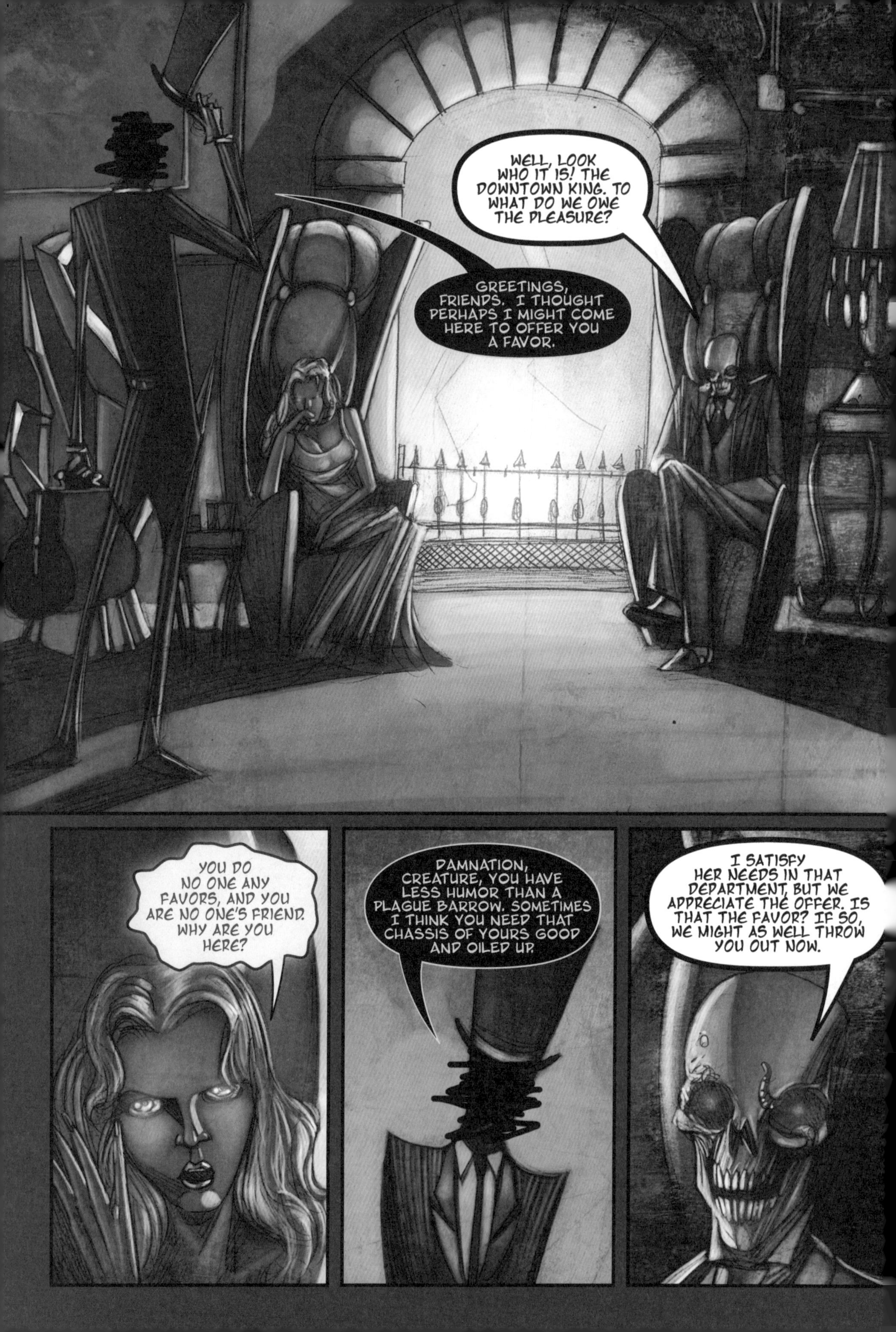
WELL, LOOK WHO IT IS! THE DOWNTOWN KING. TO WHAT DO WE OWE THE PLEASURE?
GREETINGS, FRIENDS. I THOUGHT PERHAPS I MIGHT COME HERE TO OFFER YOU A FAVOR.
YOU DO NO ONE ANY FAVORS, AND YOU ARE NO ONE'S FRIEND. WHY ARE YOU HERE?
DAMNATION, CREATURE, YOU HAVE LESS HUMOR THAN A PLAGUE BARROW. SOMETIMES I THINK YOU NEED THAT CHASSIS OF YOURS GOOD AND OILED UP.
I SATISFY HER NEEDS IN THAT DEPARTMENT, BUT WE APPRECIATE THE OFFER. IS THAT THE FAVOR? IF SO, WE MIGHT AS WELL THROW YOU OUT NOW.

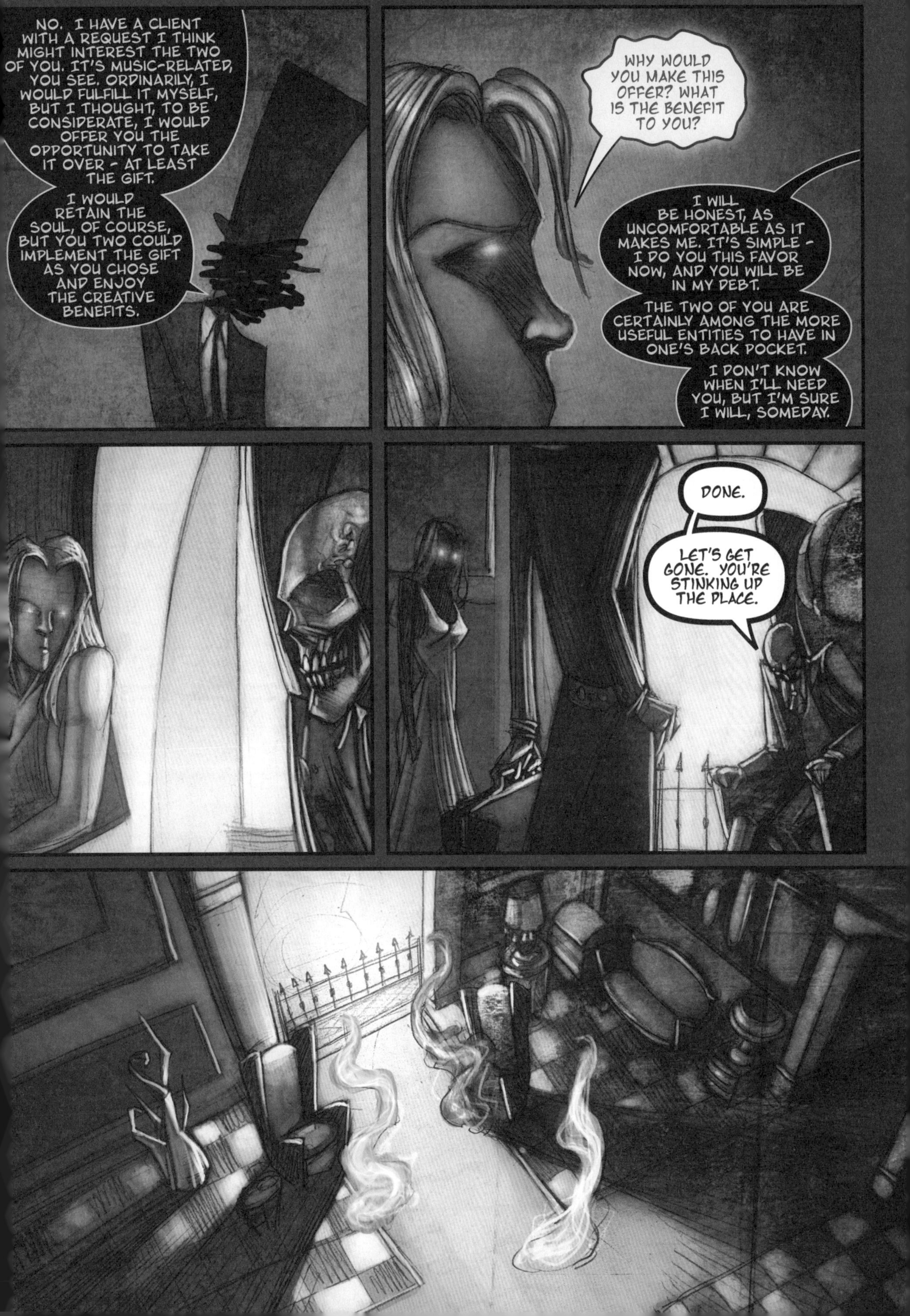
NO. I HAVE A CLIENT WITH A REQUEST I THINK MIGHT INTEREST THE TWO OF YOU. IT'S MUSIC-RELATED, YOU SEE. ORDINARILY, I WOULD FULFILL IT MYSELF, BUT I THOUGHT, TO BE CONSIDERATE, I WOULD OFFER YOU THE OPPORTUNITY TO TAKE IT OVER - AT LEAST THE GIFT.
I WOULD RETAIN THE SOUL, OF COURSE, BUT YOU TWO COULD IMPLEMENT THE GIFT AS YOU CHOSE AND ENJOY THE CREATIVE BENEFITS.
WHY WOULD YOU MAKE THIS OFFER? WHAT IS THE BENEFIT TO YOU?
I WILL BE HONEST, AS UNCOMFORTABLE AS IT MAKES ME. IT'S SIMPLE - I DO YOU THIS FAVOR NOW, AND YOU WILL BE IN MY DEBT.
THE TWO OF YOU ARE CERTAINLY AMONG THE MORE USEFUL ENTITIES TO HAVE IN ONE'S BACK POCKET.
I DON'T KNOW WHEN I'LL NEED YOU, BUT I'M SURE I WILL, SOMEDAY.
DONE.
LET'S GET GONE. YOU'RE STINKING UP THE PLACE.

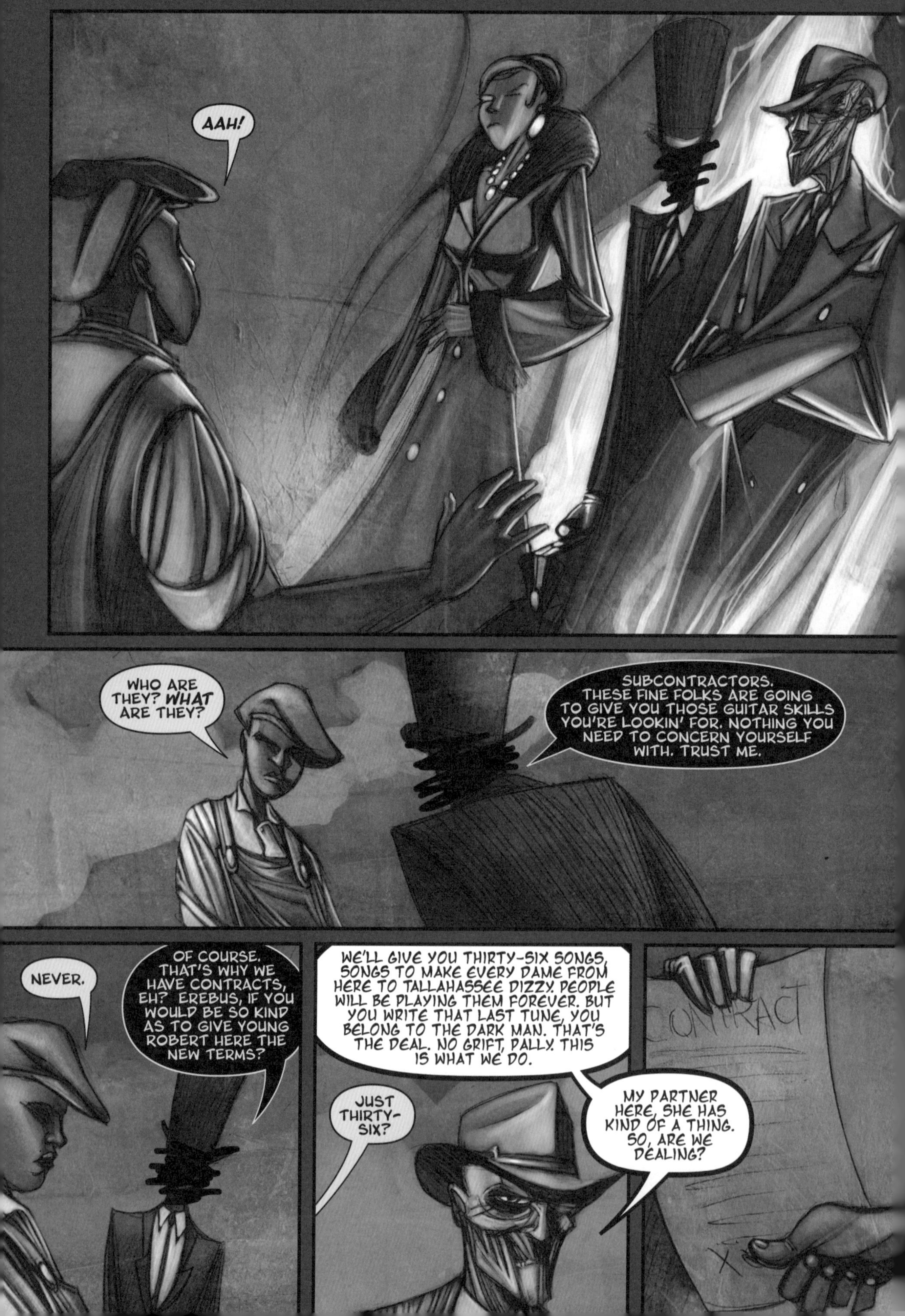
AAH!
WHO ARE THEY? WHAT ARE THEY?
SUBCONTRACTORS. THESE FINE FOLKS ARE GOING TO GIVE YOU THOSE GUITAR SKILLS YOU'RE LOOKIN' FOR. NOTHING YOU NEED TO CONCERN YOURSELF WITH. TRUST ME.
NEVER.
OF COURSE. THAT'S WHY WE HAVE CONTRACTS, EH? EREBUS, IF YOU WOULD BE SO KIND AS TO GIVE YOUNG ROBERT HERE THE NEW TERMS?
WE'LL GIVE YOU THIRTY-SIX SONGS, SONGS TO MAKE EVERY DAME FROM HERE TO TALLAHASSEE DIZZY. PEOPLE WILL BE PLAYING THEM FOREVER. BUT YOU WRITE THAT LAST TUNE, YOU BELONG TO THE DARK MAN. THAT'S THE DEAL. NO GRIFT, PALLY. THIS IS WHAT WE DO.
JUST THIRTY-SIX?
MY PARTNER HERE, SHE HAS KIND OF A THING. SO, ARE WE DEALING?
CONTRACT

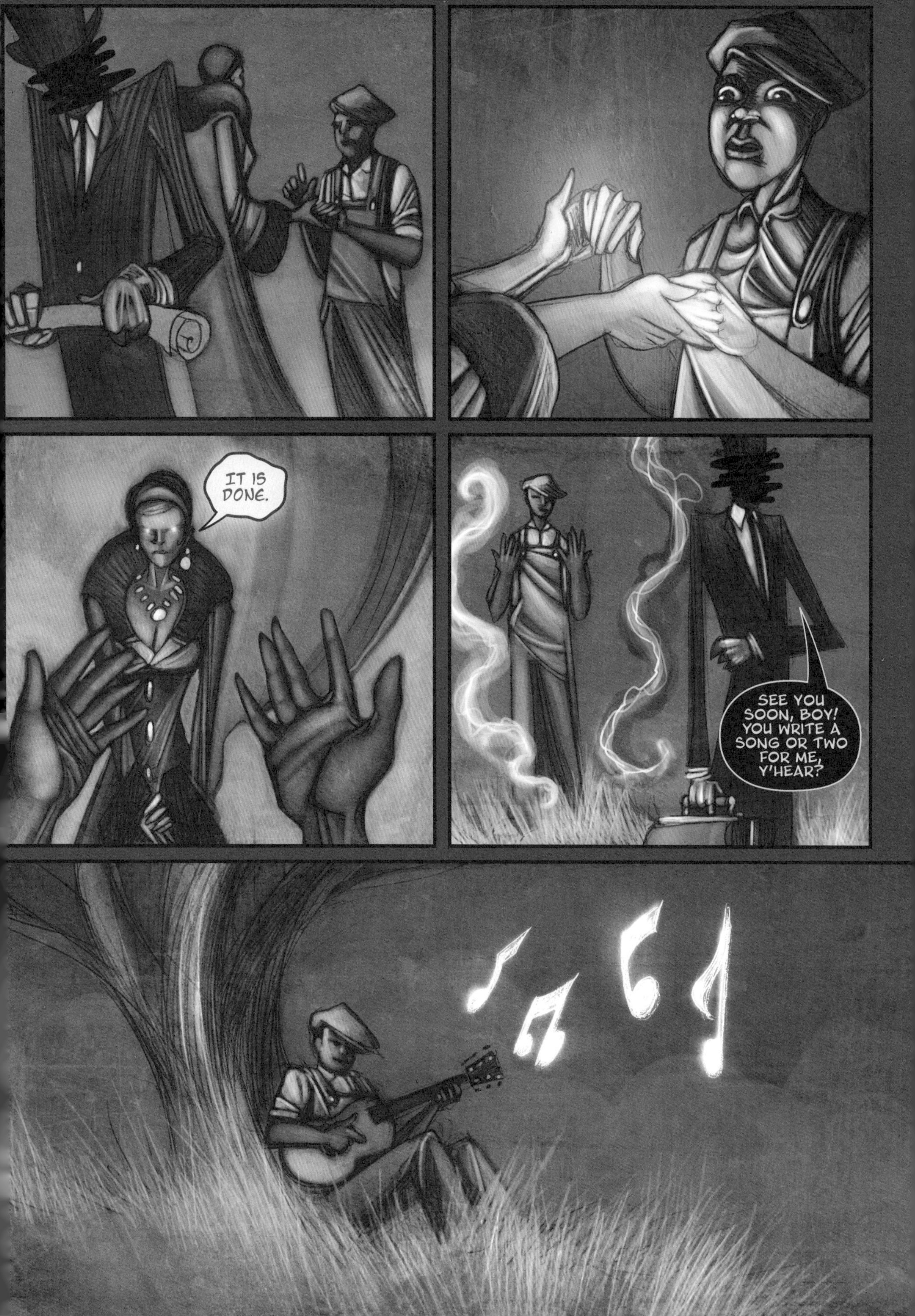
IT IS DONE.
SEE YOU SOON, BOY! YOU WRITE A SONG OR TWO FOR ME, Y'HEAR?

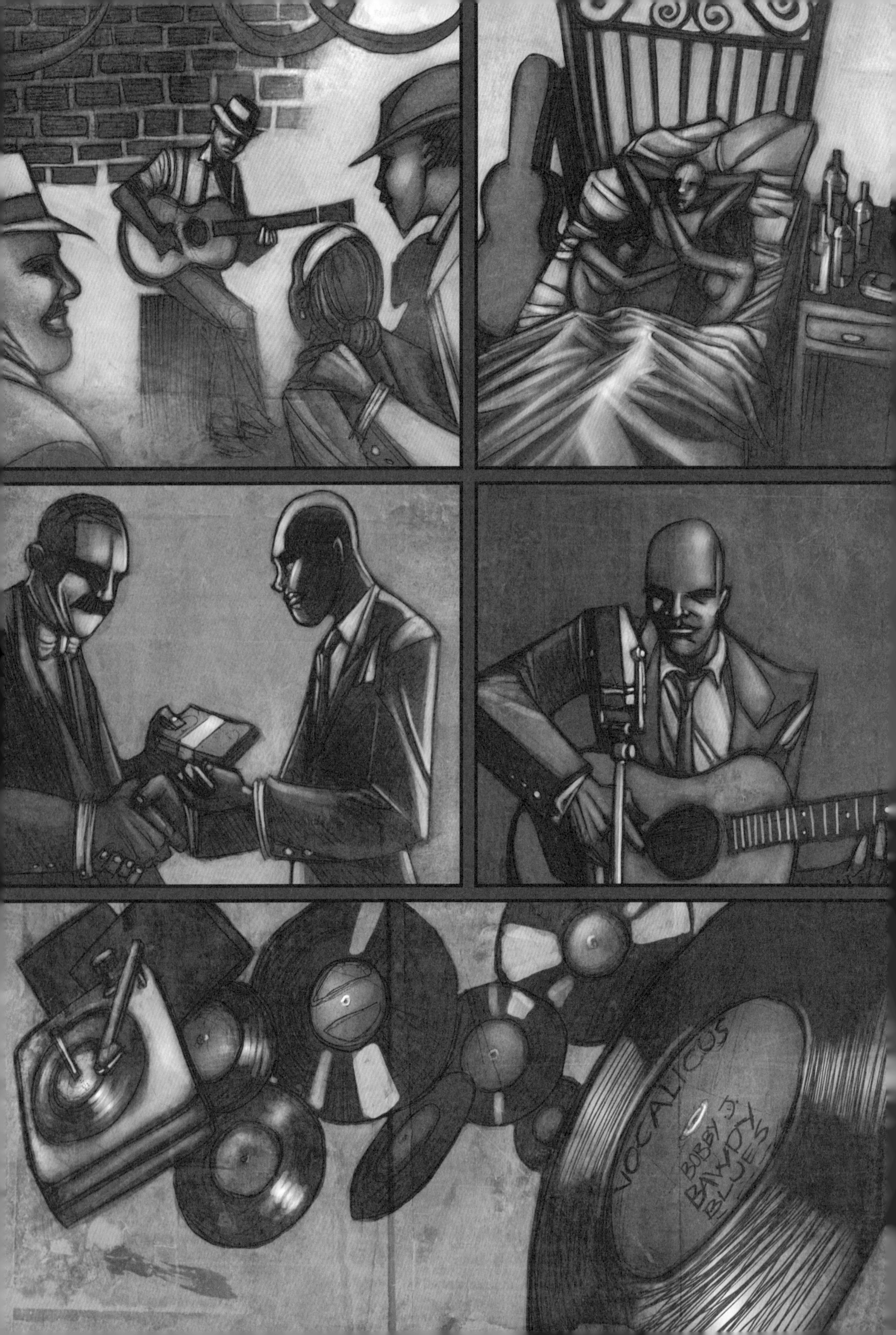
BOBBY J.
BLUES

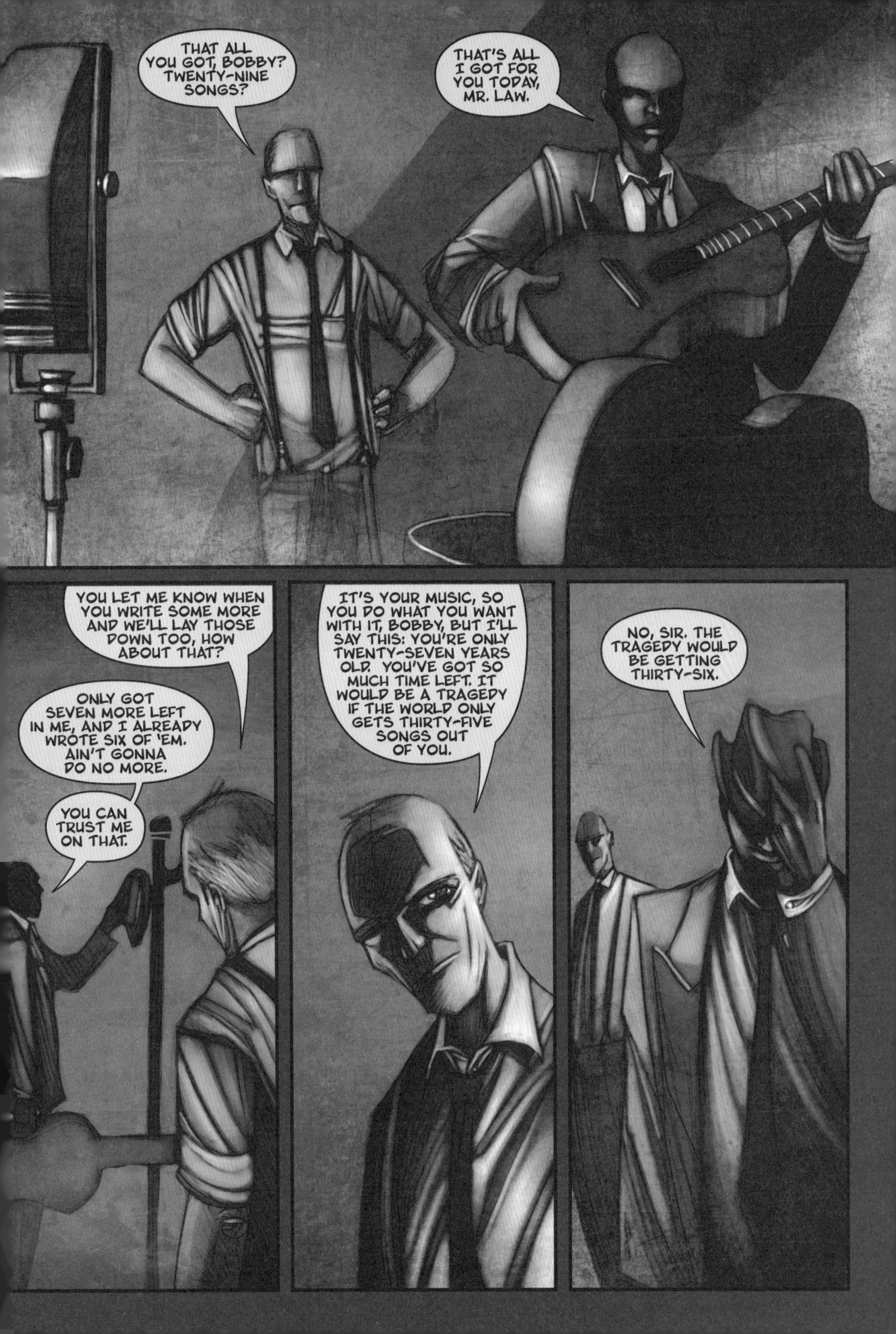
THAT ALL YOU GOT, BOBBY? TWENTY-NINE SONGS?
THAT'S ALL I GOT FOR YOU TODAY, MR. LAW.
YOU LET ME KNOW WHEN YOU WRITE SOME MORE AND WE'LL LAY THOSE DOWN TOO, HOW ABOUT THAT?
ONLY GOT SEVEN MORE LEFT IN ME, AND I ALREADY WROTE SIX OF 'EM. AIN'T GONNA DO NO MORE.
YOU CAN TRUST ME ON THAT.
IT'S YOUR MUSIC, SO YOU DO WHAT YOU WANT WITH IT, BOBBY, BUT I'LL SAY THIS: YOU'RE ONLY TWENTY-SEVEN YEARS OLD. YOU'VE GOT SO MUCH TIME LEFT. IT WOULD BE A TRAGEDY IF THE WORLD ONLY GETS THIRTY-FIVE SONGS OUT OF YOU.
NO, SIR. THE TRAGEDY WOULD BE GETTING THIRTY-SIX.

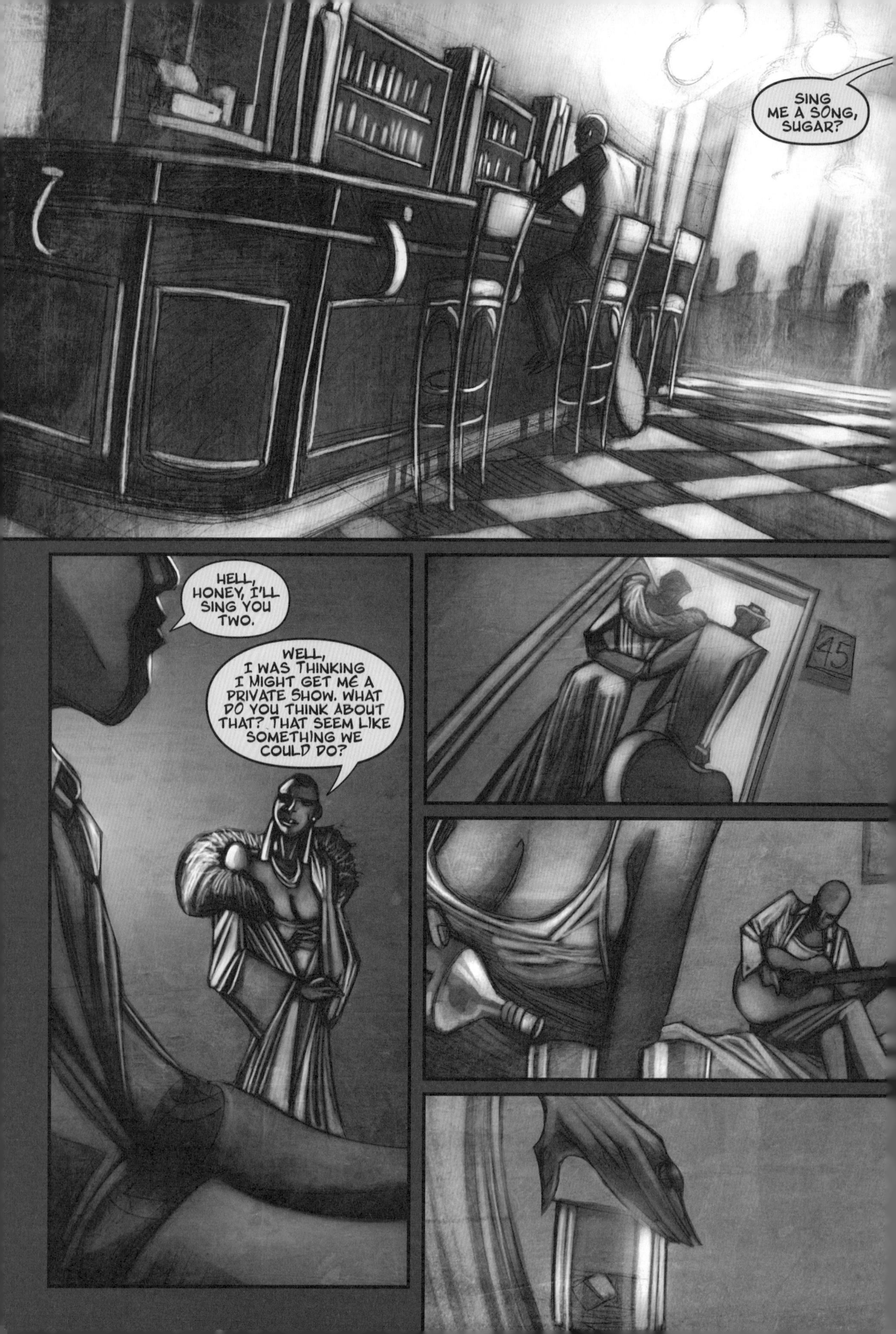
SING ME A SONG, SUGAR?
HELL, HONEY, I'LL SING YOU TWO.
WELL, I WAS THINKING I MIGHT GET ME A PRIVATE SHOW. WHAT DO YOU THINK ABOUT THAT? THAT SEEM LIKE SOMETHING WE COULD DO?
45

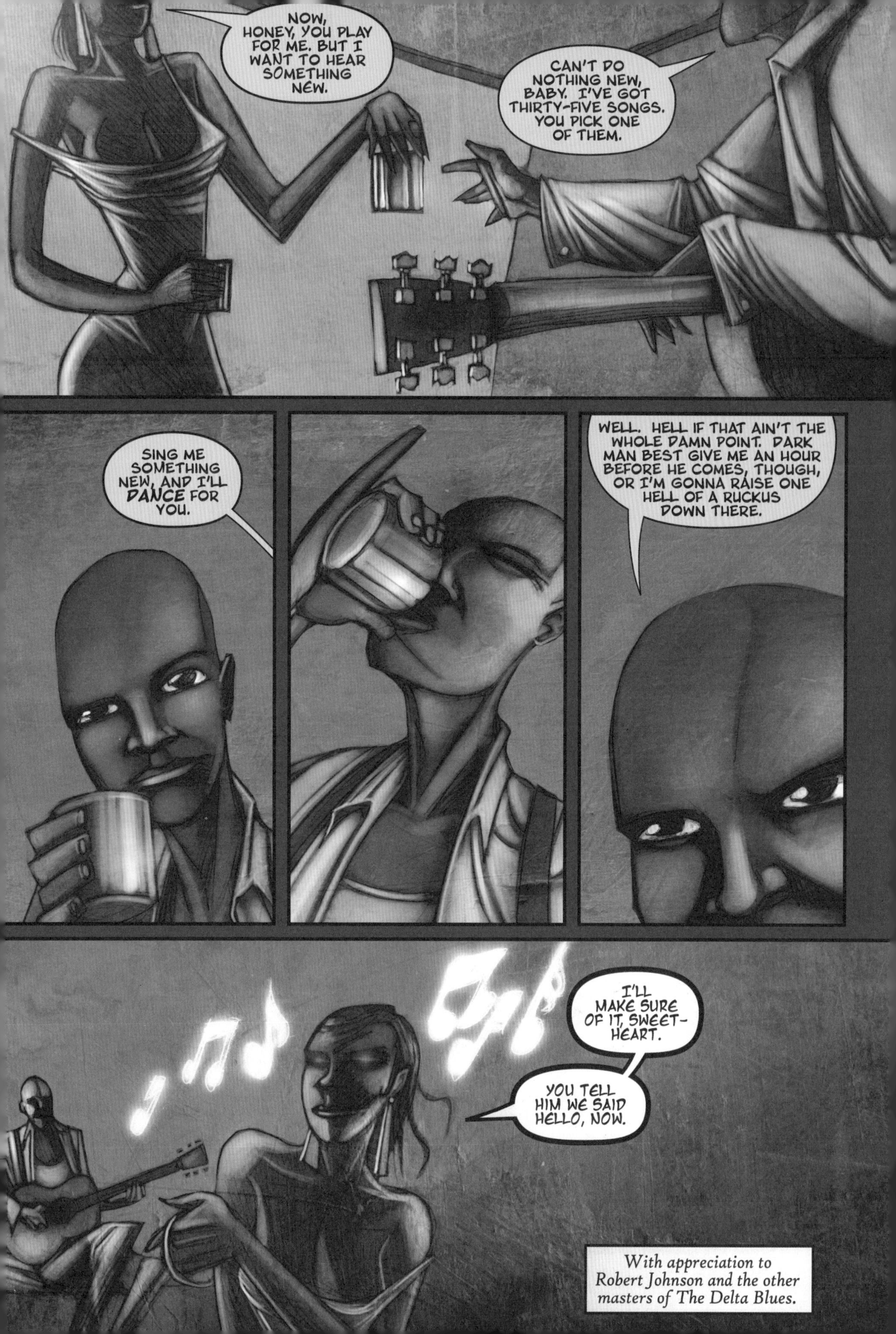
NOW, HONEY, YOU PLAY FOR ME. BUT I WANT TO HEAR SOMETHING NEW.
CAN'T DO NOTHING NEW, BABY. I'VE GOT THIRTY-FIVE SONGS. YOU PICK ONE OF THEM.
SING ME SOMETHING NEW, AND I'LL DANCE FOR YOU.
WELL. HELL IF THAT AIN'T THE WHOLE DAMN POINT. DARK MAN BEST GIVE ME AN HOUR BEFORE HE COMES, THOUGH, OR I'M GONNA RAISE ONE HELL OF A RUCKUS DOWN THERE.
I'LL MAKE SURE OF IT, SWEET-HEART.
YOU TELL HIM WE SAID HELLO, NOW.
With appreciation to Robert Johnson and the other masters of The Delta Blues.

Great Graphic Novels You're Bound To Enjoy...

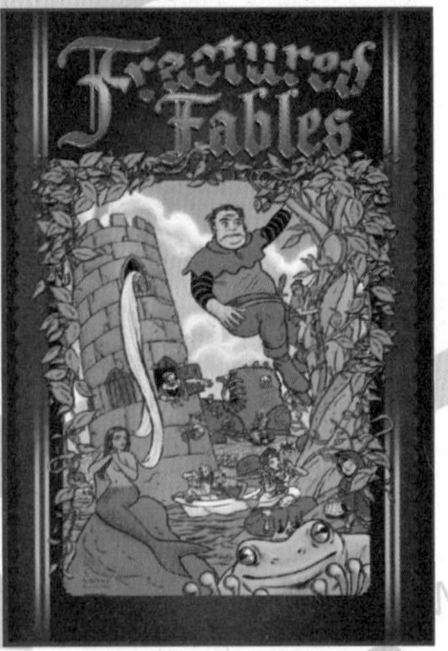
Fractured Fables

VARIOUS ARTISTS
ISBN: 978-1-60706-269-1

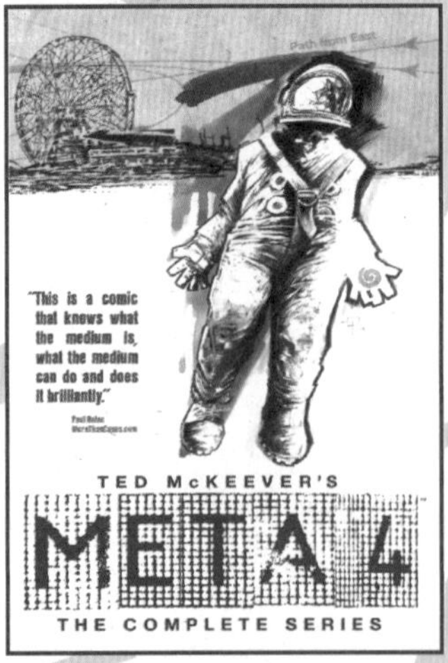
"This is a comic that knows what the medium is, what the medium can do and does it brilliantly."
TED McKEEVER'S
META 4
THE COMPLETE SERIES

TED McKEEVER
ISBN: 978-1-60706-383-4

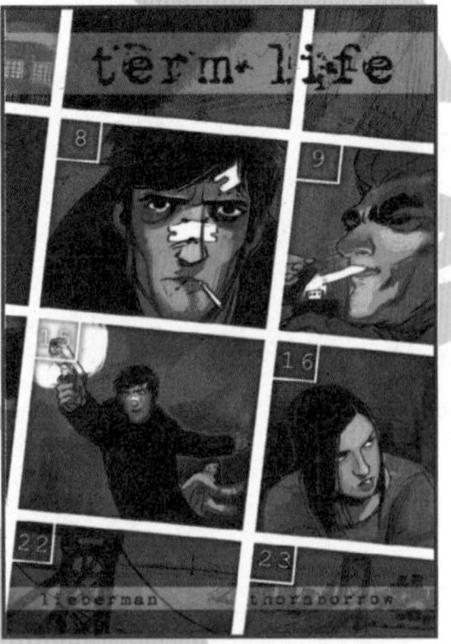
term life
8
9
16
22
23
lieberman
thornborrow

LIEBERMAN/THORNBORROW
ISBN: 978-1-60706-350-6

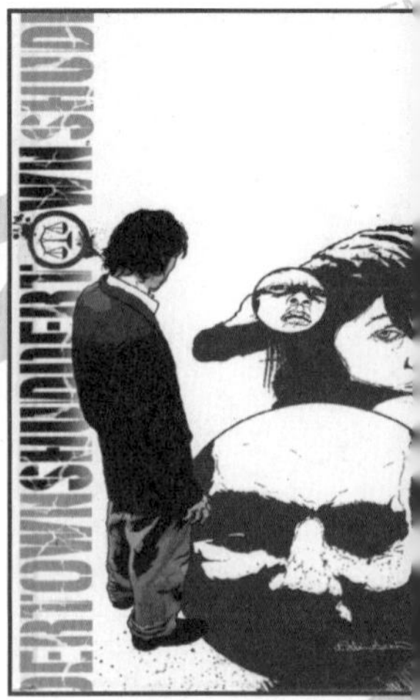

SPENCER/GEEN
ISBN: 978-1-60706-3

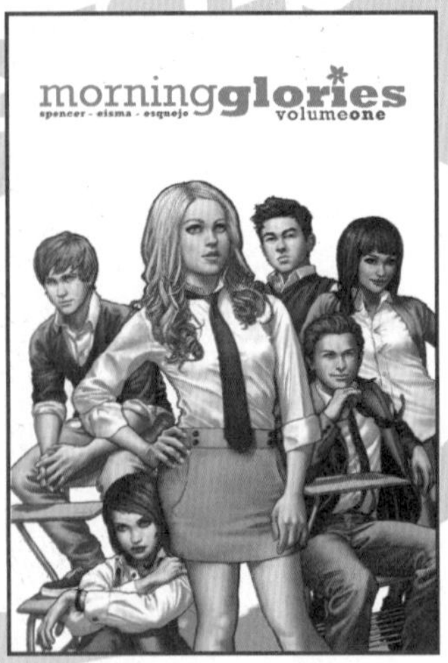
morningglories
spencer · eisma · esquejo
volumeone

SPENCER/EISMA/ESQUEJO
ISBN: 978-1-60706-307-0

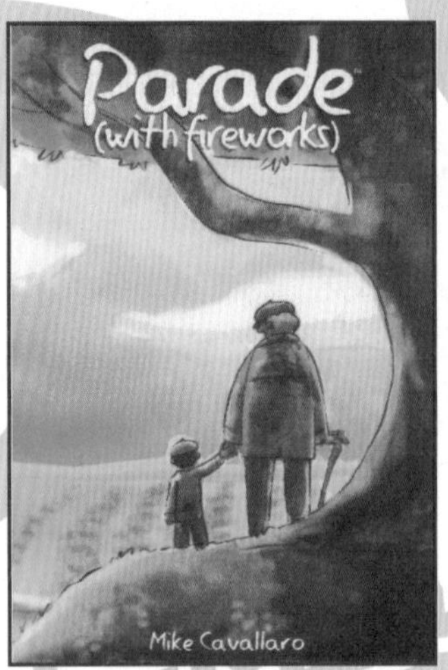
Parade
(with fireworks)
Mike Cavallaro

MIKE CAVALLARO
ISBN: 978-1-58240-995-5

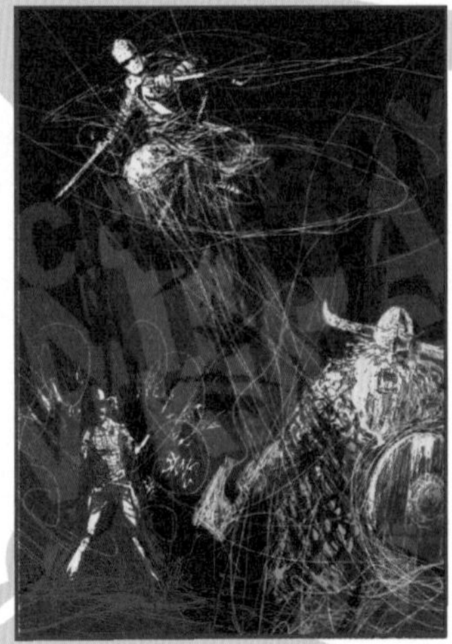

LIEBERMAN/ROSSMO
ISBN: 978-1-60706-344-5

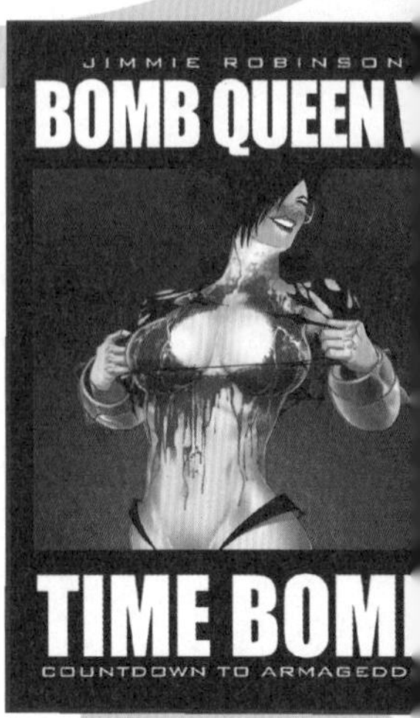
JIMMIE ROBINSON
BOMB QUEEN
TIME BOM
COUNTDOWN TO ARMAGEDD

JIMMIE ROBINSON
ISBN: 978-1-60706-189-

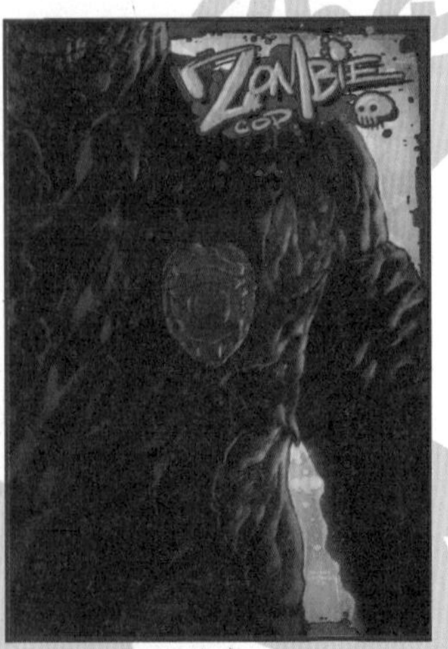
ZOMBIE
COP

MARIOTTE/KUDRANSKI
ISBN: 978-1-60706-023-9

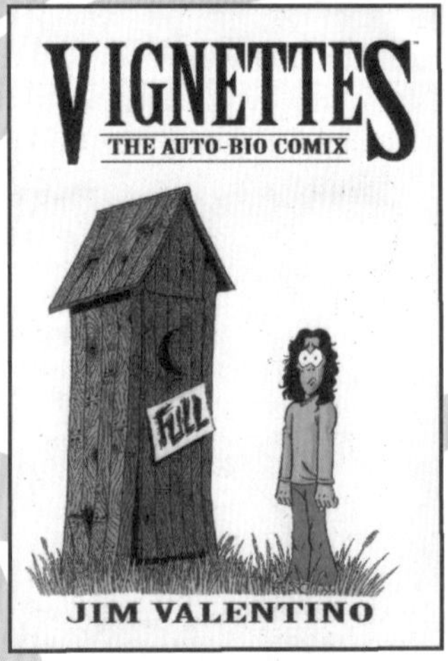
VIGNETTES
THE AUTO-BIO COMIX
FULL
JIM VALENTINO

VALENTINO
ISBN: 978-1-58240-979-5

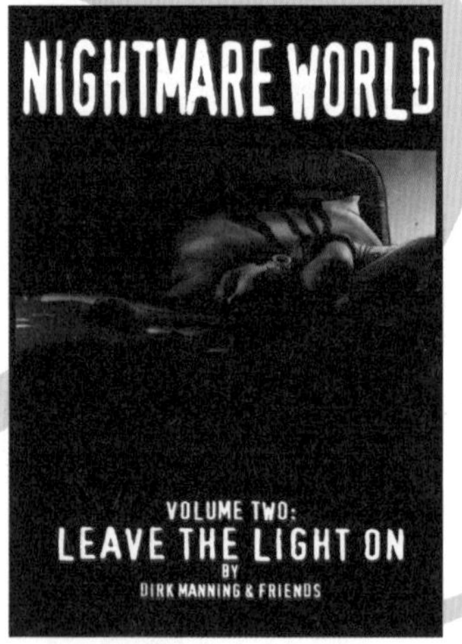
NIGHTMARE WORLD
VOLUME TWO:
LEAVE THE LIGHT ON
BY
DIRK MANNING & FRIENDS

MANNING/VARIOUS
ISBN: 978-1-60706-156-4

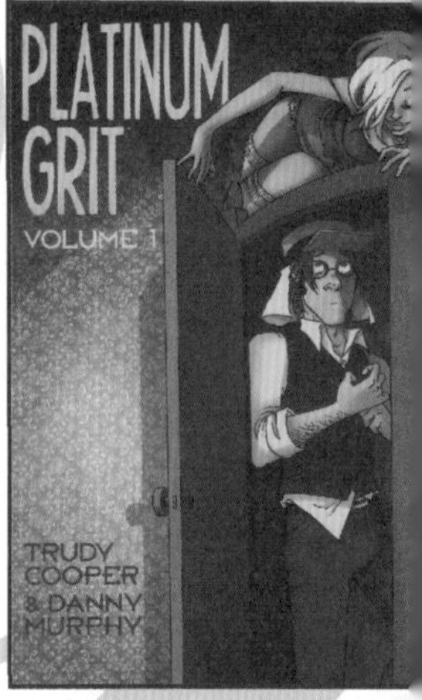
PLATINUM
GRIT
VOLUME 1
TRUDY
COOPER
& DANNY
MURPHY

COOPER/MURPHY
ISBN: 978-1-60706-35

FOR MORE INFORMATION ABOUT ALL *Shadowline* BOOKS AND WEB-COMICS PLEASE JOIN US AT

www.ShadowlineOnline.com